PC-DOS

Introduction to High-Performance Computing

Peter Norton

A Brady Book
Published by Prentice Hall Press
New York, New York 10023

PC-DOS: Introduction to High-Performance Computing

A Brady Book
Published by Prentice Hall Press
A Division of Simon & Schuster, Inc.
Gulf+ Western Building
One Gulf+ Western Plaza
New York, New York 10023

PRENTICE HALL PRESS is a trademark of Simon & Schuster, Inc.

Manufactured in the United States of America

4 5 6 7 8 9 10

Library of Congress Cataloging in Publication Data
Norton, Peter, 1943–
    PC-DOS, introduction to high-performance computing.

    Includes index.
    1. PC DOS (Computer operating system) 2. IBM Personal Computer—
Programming. I. Title. II. Title: P.C.-D.O.S., the guide to high-performance
computing.
QA76.6.N685 1985   001.64'2   84-24355
ISBN 0-89303-752-4

Contents

Miscellaneous Notes About This Book

You might be interested in learning about the computer equipment that was used to write this book.

While the research for this book involved every model of IBM PC and several other computers, the actual writing was started on a regular PC with 512K of memory, and a 10 megabyte hard disk (in the standard IBM PC expansion unit) for storage. Later revisions of this book were done on the remarkable AT model of PC, and these very words reside on the 20 megabyte hard disk inside the AT.

The manuscript for this book was printed out on one of the most impressive and worthy computer printers currently available, the Hewlett-Packard ThinkJet. The ThinkJet is not a letter-quality printer (instead, it produces a standard dot-matrix style typeface), but it makes up for that by being remarkably quiet, fast, and compact. Overall, an excellent piece of design.

Literally every version of DOS, from 1.00 through 3.10 was used in the research of this book.

An interesting hodge-podge of software was used to write this book. I have yet to convert to using a full-fledged word processing program, so this book was completely composed with an excellent editing program called Vedit, from CompuView Systems of Ann Arbor, MI. Spelling checking was done with WordProof from IBM, a high-performance spelling checker with a huge vocabulary and excellent features. WordProof has received widespread acclaim, much deserved in my opinion. LP, one of the Norton Utilities programs, was used to format and print out this book's manuscript. TS, the text-searching component of the Norton Utilities, helped considerably in checking the draft manuscript.

Software and hardware, I love it all.

Limits of Liability and Disclaimer of Warranty

The author(s) and publisher of this book have used their best efforts in preparing this book and the programs contained in it. These efforts include the development, research, and testing of the theories and programs to determine their effectiveness. The author(s) and publisher make no warranty of any kind, expressed or implied, with regard to these programs or the documentation contained in this book. The author(s) and publisher shall not be liable in any event for incidental or consequential damages in connection with, or arising out of, the furnishing, performance, or use of these programs.

Note to Authors

Have you written a book related to personal computers? Do you have an idea for developing such a project? If so, we would like to hear from you. Brady produces a complete range of books for the personal computer market. We invite you to write to Terrell Anderson, Senior Editor, Brady Communications, Inc., General Reference Group, Simon&Schuster Building, 1230 Avenue of the Americas, New York, New York 10020.

Trademarks

- IBM, IBM Personal Computer, AT, and TopView are trademarks of International Business Machines Corp.
- Microsoft, MS, MS-DOS, XENIX, MultiPlan, and Microsoft Word are trademarks of Microsoft Corp.
- Compaq, Compaq-Plus, and DeskPro are trademarks of Compaq Computer Corporation.
- Data General, DG, and DG-1 are trademarks of Data General Corp.
- WordStar is a trademark of Micro Pro, Inc.
- Volkswriter is a trademark of Lifetree Software.
- Bellesoft and ES/P are trademarks of Bellesoft, Inc.
- Framework and dBASE are trademarks of Ashton-Tate.
- PC-File is a trademark of Buttonware.
- Lattice is a trademark of Lattice Inc.
- CP/M and CP/M-86 are trademarks of Digital Research.

- UCSD and p-System are trademarks of the Regents of the University of California.
- Prokey is a trademark of Rosesoft.
- Sidekick is a trademark of Borland International.
- JET is a trademark of Tall Tree Systems.
- The Norton Utilities, UnErase, and DiskLook are trademarks of Peter Norton.
- VisiCalc is also a trademark, whose ownership has had a rocky history. It now seems to be permanently in the hands of Software Arts.

About the Author

Peter Norton was raised in Seattle, Washington, and educated at Reed College in Portland, Oregon. During the past 20 years, he has worked with a wide variety of computer equipment from personal computers to the largest main-frames, and he has worked on every kind of software from the most intricate system programming to thoroughly mundane commercial applications.

Shortly after he began working with microcomputers, he created, for the IBM PC family of computers, the now-legendary Norton Utilities software package, and wrote the best-selling book "Inside the IBM/PC," which is widely recognized as the best popular explanation of the technical inner workings of the IBM Personal Computer.

Although Mr. Norton continues to develop software for small computers, his work now concentrates on writing about the use of personal computing.

Mr. Norton lives by the beach in Venice, California, and still hasn't learned how to roller skate.

Introduction and How to Use This Book

This book is about getting started using PC-DOS, the Disk Operating System for the IBM Personal Computer family. It is also about much more.

There are two parts to this book, although you won't find them laid out in two separate sections. One part teaches you the most basic things that you need to know about getting started with DOS, and then getting the most out of it. The other part tells you things that any user of a small personal computer needs to know in order to be wily, smart, and effective with your little machine. The first part will tell you things like how to make good use of the commands that are built into DOS. The second part will tell you things like how to choose intelligently among the hundreds of programs offered for sale.

One of the things that sets this book apart from many others is that it is full of practical advice about how to do things, about what works and what doesn't, about what to buy, about what to use. This advice is based on a solid foundation of four things from the author's experience:

- over a decade of experience with all sorts of computers;
- fairly recent conversion to working with a small computer, so that the experience of being a beginner isn't lost in the swamps of time;
- heavy, full-time use of a personal computer for the last few years; actually it isn't quite accurate to describe it as full-time use—its been more like ten hours a day, six or seven days a week, so that I've compressed lots of personal computer experience into a short time.
- a healthy dose of common sense.

We won't go into all the technical details of using DOS. Your computer's manuals will do that nicely. What we will do for you is help

you understand what those manuals are about and help you get started. And we'll do something that your computer's manuals cannot, or dare not, do—give you advice about what's good and bad in software that you consider buying.

Perhaps you are the enthusiastic first-time owner of a personal computer. Perhaps your work is forcing you to use a computer that you aren't really sure you want to deal with. Perhaps you are considering getting a small computer, and you want first to learn a little of what computers are all about (and how to spend your money wisely). If you fit into any of these three descriptions, then this book is for you.

This is a help book for beginning computer users, people who will be working the **IBM PC** family of computers. How can you get the most help from it?

- *Pay attention to the cartoons.* Some of them are just for fun, but most of them have important messages to help you understand your computer.
- If you are completely new to computers and don't understand them at all, read Chapter 2, which explains the most funda-

mental ideas about how a computer and its operating system, DOS, work. Also, make use of the narrative glossary in Chapter 23; it defines some of the most commonly used technical terms about computers, and ties the definitions together into a narrative form.

● Check out the chapter headings. They will guide you into the material you need. To get going with DOS, look to Chapter 3, "Getting Started," Chapter 4, "Fundamentals of DOS commands," Chapter 5, "Overview of Elementary Commands," and Chapter 6, "Overview of Advanced Commands." The use of disk storage is at the heart of using your computer, so when you need information to understand your disks and files, look to Chapter 9. For advice on choosing software, using programming languages, and avoiding expensive mistakes, look to Chapters 10, 18, and 19. For tricks and tips and danger areas, see Chapters 11 through 16.

Most of all, this book is here to help you through the small traumas of beginning to use your computer. Every new experience brings its pleasures and pains—and the pains tend to come first. The problems of "computer phobia" are now legendary. Whether you are a reluctant beginner or a starting enthusiast, this book will help make your transition into the use of DOS easier. Computers are now for everybody.

Before we end this chapter and plunge into DOS, we should mention DOS version numbers. A complex computer program like DOS grows and expands and evolves, so there are various versions of DOS, in four series, numbered 1, 2, 3, and 4. The 1-series (which included versions known as 1.00, 1.10, and 1.25) is now mostly obsolete, and is no longer in widespread use (though we'll offer help and advice specifically for folks who are using a 1-series version). The 2-series (DOS 2.0, 2.1, etc.) added many commands and features that really set the pace for all following versions of DOS. The 3-series (DOS 3.0 and 3.1) added an important new feature, network file sharing, but didn't change much in character from the 2-series. The 4-series will probably add a feature known as multi-tasking, which allows the computer to work on more than one task at a time. Most of what we discuss in this book applies to any version that you will be using; but to be helpful, we'll mention where there are important differences between the versions.

There are several ways you can find out which version of DOS your computer has. One is to look at the manual that comes with DOS. It will have the version number on the cover or title page. There are two ways to get your computer to tell you which version of DOS it has. When you start up your computer with DOS, ordinarily the version number is reported at the beginning. Also, there is a command, called VER, which asks DOS to report its version number to you. We'll discuss how to start your computer with DOS and how to use the VER command later in this book.

Before we go on, let's pause to explain two terms: DOS and the IBM Personal Computer family.

DOS is the name used by IBM for the most widely used operating system for the IBM PC family. The term DOS stands for "Disk Operating System," but everybody calls it simply DOS. DOS was created for IBM by Microsoft, a leading company in software for personal computers. Microsoft also provides versions of DOS for many other computers; these other versions are usually called MS-DOS (short for Microsoft DOS). To distinguish our IBM version, many people call it PC-DOS. In fact, our version has been called PC-DOS so often, that it's become popularly believed that PC-DOS is IBM's official name for it. Not true. But also not important, to be honest about it. Whether you call it DOS, PC-DOS, or MS-DOS, we're really talking about essentially the same thing. The differences between DOS for one computer and DOS for another are quite minor.

This book is for use with the IBM Personal Computer family and the IBM version of DOS. When there are differences between one version and another, we'll be following the IBM version.

There are several models of IBM Personal Computer, and so we call them collectively the IBM PC family. This family includes the original model of PC, the PC-XT model (which introduced large-capacity hard disks to the family), the PC*jr* (which made PCs much more affordable), the Portable PC, and the high-performance PC-AT model. IBM also makes other models, some of them quite specialized.

The PC family, though, has broadened beyond what IBM itself offers. Other companies have manufactured computers that are highly IBM-compatible which also have a combination of features that aren't exactly matched by any IBM model. Notable among these extended members of the PC family are the Compaq, Compaq-Plus, and Deskpro—all from Compaq Computer Co.—and the DG-1 lap-sized PC from Data General.

All of these machines can be considered legitimate members of the full PC family. They all use the same DOS operating system that we'll learn about in this book.

2

Basic Computer Concepts

If you are going to use your computer successfully, you need to have a working idea of what it is and how it functions. By this I don't mean the computer technician's understanding of what's going on under the cover of your machine. I mean a simple, practical, working idea of what's what—just the sort of understanding that you need to have of a car in order to be a safe driver; not what a car mechanic needs to know, but what a car driver needs to know. As the "driver" of a small computer, you have to have an elementary idea of what's going on in your machine. In this chapter we'll try to lay out for you that kind of understanding of basic computer concepts.

We'll set it out in four parts: First, the metaphor of the computer as an office worker. Then we'll consider what a computer can do and what it can't. Next we'll look at the importance of an operating system, like our DOS. Finally, we'll wrap up this chapter with a very practical matter—the two quite different ways that you can use your computer.

2.1 The Computer as Worker

The best way that I know of to comprehend how a computer works, to make sense of its various parts, and to understand how they work together, is to draw an analogy between the computer and a human office worker (and a not very bright one at that). In many ways, a computer is remarkably like someone doing simple clerical office work.

Let's suppose you are at work, and your boss introduces you to someone who will be your new personal assistant—someone whose only task is to help you with your work. But, the boss tells you privately, your new assistant isn't very bright. Conscientious, yes; hardworking, yes; but bright, intelligent, and imaginative? Absolutely not. This helper will do whatever you ask to be done, but has to be given

5

instructions in laborious detail. A worker with lots of energy, but absolutely no initiative, no common sense, and no independence.

You don't need us to tell you the identity of your new assistant—you know already it's your computer. Well now, let's consider what your computer assistant has to offer, what it needs to get any work done, and what you'll have to do to get any useful work out of it.

Your computer has, as they say, an "electronic brain." This brain (and as we'll see, it's a pea brain, for sure) is called various things in computer terminology. It is the central processing unit, or CPU, or just the processor, for short. This is the most central and fundamental part of a computer; and sometimes people refer to this one part of a whole computer system as being the computer itself. That is pretty accurate, but naturally it can be confusing to call this one part the computer, so we'll call it the microprocessor.

Your computer's processor is quite analogous to the brain of a not-very-bright person. It is a fair analogy—the computer's processor, like a person's brain, is the part that has the ability to comprehend and carry out your instructions.

So far, we have the worker's brain: the computer processor. What comes next? If your assistant is going to get any work done, it needs a work place. For an office worker that would be a desk. What part of your computer is its work space, its desk? It might surprise you that it is the part that we call the computer's memory.

Now, we all know that a person has a memory, and most of us have heard about a computer also having something known as its memory—so it is natural to think that the computer's memory is analogous to our memory. Wrong. Our memory is—as stupid as this sounds—where we remember things; it is our brain's more or less permanent record of information. But the memory of a computer is not a permanent record of anything. Instead, the computer's memory is the part that it uses as a work space. The memory is where the computer places the information it is working on while it is doing the work. This is just like the desk of an office worker. When work is being performed, it is spread out on as much of the desk as is needed. When the work is finished, it is cleared off the desk, ready for another task. So it is with the computer's memory. The computer uses its memory on a temporary basis. When the current job is done, the memory can be cleared for another task.

This analogy of the computer's memory and an office worker's desk goes even further. While in principle all of your desk is work space, part of it is probably taken up by a telephone or a pencil cup. It is the same way with a computer's memory. Certain parts of it are dedicated to one specialized use or another; but on the whole, most of the memory is available as working space for the computer.

Some things that you do at a desk take up very little space. To scribble a letter, you don't need much space. But if you are writing a report, you need more space—space for your writing pad, for your notes, for a dictionary. Nearly any desk has room for that sort of work. If you are doing a very complicated task—let's say a complex accounting job that requires looking information up in all sorts of accounting books and journals—then you need much more space. Maybe more space than there is on an ordinary desk.

Things work the same way with a computer. First, the more complicated the task, the more memory the computer needs for working space. Second, like desks, computer memory usually comes in some rather standard sizes. For a computer, the size of its memory is usually measured in "K," or thousands of characters of memory capacity. One K is 1,024 characters (bytes, in computer terminology); for convenience, we can think of each K as simply a thousand characters—the amount of space taken up by 150 words of English. That's about the size of this paragraph. A typical size for home hobby computers is around 48K of memory. Personal computers for professional use usually start at 128K and often have 256K or even more, though in the past 64K was common for professional-class PCs. These are the most common work space sizes for personal computers—64K, 128K, and 256K. Larger sizes are available, and it is not unusual for a personal computer to have 512K. The standard models of the PC family can accommodate up to 640K of memory, and the advanced AT model can handle 3,072K bytes (which is called, when the numbers get that big, 3 megabytes).

There is another way that a computer's memory is like a worker's desk. For common simple tasks, not much of the memory/desk is used. For more complex jobs, more will be used until, finally, some job will be too large to fit into the available space. This is why it is good to have plenty of memory in your computer. Since memory is relatively cheap, having plenty is inexpensive insurance against having a problem that is too large to fit. As with an office worker, having more work space generally doesn't affect how fast the work gets done—that relates to the worker's brainpower. The size of the work space mostly affects how large and complicated a job can be done.

Naturally you wouldn't get your assistant a desk the size of a football field, and you don't need to get your computer more memory than can be put to good use. For some guidance on what might be enough for your computer, see Chapter 19.

So far in understanding the parts of our computer, we've covered the processor (brain) and the memory (desk/work space). What about the rest of the computer parts? Let's consider what disk storage represents to your computer.

Disk storage is the computer's equivalent of the office worker's filing cabinet. Disk storage comes in several forms: as flexible "floppy" diskettes, as rigid disk cartridges, or in the form of permanently mounted, non-removable fixed "hard" disk systems. They may be called disks, diskettes, fixed disks, hard disks, Winchester disks, cartridges, or mini-disks. Functionally, they all do the same job for our computers—they act as a place to store information, which could be either data or programs, when the computer is not actually working on it. When the computer is working on the data, the data is in memory (on the desk top, so to speak), and not in the disk storage.

Disk storage acts like a filing cabinet for the computer, and it even borrows some of the terminology of filing cabinets: inside disk storage, our information is organized into "files." Each file contains whatever kind of data is appropriate to its purpose. This might be written text, accounting numbers, or sets of instructions (programs) for the computer. When the computer needs information from a file, it "opens" it, reads or writes it, and then "closes" the file. Here the computer terminology closely matches what human workers do with files. There is only one major difference in the way a computer uses a file and the way a person does. If you or I were to work with a file from our filing cabinet, we would place the whole file folder on our desk to work with it. The computer's way of using a file is a little

different—it works with small parts of a file at a time, similar to what we would do if we took only a page at a time from a file folder. Part of the reason a computer works this way is to reduce the amount of memory needed to get its work done.

Like people, computers can, in a sense, read and write, and also talk on the telephone. Computers do this through what are called input/output devices, or I/O devices, or peripheral devices. A personal computer usually has a display screen to write information onto, and often a printer as well. A printer is the computer's equivalent of having a typewriter at hand. The computer does most of its reading (other than reading from its disk filing cabinet) from its keyboard—it "reads" what we type on the keyboard. The computer also can use the telephone to talk to other computers or to distant peripheral devices—such as writing through a telephone line to a printer that is located somewhere else. To use a telephone, a computer needs special parts to connect it to the phone lines. These special parts are called a communications adapter and a modem; they perform the translation necessary to change computer talk into telephone talk. These parts, the adapter and the modem, may be built into your computer, or they may be separately attached parts.

There are many possible kinds of I/O devices, or peripheral devices, that can be connected to your computer—many of them

designed for very special purposes. There are special printers designed to draw pictures called graphics printers or plotters. There are special input devices that the computer can read—such as a light pen (which can read a position on the display screen), a joy stick (mostly used for games), or a mouse (which is a joy stick for people who are too serious to play games). And naturally there is much, much more. The disk storage on a computer is also an I/O device—we just discussed it separately since it has its own special importance.

So that is basically the full set of a computer's parts—the processor (brain), the memory (work desk), the disk storage (filing cabinet), telephone (adapter and modem), typewriter (printer), and so on. That is the hardware, the physical computer as worker. What about the computer software we hear so much about?

Our analogy of the computer as a faithful but not-very-bright office worker helps to explain software—computer programs—as well. A person normally has a general education, general mental skills, and knowledge that we call job skills. A computer, like an imbecile, has few job skills of its own. But the computer, like a loyal and dim-witted assistant, can do anything that we can explain how to do in meticulous detail.

The computer doesn't know how to do anything by itself; it needs programs to tell it what to do—as if our office assistant could do nothing but follow an elaborate manual of office procedures. To accomplish any work, the computer must first turn to its disk file for the program instructions that will tell it exactly what to do.

When we use the computer, the first step to get it to work is to tell it which program, which book of instructions, to follow. The program could be anything that people have taught computers to do—from accounting calculations to game playing. Some of the programs we run on our computers are aids to make it easier for us to write further programs.

One of the programs that a computer can run is a master program—a program that makes it easier to run other programs. This master program is called an operating system, and it is the computer's analogy to a human worker's general education, or an office worker's general office skills. If you or I were working as clerks in an office, we would be expected to have training in specific jobs—like a computer has programs for specific work—but we would also be expected to know how to do common ordinary things, like how to sharpen a pencil, or even how to find things in a filing cabinet. The kinds of very basic skills are given to a computer by its operating system. The operating system takes care of the most ordinary tasks that all programs need to carry out, including the very important task of taking care of the filing cabinet, the computer's disk storage. The main subject of this book is an operating system, one particular one: the Disk Operating System, called DOS, from Microsoft.

So now, I think, we are ready to see how a personal computer works as a whole, keeping our analogy to the dumb-but-faithful office assistant in mind.

When we first need our computer, we turn it on—it reports to work. The first task we give it is to start up its operating system. Our office assistant has forgotten everything overnight, so its first task in the morning is to take its general instruction manual (operating system) out of the filing cabinet (disk storage), and place it ready on its desk (computer memory).

Once the computer is running—the office worker is ready for work—we can tell it what to do first. We give it the name of a program, which might be a word processing program, like Microsoft Word, for us to write with; or a spreadsheet program, like Lotus 1-2-3, for us to do financial planning with. With the name of the job to be done, our worker takes the specific instructions (program) out of the filing cabinet (disk) and gets it ready on its desk (memory). For a while, we have our computer do that kind of work; when we're done, it puts the program away. When we want to do something else, we give our computer assistant the name of another program—and so it goes. As the computer works for us, it uses its disk storage to fetch and save our information. It uses the display screen to speak to us; it uses the printer to give us a written record; it uses the keyboard to take our commands. It may use the telephone to pass information to and from another computer. But whatever the computer does, it is just a simple helper for us.

Like my example of a dim-witted assistant, there are times when the computer can be very helpful, and times when it is more of a nuisance than an assistant. We have to teach it how to do things (which is laborious), and we have to learn the limitations of its ways (which can be equally time-consuming). For some things it helps; for others it doesn't. But on the whole, it can be very useful.

2.2 What a Computer Can and Can't Do

There are some things that a computer can do, and many, many things that it can't. Even more important, there are many things that you might try to do with a computer, that are better done by hand.

First, let's consider what the computer can do, and do well. It's a real whiz at arithmetic—fast and unfailingly accurate. Arithmetic is what computers do best; in fact, when you are using a computer for something else, like writing a letter with a word-processing program, most of what the computer is doing, behind the scenes, is arithmetic. So when we need arithmetic done, the computer is just dandy at it. The computer's most famous and best success with arithmetic has been with "electronic spreadsheets," the sort of program pioneered by VisiCalc and improved by Multiplan and Lotus 1-2-3.

VisiCalc is a fine example of computing at its best—it is quick and handy, and it makes it possible for many people to do all sorts of financial planning and numeric calculations, which they wouldn't have even tried before there were programs like this. Doing the kind of work that VisiCalc does by hand was so difficult that we might as well say it was impossible.

The next thing that computers are very good at is record keeping — but only certain kinds of record keeping. With their large disk storage, computers can save large amounts of data. Under the right circumstances, computers can be efficient about searching out just the information that we need. But it is also true that many kinds of simple record keeping are more work to keep on a computer than to keep by hand. This is something really worth knowing. Once you fall even a little in love with what a computer can do, it is easy to become infatuated and try to get it to do everything for you. Beware. You wouldn't turn to your computer to add 2 + 3, but you would use your computer to add up the square roots of a hundred numbers— that's more in its line of work. So it goes with record keeping. If you have any information that is reasonably easy to keep organized by hand, then it would probably be more work to use your computer to keep track of it. On the other hand, when your manual records get out of hand, it's time to call in the computer.

We people are still learning how to master the talents of computers, and so we are expanding the range of things that it is practical to have computers do for us. Some things that don't fit into a computer's natural skills of arithmetic and record keeping have turned out to be very good things to have a computer do anyway. The best example of this is word processing, which means computer work related to the written word—accepting written text, changing (editing) it, keeping track of it, checking its spelling and grammar, and formatting it into tidy printed pages. This is the kind of work that the computer learned (through our programming) how to do fairly recently. And yet it has become one of the computer's greatest successes. There are now, and will be in the future, many jobs a computer can do well, even though they don't involve much computation.

There are some things, though, that computers can't do now, and may never be able to do, and that is anything that involves intelli-

gence and judgment. Computers do very well by rote, but when a task calls for imagination, intuition, and the like, it is, at least for now, a job for people—perhaps a job at which a computer can assist, but still a job for humans.

You can expect your computer to be able to do anything that is mechanically straightforward, but you can't expect it to do anything that involves judgment. And you can expect to have success with your computer in any work that is in the right scale—neither too big for your computer to handle, nor too small for it to be worth putting on your computer.

2.3 The Importance of an Operating System

So far, we've seen roughly what a computer is and the sort of things that it can do, and we've had a little bit of an explanation of the role of the computer's operating system—DOS—but that is all. It also seems that the operating system is no big deal. Actually, the operating system is a very big deal, for several reasons.

The first reason why an operating system is very important is because it sets the environment in which you interact with the computer and the environment in which your programs work. The operating system establishes the character of how your computer works, just as much or more than the particular kind of computer you have does. Likewise, the operating system sets many of the practical limits of your computer's usefulness, just as the specific hardware does.

The operating system, in effect, completes your computer. Without it, your computer is a useless hunk, like a car with no fuel. With it, your computer takes on both life and a particular character. Your friends who grew up in big cities have a different character and style, on the whole, than your friends who grew up in the country. With one operating system, your computer will have one style, and with another system, another style. Because this style will permeate much of your interaction with your computer, the character of your operating system affects how you use the computer.

There are other reasons why your operating system is important. Computer programs will not work with any operating system. Programs generally have to be matched to their operating system, and this means that the list of programs available for your computer is heavily influenced by the popularity of the operating system that it uses. Thanks partly to the enormous success of the IBM Personal Computer—which pioneered the DOS operating system—and partly to the strong reputation of Microsoft, DOS has become the dominant operating system for the current 16-bit generation of computers. In many ways it does not matter to us if our operating system is better or worse than some other system; what does matter deeply is how popular it is—that is, how many programs are available for it, and how many different computers use it. The popularity of our operating system mostly determines how good a choice of program tools we have available to us. Thank heavens that we have, in DOS, a runaway popularity winner.

There is yet another reason why our operating system is important to us—the future. It is possible for an operating system to be open to the expected future of computing, and it is possible for an operating system to cut itself off from the expected future. Again, fortunately for us, DOS has a well-planned and orchestrated future ahead of it, based upon a compatible family of operating systems.

When—not if, but when—you change from one personal computer to a newer one, you do not want to have to discard all of the computer skills and experience that you have acquired. Here again, DOS is a plus for us, because by being the dominant operating system in its part of the computer world, we are ensured that it is very likely that our future computers will use either DOS or a big brother to DOS; thus salvaging the usefulness of our skills and probably our programs as well.

2.4 Two Ways of Using a Computer— Interactive and Batch

Before we finish this chapter on computer fundamentals, you should learn about a subject that will become increasingly important to you as your use of a personal computer widens—the two basic ways of using a computer.

When you first start using your computer, you will probably be giving it your full attention. You will be working with the computer interactively, which means that you do something (type something at the keyboard), and then the computer does something (shows a result on the screen), and you type something else, and so on, and so on. This is interactive computing, one of the two fundamental modes that computers can operate in. This interactive mode may seem so natural to you, that you may wonder why you might ever want the computer to work in any other way.

But, the simple fact is that when you are working with the computer interactively, the computer is keeping you busy just as much as you are keeping it busy. This isn't always ideal.

When you need some computer help with your work, it is natural to have an interactive computer. But there are some things that we want the computer to do, that do not require our attention. This is when the computer does its work more or less on its own, unattended by us, and, thankfully not needing our attention. This style of computer operation is called—for historical reasons—batch mode.

So your computer can be working either in interactive mode or batch mode. There isn't a strict division between the two—it's just a matter of degree of how much attention your computer requires when it is doing some work.

There is a very good reason why we are pointing out to you that computers can, under the right circumstances, work on their own unattended.

You may begin using your computer only occasionally, but it is inevitable that as time goes by, you will want your computer to do more and more work for you. Does this have to take up more and more of your own time? Not if you are aware of the possibilities of the computer's unattended batch processing capability.

As an example, consider an accounting program that I use. One of its operations is quite lengthy. Unfortunately for me, when this program is doing its lengthy operation, it repeatedly asks me if I want it to continue (I always do). The darned thing won't carry on without me. This wastes my time just sitting around telling it to get on with its business. Ugh. If this nasty program had been written with a batch mode in mind, it would be enormously more useful to me.

The moral of this story is twofold. First, you should be aware of the possibilities of unattended batch operation, and second you should be careful in buying, or writing, programs to see that they do not unnecessarily require attention from people. People have better things to do than pay attention to fussy programs.

The secret of successful batch operation lies in two things—programs that don't require unnecessary interaction, and the good use of DOS's batch processing files, which you will find discussed in Chapter 11.

This, then, has been a quick course in the fundamentals of computers, with emphasis on the parts that are most likely to end up being useful to you. Next we'll move on to how you get started with DOS.

3

Getting Started With DOS

Things often seem topsy-turvy when you start some new endeavor. The way it usually works is that you need to know everything at once. What do you learn first? What do you do first? It usually seems that before you can learn one thing, you need to know everything else. We'll grapple with this problem as we learn how to get started with DOS.

3.1 The Best Way to Start

The best way to start using DOS and your computer is not to do it alone. If you can get someone who knows the ropes and isn't impatient, get your friend to lead you by the hand through these basic steps. With the help of someone experienced, you can skip over the rest of this chapter.

The next best way to start is to read on.

3.2 What You Have to Do Once You Know How to Do It

There are some fairly urgent things that you need to do "before you get started." Not really before you get started, but still quite early in the game. You can't—or shouldn't try to —do these early steps, which have to do with safeguarding your DOS system, before you are at least slightly comfortable with your computer.

So that you don't feel lost, here is what we are working towards: first, we're going to gain a little working knowledge of what DOS does when we work with it. Second, we're going to learn to do the most preliminary steps that are needed to get going—getting diskettes ready for use (called formatting), and making copies of our data, so that we don't have to worry about damaging our only copy.

Once we have an idea of what we are doing, we are going to do the most basic diskette operations: formatting, copying, testing, and, of course, using the diskettes.

Before we are ready to get down to work, however, we need to understand some things.

3.3 What You Need to Know First

The very first things you need to know are these, which we'll talk about in this section:

- how DOS settles in at its desk when it begins its working day
- how you tell DOS to do some work
- what are the dangers of starting out
- how the safeguards to these dangers work
- what setting up diskettes is all about

Let's begin with what DOS does when it starts its working day. When your computer "wakes up" it doesn't know very much, since it doesn't have an ordinary program loaded into it. Your computer does have two special programs built into it, so it does know how to do two things—one is how to do a little self-testing, to see that things are in working order, and the other is a program that knows how to start up DOS. This start-up program is usually called a bootstrap loader, since it "pulls DOS up by the bootstraps." This simple start-up program reads the very first part of a diskette, where DOS has left a program that knows how to get DOS all set up.

This bootstrap operation works in three interesting stages. First, there is the tiny program built into your computer. It doesn't know anything about DOS—it just knows how to read the beginning of a diskette and run it as a program. This tiny program built into the computer doesn't know, or care, if it is starting DOS or some other operating system. It just reads the beginning of a diskette, where DOS's own starting routine is.

The second part of this start-up routine, which is part of DOS, is just smart enough to get the rest of DOS going; it reads the rest of DOS from the disk, and, voila—DOS is running.

All this, however, goes on behind the scenes. We don't see the details, we just watch the computer working away until DOS is started up. When DOS is ready to start, it first asks us to tell it the current date and time. It is a very good idea to faithfully put in the right date and time, because that lets DOS keep track of when our data is created or changed (which can become very important later).

The exact form that DOS asks for the date and time may vary slightly from version to version, but this is typical. DOS displays this on your screen and waits for you to key in the date:

```
Current date is Tue 1-01-1980
Enter new date:
```

You key in the date, using the hyphen (-) or the slash (/) to separate the year, month, and date. After you do this, DOS does the same thing for the time:

```
Current time is 0:00:12.34
Enter new time:
```

Again, you key in the time, using a colon (":") to separate hours, minutes, and seconds. DOS uses a 24-hour clock, which means that if the time is past noon, you enter an hour of 12 or more. For example, 2 P.M. is 14, and so forth so you would type "14:00" at 2 P.M.

It might be getting a little ahead of ourselves, but I ought to mention that your computer can be equipped with hardware that will automatically set the date and time. The AT model of IBM PC comes with this feature, and it can be installed in most PCs; if so, you might find that the time and date are set automatically for you. Also, there is a way to bypass these starting operations, which we'll discuss later. I don't want to get lost in the details of how these things can be made different than what I'm showing you here. I just want to warn you that if your computer is set up with certain hardware or software, the start-up messages could be quite different.

After these preliminaries, DOS announces that it is ready for work, with a few messages that usually give the brand of your computer and the version of DOS. This is a typical example:

```
The IBM Personal Computer DOS
Version 3.10 (C)Copyright IBM Corp., 1981, 1982, 1983, 1984, 1985
```

This is what we call DOS's starting message, and in Chapter 21 we'll show you how you can change it, if you want to.)

There is one thing you should pay attention to, right away, and that is the version number. If you don't already know which version of DOS you are using, look at the version displayed. (Our example shows version 3.10; yours might be 2.00, 2.10, or something else.) It will help, as you read this book, to know which main series your DOS belongs to: the 1-series, the 2, the 3, or the 4. Our example above, version 3.10, is, of course, from the 3-series. Later in the book we'll mention where there are important differences between one series and another, so it will help if you know which you have. If you have

DOS UP AND READY TO GO!

a DOS manual at hand, it will tell you which version it is on the cover or title page.

This is, in simple terms, how DOS begins its working day. Next let's see how we tell DOS to do some work for us. The process works as a simple, and very terse, dialogue between DOS and us. DOS tells us that it is ready for a command, and then we tell DOS what to do. DOS tells us that it is ready for a command by displaying the DOS "prompt," prompting us to put in a command.

The typical prompt looks like this:

```
A>
```

That's a capital letter A followed by a "greater than" symbol. The "A" part of the prompt indicates which disk drive DOS is currently using. It might be a letter of the alphabet other than A, but the effect is the same. (We'll go into what this letter means in the next chapter on elementary commands.)

If we see the DOS prompt, "A>" or "B>" or whatever, then we are talking to DOS, and DOS wants us to tell it what to do—DOS wants a "command," an instruction of what to do next. On the other hand, if we see something else on the display screen, then it isn't DOS waiting for a command, it's some program, asking us for instructions.

What are DOS commands and what can they do? A command, in simple terms, is the name of a program that you want the computer to carry out. That program command might be the name of one of your own programs. Or it might be the name of a program that you have bought—like VisiCalc or WordStar. Or it might be a program that is a part of DOS itself—like the command TIME, which changes the setting on DOS's clock. Finally, it might be the name of a special kind of DOS program called a batch execution file, which we'll cover in Chapter 11. You might say that there are four kinds of commands—our own programs, commercial programs, DOS's own programs, and DOS batch programs. But this is just dividing commands up into four logical categories for us to think about. There is very little basic difference between these four. At heart, they are all just programs that we can get DOS to carry out for us.

In Chapter 4 we'll start looking more closely at what commands are, and we'll find out which commands can be used at any given moment.

How do we get commands to work? We key in the name of the command and press the computer's enter key. DOS takes it from there—figuring out what sort of command it is, finding the program, and making the program work. DOS does all this for us. All we have to do is type in the command name.

So far, we've seen how DOS gets started, and how it takes commands from us. Now, what are the dangers? And how do we protect ourselves from them?

The dangers are few, and they mostly are about losing our data. It's pretty hard to break the computer itself, short of dropping it out the window, or pouring coffee inside it. If you were driving a car, rolling along at a good speed, and then suddenly shifted into reverse, you'd break your car. Driving into a tree would do a lot of damage, too. With a computer, however, you can't break it by "bad driving." You can damage your computer by physical abuse, not by typing the wrong thing at the keyboard.

No, the major danger we face as users of a computer is of losing our only copy of some information. We can lose data in two ways. One is by physically damaging a diskette that stores the data—the equivalent of taking a phonograph record and breaking it. The other is by telling the computer to throw data away—the equivalent of taking a cassette recording of some music and erasing it. There are ways you can reduce the chance that you'll do the computer equivalent of breaking a record or erasing a tape, but the most important safeguard against losing data is simply to have other copies.

That is the simple reason why the first thing to do when you get your computer is to make copies of your DOS diskette, so that you can start working with the copy—with the safe feeling that if you do anything wrong, the original is safe.

There is one more thing to learn before we can begin—we need to know the basics of setting up diskettes. We make copies of our diskette data, including the DOS diskette, onto blank diskettes. But a blank diskette can't be used just like that—it has to be "formatted." What is formatting? It is something like taking a blank piece of paper and ruling lines on it, so that we have guidelines to make our handwriting even. A blank diskette is just that—blank—but our computers need the equivalent of guidelines written onto the diskette, to create a framework for our data. Formatting a diskette creates this framework, the guidelines for writing on our diskettes. With a formatted diskette, we can copy our data onto the diskette.

When a disk is formatted, it can include a copy of DOS or not. That may seem odd, but that is the way that it is. (We'll get a clearer idea of why in Chapter 9 when we learn more about diskettes.) Why would we want or not want a copy of DOS on our diskettes? If we format our diskettes with DOS, then we can start our computer system using these diskettes. That can be very handy. Any diskette that you have put DOS onto can be used to start your system, so you don't have to look for a special start-up diskette; any disk with DOS on it will do. On the other hand, having a copy of DOS on a diskette takes up some space on the diskette, so that there is less room for our own data.

When we get deeper into the subject, we'll learn how to decide when it's a good idea to put DOS onto a diskette, and when it's better not to. We'll see more about that in Chapter 5, on elementary commands, and in Chapter 9, on diskettes, including the advantages and disadvantages of a shortcut called DISKCOPY.

For now, we'll follow the simplest and safest rule—we'll put DOS on all of our diskettes.

With that background out of the way, let's proceed to safeguard and play with our DOS.

3.4 The First Things to Do

Now we're ready to start up DOS for the first time, make safekeeping copies of your DOS, and start playing around.

DOS IS SAFE WHILE A COPY DRAWS THE FIRE...

To begin, you'll need four things. The first, naturally, is your computer. The second is the computer's introductory Guide to Operations to check to see how each operation is done for your particular computer. The third is the DOS diskette that came with your computer's DOS manual. The fourth is a few blank diskettes.

With these parts ready, place the DOS diskette in your computer's first disk drive opening, close the hatch, and then turn your computer on. For most computers, it will take a short while for the computer to warm up and then to test itself. When that is done, the computer will begin reading the DOS diskette; and DOS will start, as we described in the last section, by asking you for the date and the time, like this:

```
Current date is Tue 1-01-1980
Enter new date: XX/XX/XXXX   (we type in where the X's and /'s are)


Current time is 0:00:12.34
Enter new time: XX:XX        (here, too, we type where the colon and X's are)


The IBM Personal Computer DOS
Version X.YY (C)Copyright IBM Corp., 1981, 1982, 1983, 1984, 1985
```

When that is done, DOS is ready for us to start work, and DOS will give us the command prompt, which will be

A>

The next thing we want to do is to format some diskettes, so they are ready for use. Formatting diskettes is a very basic and everyday operation, so we might as well get some practice at it.

If you have read any of your computer's Guide to Operations manual, you've probably seen the discussion of what you do if you have one or two diskette drives. DOS and your computer need to have two diskette drives to work with, so that we can do things like copy data from the diskette in one drive to another diskette in the other drive. Your computer probably has two diskette drives. But what if it has only one? DOS solves this problem by pretending that the computer has two anyway. It pretends that there are two drives by first treating the one disk drive as the first drive (known as the "A" drive), and then treating the same drive as if it were the second drive (known as the "B" drive). If you actually have two disk drives, then the two just merrily work away. If not, every time that DOS switches from treating the one real drive as A or B to treating it as the other, DOS stops and tells you to change the diskette from the one that is supposed to be in the A drive to the diskette that is supposed to be in the B drive (or vice versa). So, with only one disk drive, DOS switches the use of it back and forth between the two drives that it needs, A and B.

From now on, we'll always refer to your computer's diskette drives as A drive (the first one) and B drive (the second one). If you only have one real drive, DOS will take care of maintaining a pretense that there are two drives, as long as you cooperate by switching the diskettes in and out of the one drive. (When this happens, you'll quickly learn why you should have two drives.)

Now we are ready to format some diskettes. First, we have to give DOS the command to format them. The command looks like this (we'll explain the parts of it in a moment):

FORMAT   B: /S

There are three parts to this command. First, there is the command itself, "FORMAT". Then there are two parameters, which tell FORMAT just how to operate. The first parameter, "B:", tells the FORMAT command that the diskette to be formatted is in the B drive. The second parameter, "/S", tells the FORMAT command that we want it to place a copy of DOS onto the formatted diskette. (As we mentioned before, a diskette can have a copy of DOS on it or not, which means that the disk can or can't be used to start up DOS; we'll see more about this in Chapters 4 and 8.)

With this done, we press the enter key and the FORMAT command begins working. When FORMAT is ready to start formatting our diskette, it will stop and ask us to put our diskette into the B drive, and then press a key (it may tell us to press any key, or it may tell us to press the "enter" key in particular—that's one of the minor differences among different versions of DOS).

After we do that, the FORMAT command program will work away, formatting the diskette. When it is done, it will give a little report on its work. The exact nature of the report depends on your computer and the kind of diskettes that it uses, but this is typical:

```
Formatting...Format complete
System transferred

  362496 bytes total disk space
   40960 bytes used by system
  321536 bytes available on disk


Format another (Y/N)?
```

We should take this opportunity to format several diskettes, so answer "Y" to the question about formatting another. After that, FORMAT will remind you to put a new diskette into the B drive, and also tell you to press "enter" or to press any key.

In addition to the messages you see here, you may get another message from the FORMAT operation, something like this:

```
1024 bytes in bad sectors
```

What is that all about? Is it anything to worry about?

Disks sometimes have flaws in them, and the flaws are detected in the formatting process. DOS safely keeps the flawed parts of the disk from being used by marking them as "bad sectors." That's what we see reported in this message. It's best, of course, if our disks don't have any flaws, or bad sectors, on them; but for most purposes, though, you don't have to worry about this "bad sector" message. It's just DOS protecting us from problems.

Keep doing this formatting until you have a small working supply of diskettes. They will come in very handy shortly. After you have enough, maybe four or five, answer "N" so that the FORMAT command will come to an end.

At this point we now have several diskettes, each formatted, and each with a copy of DOS. Having a copy of DOS means that the system can be started from that diskette; but it does not mean that all the parts and tools of DOS are copied onto the diskette—just the most fundamental parts. Our next step is to copy everything from our original DOS diskette onto one of these new diskettes. This will become our main working copy of DOS, so that we can put the original copy of DOS away for safekeeping.

So far we have experimented with one single DOS command: FORMAT. Now, we'll get a chance to try another one, the COPY command. COPY is a command that does several different and interesting things for us, as we'll see in Chapter 5. In fact, many of the commands that make up DOS have more than one use. For now, the feature of the COPY command that we will use is its most simple and straightforward: copying data from one diskette to another.

The COPY command, as we use it to copy everything that is on the diskette in drive A to the diskette in drive B, is done like this:

```
COPY    A:*.*    B:
```

While we'll put off understanding the details until the next chapter, we can easily see the main parts of what is going on; and it's not much different from what we saw with the FORMAT command. There are three parts here: the command name (COPY) and two parameters separated by spaces. In this case, the first parameter indicates what to copy from. It says, with the "A:" part copy from drive A, while the "*.*" part is a way of saying copy everything that's on that diskette. The second parameter, "B:", says to copy to drive B. While the first parameter had a "*.*" part to indicate that everything was being copied, the second parameter doesn't have any such specification. Why? Because it's implied that whatever is found on A should be copied as is to drive B. We'll dig deeper into how these things work in Chapter 4.

If we type this command in and press the enter key, then DOS's COPY command will dutifully copy everything it finds on the diskette in drive A to the diskette in drive B.

Do exactly this, and then you will have in drive B a diskette with a copy of everything that was on the diskette in drive A. We can use this new diskette as our working copy of DOS. We can now put the original copy of DOS away without having to worry about doing it any harm.

This finishes a short lesson on how to get started in DOS. It has done several things for us. For one thing, it "got our feet wet." Without having to understand too much about DOS, we've been able to put it to work a little and get a useful result out of it—namely we've got some formatted diskettes to work with, and we have a copy of the DOS diskette to use. What we're ready for now is how to understand the principles behind what we've done and more about the commands of DOS, ordinary and advanced. This will occupy us for the next three chapters.

4

Fundamentals of DOS Commands

Before we can move on to start really looking at the DOS commands, we have to learn the fundamentals of how they are laid out and used. In this chapter we'll pause to master the basics of DOS commands.

4.1 Keeping Track of Drives

Our real goal in this entire book is to get you comfortable with DOS—to speed you, as quickly as possible, toward thinking of DOS as an old friend, an old tool, which you use with ease and hardly a second thought. One of the things that will help you most in getting comfortable with DOS is to understand how important disk drives are to DOS.

DOS is, after all, a Disk Operating System; and disks are very much at the core of the way DOS operates and the way it organizes itself. If we want to understand DOS, we need to understand the way that DOS thinks about disks.

One of the first things we need to realize about how DOS works, is to realize that DOS is focused more on the disk drive than on the diskette that is in the drive. Your computer probably has one or two diskette drives in it and maybe a large-capacity hard disk system. DOS needs a consistent and uniform way of keeping track of this disk gear, and it does this by giving a letter code to each of the drives. The first drive is referred to as A, the second as B, and so forth. Your computer likely has at least two drives; but if it doesn't, as we mentioned in the last chapter, DOS will turn your one drive into a let's-pretend pair of drives, A and B. Many DOS command operations need two disk drives, and, when there is only one drive, it is easier and more consistent for DOS to fake having a second drive, a B drive, than to try doing everything with only an A drive.

By the way, if your computer has a large-capacity hard disk system, it will probably be known as drive letter C, while the letters A and B will stand for two floppy diskette drives (or one diskette drive masquerading as two, as we mentioned.) The XT model of IBM Personal Computer, and most AT models, have these large-capacity, non-removable hard disks (IBM calls them "fixed disks", because, unlike floppy diskettes, you can't take them in and out). If you have a hard disk, then most of the work that you do with the computer will be centered around drive letter C, which identifies the hard disk. But when you do operations that involve floppy diskettes, however, you'll be using letters A and B.

If we have a diskette that we want to work with, and we put that diskette in our A drive, then we'd tell DOS to look to the A drive to find what is on that diskette. We'd get the same result if we put the same diskette in the B drive and told DOS to look there. The idea is simple—DOS doesn't know what we're doing with diskettes, which we might be switching around behind its back. But DOS does know what's what with the disk drives, so that is where DOS's focus is.

This means that whenever we do anything with data or programs on a disk, we have to let DOS know which drive we want it to look to. This is done by giving the drive letter, followed by a colon, like this:

    A:

That told DOS to work with drive A; we'd do the same for drive B or C, like this:

    B:

    C:

(By the way, DOS will happily take either an upper- or lowercase letter and treat them the same. In our examples, we'll always show things in uppercase, but you can type them in either way at your convenience.)

When any of your computer manuals refer to the drive specification, what you see above is what they are referring to: the drive letter followed by a colon. So "A:" or "B:" is a drive specification.

Since much of what we do with the computer involves disk data, it could be a real nuisance to have to keep typing in the drive specification, A: or B: or whatever, all the time. DOS simplifies the process by having a default drive. DOS keeps track of the current default drive; and any time we refer to a disk, or one of our programs refers to a disk, without giving a drive specification, then DOS assumes we

intend to use the default drive. This idea can be enriched even further with a concept called the default directory; we'll cover that topic in the last section of Chapter 8.

We've already mentioned that DOS prompts us for commands with something like this:

A>

You're probably ready to guess that the "A" in this prompt tells us that A is the current default drive. If the default drive were changed to B, then DOS's prompt would be

B>

This is really quite clever if you think about it. If the default drive can be changed, it would be very helpful for DOS to give us reminders of where the default is now. But it would be a nuisance to have DOS repeatedly putting a message on the screen like "The default drive is now X." The DOS command prompt is a compact, handy, and unobtrusive way for DOS to remind us of the default drive.

What if you want to change the default drive? (We'll postpone talking about why you would want to change it; that makes sense only after you have a feel for how you use DOS.) There is a very simple way to change the default drive: just type in a drive specification as a command by itself. DOS takes that to be a command to change the default drive, and away we go. Here is a dummy example:

A>   (DOS prompts us, saying the default drive is A)

   B: (we enter a B drive spec, with no command)

B>   (DOS has now changed the default drive)

By the way, if your computer has a large capacity hard disk in it (what IBM calls a fixed disk), then that's probably the disk you'll be working with the most. Usually a fixed hard disk is known as drive C. If we have a hard disk, then we probably want it to be our default drive; we make C the default drive with a command like this:

   C:

We can switch back to the A drive, and have it be our default, in the obvious way, like this:

   A:

Whenever we are working with disks, we have a free choice of using the default drive or specifying the drive. We can specify the drive even if it is already the default drive—there is no harm in that. If for any reason we want to be very specific about things, we can indicate the drive we want to use, and it will work just fine, default or not.

Most of the time, though, having a default drive is a real convenience, because it cuts down on the keystrokes we have to type in.

4.2 Where Commands Come From

The next thing that we need to know about commands in general is where they come from. All commands that we ask DOS to carry out are, in one way or another, programs. The question is, then, what kind of programs are they, and where are the programs located.

This brings us to a topic that DOS calls internal and external commands.

There is a problem inherent in DOS having a nice, large number of services, or commands, available for us to use. On the one hand, we would like to have these command services on tap, instantly, at all times. But to do this, the programs that provide these services would have to be resident in memory, our working desk top, which means that they would be taking up some of our working memory space all the time, both when we were using them and when we were not. So, on the other hand, we would like to have as little as possible of our memory, our working desk top, taken up by these command programs.

This is an obvious conflict, and to resolve it DOS has worked out a compromise. A handful of the command programs that are the smallest and most useful are made a resident part of DOS, which means that they are in memory all the time once DOS has been read off the disk and started up. These are called the internal commands since they are internal to DOS. All of the other command programs are called external, and they are kept in the disk "filing cabinet" until the time comes when they are needed.

The internal commands are built right into DOS, so there is no question that they are a part of DOS. The external commands are also provided with DOS, and they are rightly considered to be a part of DOS as well. But, actually, any program that can be used from the disk can work just like all of the DOS commands. So there is only a fuzzy distinction between the external commands that are DOS commands and all other programs, which are also a form of command. Shortly we'll see a list of the commands that are internal and those that are external.

Depending upon which kind of command we happen to select to use, DOS will either be able to carry it out immediately, or else it will have to look into its disk filing cabinet for the command program. The practical significance of this is that the command's program must be on the disk when DOS goes looking for it. At first this may seem a silly point, since you expect to have your DOS diskette in a disk drive. But soon you'll learn that it isn't that simple. Unless you have a large-capacity hard disk system, you'll soon be using more command programs than will fit onto a single diskette. In fact, all of the parts of your DOS probably take up more than one diskette as it is. What do you do when you have more programs than you can keep on one diskette?

The answer is very simple: you organize your diskettes functionally, combining all the parts that you need to carry out one kind of work, leaving other programs off each diskette. In Chapter 13 we'll give you some advice about doing just that. Right now, the important point is that DOS can only carry out those commands for which it has access to the programs. The internal commands are always on tap, and you can ask for any external command whose program disk is currently loaded.

Of course, all it takes to get access to other commands is a change of diskettes. You take out one diskette, put in another, and you can have a whole new set of commands at your service. But DOS can't do that for you. So, if you ask for a command that isn't internal, and isn't on your current diskettes, then DOS can't perform the command. Instead, DOS will tell you something is wrong by displaying this message:

`Bad command or filename`

At first you might be confused by this message, which is part of the reason why we're discussing it. As you learn more about how external commands are stored on disk, you'll see that a command's name is the same as the name of a file on a disk, which explains the "or filename" part of the above message. The important thing for you to know is that when you see the above message, DOS is telling you that it couldn't find a command program that matched the command name that you entered.

There are two reasons why DOS might not be able to find a command you have entered. One reason, which we've been discussing, is that the command program is on another diskette. The other reason, which you have to be prepared for, is a simpler one: you typed the command name wrong. So, the first thing that you should do when you get the "Bad command" message, is to check what you typed as a command name—it may not be what you intended.

There are several common reasons why DOS might reject a command we give it. The most obvious reason is that we mistyped the command name—typing CIPY instead of COPY, for example. Other common mistakes include not having a space between the command name and any parameters that follow, or putting in a semicolon, ";", when we meant to type a colon, ":". If DOS rejects your commands, check carefully for simple typing mistakes.

4.3 Common Command Notation

There is a standard format for asking DOS to carry out commands, a notation or syntax to the way we are supposed to enter commands. This section will explain the normal way that DOS commands are requested. Unfortunately, there is a little too much variety in the way that you can enter commands, which can lead to some confusion about the best way to express commands. We'll try to clear all that up here.

First, all commands start out in this basic format:

`COMMAND-NAME    PARAMETERS-IF-ANY`

For example, when we set up our DOS diskettes in Chapter 3, we used this COPY command:

`COPY    A:*.*   B:`

The command name was "COPY" and two parameters were needed, the first indicating what to copy from ("A:*.*") and what to copy to ("B:").

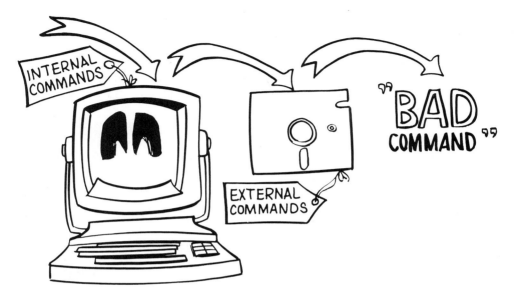

THE SEARCH FOR A COMMAND PROGRAM.

So far, we have the most basic part: a command begins with the name of the command, followed by whatever parameters are needed.

Some kind of punctuation must be used to separate the command name and the parameters. In our examples, we've always used spaces, but DOS allows other things to be used for punctuation—commas, semicolons, and some other symbols.

It is best, for various reasons, to use the space character, the comma, or the semicolon. You'll probably get the best results and have the fewest problems if you always use the blank space character to separate commands and parameters, except for one special circumstance, which we'll discuss next.

While most commands need only one or two parameters, some special command programs, such as compilers for programming languages, need a longer list of parameters, some of which may be left off. For this kind of command, there is a very useful convention: each of the parameters is separated by a comma. If a parameter is left off, then two commas appear in a row. When no more parameters follow (even if there might be more), a semicolon indicates the end of the list. Here is an example showing how this is done:

```
COMMAND  1st,2nd,,4th,,6th;
```

You'll notice that the third and fifth parameters don't appear, but the commas serve to hold their places, so that it is clear that the 4th parameter *is* the 4th parameter.

When you need to specify command parameters this special way, feel free to do so—otherwise, for simplicity, I recommend that you always use spaces to separate a command name from its parameters, and the parameters from each other.

There is one more thing you need to know about how commands and their parameters are written. Some commands divide their parameters into two categories, regular parameters and what are called switches. As a simple way to understand what switches are, here are some guiding rules:

- COMMANDS indicate what is to be done (such as copying data)
- PARAMETERS indicate what the command is to be performed on (e.g., what to copy)
- SWITCHES indicate how it is to be done (e.g., should the copy be checked for correctness?)

To make it easier to separate parameters (what to act on) from switches (how to carry out the action), a special notation is used. The switch is preceded by a special character.

The standard switch identifier is a slash (/), and that's what all the programs that make up DOS itself use. Most other programs do too; just to make life more complicated, though, let me warn you that some programs identify their switches with a hyphen (-) instead. In this book, for consistency, we show the slash format, which is the normal DOS form.

You saw one example of a switch in the last chapter—we used one ("/S") when we used the FORMAT command. Usually switches are very short and simple, typically just a single letter. The idea of a switch is that it is an instruction to do or not do some variation on the basic operation. For example, the "/S" switch in the FORMAT command tells it to include a copy of the DOS on the formatted diskette. Another example: the COPY command has a "/V" switch, which tells it to Verify the copy, checking to see that it is right.

4.4 Files, File Names, and Other Wild Stuff

Most DOS commands do some operation either on an entire disk or on files that are stored in a disk. You will see that most parameters are either just a disk specification (telling the command which disk to do its operation on) or the names of some files.

We'll put off going over all the details of file names until we cover disks in more detail in Chapter 9. For now, we still need to know a little about them, because we're going to be seeing them a lot as we go over the DOS commands in the next two chapters. Here is a quick summary, which will do for now, and also give us a head start when we come to Chapter 9.

Data on a disk is organized into files. To identify the files, each one has a filename. Among all the files on one disk, the filename must be unique so that files don't get confused. The name of a file actually has two parts called the filename proper and the filename extension, or the extension to the filename.

The filename is at least one character, and it can be as long as eight characters but no longer. Filenames can be made up of letters of the alphabet, digits, and some punctuation characters (wait until Chapter 9 for details). You can't have a space character as part of a filename or any of the other punctuation characters that are used to punctuate a command and its parameters. We can use upper- or lowercase letters in filenames, but DOS treats them as if they were all uppercase. Here are some sample filenames:

`FILENAME`

`12`

`A`

`ABC123`

The extension to the filename is a short appendage added on after the filename. The two are separated by a period so that a filename and extension look like this:

`FILENAME.EXT`

The extension is three characters at most, and it's an optional part—a file must have a filename part, but it doesn't have to have an extension part. If there is no extension part, then we drop the period that is used to separate the two parts.

Here are some more examples of file names, with and without extensions, to give you more of an idea of what they can look like:

`FILENAME.EXT` (this is as big as they can get)

`A` (this is the minimum file name)

`12345678` (numbers are OK)

`NEW-DATA`   (hyphens are OK)

`NEW_DATA`   (underscores are OK too)

`ADDRESS.LST`   (an example of how a file name can indicate contents)

`JULY.83`   (another informative file name)

The intended purpose of an extension is to indicate the category that the filename falls into. It is an informal—not a mandatory—way to indicate what type of file a file is. In Chapter 9 we'll look at some of the more common categories.

It is a little confusing to have a file's complete name be called a file name, and part of that name be called a filename, (with no space), but that is the terminology that is used with DOS, so we have to live with it. Whenever you run across either term, slow down and be careful to see what is being referred to.

There is a way to refer to more than one file at a time—through a mechanism known as wild cards, or (more officially) "global filename characters."

Wild cards are a way of partly specifying a file name so that several files may match the specification. For example, in the last chapter we did a COPY command with a file specification of "*.*"—which meant any filename and any filename extension. If we had written it as "*.COM" that would mean any filename, but only the extension "COM".

There is a very useful way that wild cards can be used in a file specification, using two wild card symbols: the asterisk (*), which we've seen, and the question mark (?), which we haven't seen yet. More will be revealed in Chapter 9. For now, understand that we can use "*.*" as a way of saying any filename with any extension—or, in other words, all the files on a disk.

With this accomplished, we are ready to move on to look at some of the commands that DOS provides for us.

5

An Overview of Elementary Commands

In this chapter we'll begin going over the commands that DOS gives us to work with and control our computers. Here we'll look at the commands that are easiest to understand and the ones that are the most commonly used. We'll reserve the more complicated commands for the next chapter.

To make it easier to understand, we'll cover them grouped by topic rather than alphabetical order. What we won't do here is to cover the precise details of how the commands work—that's a subject that belongs to your computer's manuals, particularly since some of these commands vary a little from version to version. What we will do here is to make sense of these commands for you, and give you tips and handy hints about how to get the most from these commands (and how to avoid problems with them, as well). Try them as we go along.

5.1 The Time Commands—DATE and TIME

DOS keeps track of the date and the time of day, which is very handy. It is handy for all sorts of reasons, and one of the best reasons is that every time you create, or change, some information on a disk, the disk file is marked with the current date and time. This can be extremely valuable to you for answering questions like, "which of these files did I work on last week?" or, "which of these diskettes has the latest changes to my report?"

I have occasionally found it a lifesaver to know that all of my files have an accurate date and time stamp on them, and there is hardly a day when I don't find it at least useful to see time stamps on my files. (Later in this chapter we'll learn how you see these time stamps when we cover the DIR command.)

To make it possible for us to enter or change the date and time, DOS has two special commands called, naturally, DATE and TIME. These commands work independently so that you can enter or change either one without affecting the other. By the way, when DOS starts up, it automatically invokes both DATE and TIME as part of its start-up procedures. We saw this in action in Chapter 3 when we described how DOS begins operation.

Both DATE and TIME work the same way, and both can be used two ways. The first way, which we might call interactive, happens when we just enter the command name, like this:

`DATE`

DOS then responds by telling us what its current record of the date (or time) is, and asks us for a new date (or time), like this:

`Current date is Tue 01-01-1980`

`Enter new date:`

At that point, we can either enter a new date (time), or just press enter to leave the date (time) unchanged.

The other way to use the DATE and TIME commands is more direct. If we key in the command name, followed by the date or time, and press enter, then DOS will change the date or time without displaying or requesting anything else. Here is an example of how we would use DATE and TIME this way:

`DATE  7-4-1984`

`TIME  14:15`

Here are some tips and notes on the DATE and TIME commands:

- When we enter the date it's punctuated with either hyphens (-) or slashes (/); it's our choice. The time is punctuated with colons (:).
- You can leave leading zeros off the figures, so January can be entered as "1", rather than "01".
- When entering the date, we can leave off the century, the "19" in "1985".
- When entering the time, we can leave off the seconds, or both minutes and seconds, if we want.
- There isn't any normal way to get DOS to display the current date or time without having it wait for us to enter a new value (but there is a trick that can be used with the 2-series and later versions of DOS).

- As long as it is running, DOS keeps track of when midnight passes and, under normal circumstances, automatically changes the date.
- DOS is smart enough to keep track of leap years.

For example, we don't put "TUE" in the date. It calculates it for us.

The DATE and TIME commands are internal (except in the obsolete 1.00 version of DOS) so that you can use them at any time, regardless of what you have on your disks.

Some computer systems have special hardware functions to keep track of the date and time even when the computer is turned off. It's standard equipment on the IBM PC AT model, and it can be installed in other PCs in what's called a clock-calendar option. These clock-calendars come with many of the most popular multi-function expansion boards for PCs. This hardware, combined with the right supporting programs, can save you the trouble of entering the date and time when you start up DOS. However, you still have the option of using the DATE and TIME commands to change DOS's record of the date and time.

DOS SETS ITS WATCH AND CHECKS ITS CALENDAR.

5.2 Checking Out Your Disks—DIR, CHKDSK, and VOL

There are three commands designed to let you find out what's on your disks—DIR, CHKDSK, and VOL.

DIR is the directory listing command. It is designed to tell you the list of commands on a disk. There are several ways that DIR can be used. The most common way is to just put in the command DIR with a drive specification (or, implied, the default drive) like this:

```
DIR A:
```

This will ask DIR to list all of the files on a disk. The list will include the filename, the filename extension, the size of the file in characters or bytes, and the date and time the file was created or last changed. You will recall that we mentioned in the preceding section, in discussing the DATE and TIME commands, that files were marked with time stamps like this. The DIR command is our way to see what the time stamp is as well as each file's size.

Here is an example of what the DIR command will show us:

```
Directory of  A:
DEMO     BAT     1646   12-07-84    3:00p
README   BAT     3664   12-07-84    3:00P
LONG     BAT      941   12-07-84    3:00P
SHORT    BAT      936   12-07-84    3:00P
         4 File(s)       31232 bytes free
```

If you don't want to see a list of all of the files, but only the information on one, you can enter that file's name, and DIR will report on only it like this:

```
DIR THISFILE.EXT
```

Similarly, if you use the wild cards mentioned in the last chapter (and covered more in Chapter 9), then you can get information on just some files. For example, this command would get directory information on all files that have an extension of "BAT":

```
DIR *.BAT
```

One of the incidental things that DIR reports is the amount of space left free on a disk. You may want to use the DIR command not to see a directory listing but simply to find out how much space is available for use on a disk.

A disk can have "hidden" files on it; usually if it does, they are just secret parts of the DOS operating system (we'll see more about that in the next section and in Chapter 9). The DIR command acts as though hidden files were not there at all (but CHKDSK, which we're coming to, tells us about them).

There is one peculiarity of the DIR command that you need to know about. Most DOS commands work with wild card file specifications, like "*.*", which means "all files with any names." DIR works with wild cards as well, but it has one difference—DIR will assume a wild card where you didn't put one. So, if you enter the command

    DIR

it will be treated just as if you had entered

    DIR   *.*

and if you put in a filename, with no extension, such as

    DIR   FILENAME

it will be treated as if you put in a wild card for the extension, such as

    DIR   FILENAME.*

This special feature of DIR is rather handy, but it has one real drawback—it is inconsistent with the rest of DOS. Consistency is important in anything as complex as DOS, because it reduces the number of rules that you have to learn, and it increases your confidence that DOS will do what you think you are asking it to do. In this case, don't be worried if you find that DIR is acting a little different than all the other DOS commands. It isn't you misunderstanding things, it's just DIR doing things its own way.

There are two switches you can use with the DIR command; pause after the screen fills ("/P"), or list the files in five columns across the width of the display screen ("/W"). Both switches are intended to help you see the list of files better. Try them to see how the directory listings look.

While the DIR command shows us a list of files on a disk, the CHKDSK, or check disk, command is intended to give us a status report on our disks. CHKDSK does two main things—first it checks the disk over, to see how much space there is, how much is in use, and if there is any discrepancy in the space usage. (It is rare for there to be any discrepancy, so you may never encounter one. How and why things can go wrong with the space allocation is a very interesting subject, but one that is too technical for this book.) Then it reports to us the total space, the space in use, the number of files, and incidentally if there are any hidden files.

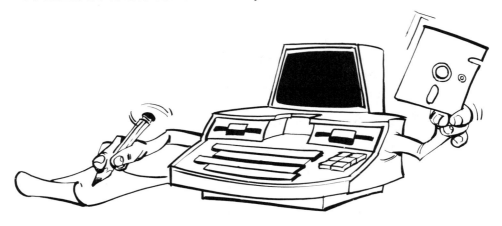

DIR LISTS THE FILES ON A DISKETTE.

CHKDSK is also prepared to repair any logical damage in the use of space. If any space has been "lost"—which is one of the possible discrepancies in the space usage—CHKDSK can recover it and also report or repair other kinds of mix-ups in the space (which is rare). In the 1-series of DOS, CHKDSK did this repair work automatically; but that can be a little dangerous. Starting with the 2-series of DOS, CHKDSK will repair the disk only if you give it permission with the "fix" switch, "/F".

This check, report, and repair operation is a very valuable one, and so it is a very good idea to routinely do a CHKDSK on all of your disks occasionally. When you set up batch files, which we'll cover in Chapter 11, it would be good to include CHKDSK in many of your batch file operations.

Like DIR, CHKDSK reports on the amount of space available on your disks, and does something else nice that is completely unrelated to its check-your-disk function: it reports on the amount of memory available in your system. Just as you might use DIR to find out about available space on disk, you can use CHKDSK to see how much memory your computer has.

We haven't had an opportunity to mention it yet, but your disks can have identifying "labels" stored on them that give them names. These volume ID labels help you keep track of the many diskettes that you'll be using (and they are even handy with hard disk systems too). In the next section we'll see how to put labels onto disks. For now I want to tell you that both the DIR and the CHKDSK commands will report a disk's volume label, if there is one.

If you just want to display the ID label on a disk volume, however, you don't need to go through the often time-consuming DIR or

CHKDSK operation. There is a special command that does nothing but report to you the volume label on a disk. It's the VOL command, and you use it like this:

```
VOL A:
```

The report it gives you is like this:

```
Volume in drive A is XXXXXXXXXX
```

DIR and VOL are internal commands, so you can use them at any time. CHKDSK is an external command and must be available on your disks to be used. VOL isn't available in 1-series versions of DOS, but DIR and CHKDSK are universal.

5.3 The Diskette Preparation Commands— FORMAT, SYS, DISKCOPY, and LABEL

Since DOS relies so heavily on the use of diskettes, naturally there are commands to prepare diskettes for use. We took a short look at one of them, FORMAT, in Chapter 3. Now we'll look closer at all four set-up commands, FORMAT, SYS, DISKCOPY, and LABEL.

Each of these four commands is external, which means that we can only use them when we have a disk in the drive that contains the command programs for these commands. LABEL isn't available with series 1 and 2 of DOS, but it is a part of all later versions.

The FORMAT command is used to do the most basic preparation of a disk for use. It is the equivalent of drawing writing guidelines on a blank sheet of paper, to make it possible to later write evenly on the paper.

FORMAT actually does two important things with a diskette—it draws the electronic "guidelines" that make it possible for DOS to work with the diskette, and it also checks for any defects in the diskette. Because diskettes are so vulnerable, they may have damaged patches on them. But a diskette with a bad patch can still be used— the FORMAT command knows how to recognize these bad patches and puts a safety fence around them. When FORMAT finds bad patches, it reports them to you, indicating their size as well as the size of the usable part of the diskette. With this done, the rest of the diskette is ready to use.

Here's an example of how the FORMAT command tells us about bad patches on a disk:

```
160256 bytes total disk space
  8192 bytes in bad sectors
152064 bytes available on disk
```

You'll notice that the second line indicates how much space was bad, while the first and third lines tell us the total possible space and the amount of space that is good and usable.

Whether or not you want to use a diskette with a bad patch is up to you. Obviously a bad patch takes up part of the space on a diskette, and makes you wonder about the quality of the rest of the diskette. But usually bad patches are small and nothing goes wrong with the rest of the diskette. If you need every bit of space that a diskette has to offer, or if you are unusually worried about risks to your data, then put aside any diskette that has bad patches when it is formatted. Normally, though, I would say that there is no problem with using a diskette with bad patches that are a small proportion of the diskette.

Usually, diskettes format without any bad patches. If you encounter them a lot, it is a sign of one of two things—either you have a bad batch of diskettes, or the recording heads on your disk drives are dirty and should be cleaned. If you suspect that the problem is dirty heads, see your computer's manuals for cleaning instructions.

When you format a diskette, you have the option of putting the DOS operating system on the diskette. The advantage of including DOS on many of your diskettes is that you can then start your system using any of those diskettes—you don't have to use just one special start-up diskette. This can be a real convenience. The disadvantage is that having DOS on a diskette takes up some of the diskette's usable space. I would recommend, for starters, that you include DOS on every diskette until you learn from your own experience which ones you do and don't want DOS stored on. At first, it is better to have DOS on all of your disks. Later you can be more discriminating—for example, putting DOS on all of your program diskettes but leaving it off your data diskettes. If you have formatted a diskette without a copy of DOS, then you cannot later add DOS to the diskette except by reformatting it (which would wipe out any data you had placed on the diskette). In general, it is better to include DOS in your formatting.

The System switch, "/S", is used to tell FORMAT to include a copy of DOS on the diskette.

When the FORMAT command sets up a diskette as a system diskette, it places three files on the diskette. Two of these files are hidden, which means that you can't ordinarily see them except through a CHKDSK command (discussed above) which reports on the number of hidden files on a diskette. The third file is not hidden—it can be

FORMAT MARKS OFF THE DAMAGED SECTION.

seen like any other file, and it is named COMMAND.COM. We'll see more about the two hidden files and the COMMAND.COM file in a moment.

Unless you are using a 1-series version of DOS, you can put a logical volume label on your diskettes when you format them. This label allows DOS to report to you what the name of the disk is whenever DOS refers to it. The label can be up to 11 characters long. Putting a label on each disk is a very good idea and I highly recommend it. The "/V" switch is used to tell **FORMAT** that you want a volume label on the disk. If you want to change labels later, you can do it with the LABEL command, as we'll see in a moment.

Our PCs work with more than one diskette format—for example, single- or double-sided diskettes. The **FORMAT** command is prepared to create disks in any of several formats. Normally you should let DOS decide which format to use, unless you know that you need a special format that is used by another computer. New computers, and later versions of DOS, can create and use diskette formats that can't be read by some earlier versions.

The switches in the format command allow you to control which type of formatting is done. There are lots of combinations of formatting, and we'd get lost if we tried to explain them all. There are only three that matter, for most practical purposes, and I'll show you the format switches used to create each one.

First—and most important for us—is formatting with a copy of the DOS operating system, which we've already discussed. You create this kind of disk by using the "/S" switch, like this:

```
FORMAT /S
```

Second, there is the format that will give us the greatest possible storage space. This is a disk formatted to the highest capacity that our diskette drives can manage, and without a copy of DOS taking up any room. We create that kind of disk by leaving off all switches, like this:

```
FORMAT
```

Third, and last, there is the "lowest common denominator" diskette. This is the diskette format that can be read by any model of PC, using any version of DOS, even the oldest PCs and the very first 1.00 DOS. This is the universal diskette format for IBM PCs. When we use it, we sacrifice storage capacity for universal use. Most software is distributed in this format, even though few PCs need this lowest common denominator. Technically this format is called single-sided eight-sector format, and you may occasionally hear those terms used. We create this kind of diskette by using the switches "/1" (for single-sided) and "/8" (for eight-sector), like this:

```
FORMAT /1 /8
```

WARNING: FORMAT is one of the most dangerous of all the commands in DOS because it can wipe out an entire diskette's worth of data at one go. If you format a diskette that has some valuable data on it, it is thoroughly gone, and nothing will bring it back. So be very careful when you format diskettes—check for sure that the diskette doesn't have something important on it before you wipe it off the face of the disk with FORMAT. On the other hand, if you have to destroy some confidential data and need to be sure that it can't be reconstructed, FORMAT is the right tool to use.

Since the FORMAT command is so dangerous, you should know how to make things safer. More than one disk has been ruined trying every command that's available to see what happens. If you have children or friends who know just enough about your computer to try the commands on it, they might unintentionally activate the FORMAT command and wipe out your disks. One way to protect yourself against this is to leave the FORMAT command off of your disks. Another safeguard is to prevent the command from being used by renaming the command file to have a filename extension other than COM. We'll be learning more about renaming files and about filename extensions in the pages to come, but for now, here is a quick safety technique. If you enter the command

```
REN  FORMAT.COM  FORMAT.XXX
```

it will prevent the FORMAT command from being used (but it will still be around, when you need it). This command

```
REN  FORMAT.XXX  FORMAT.COM
```

will switch the command back into a usable form.

If you want to protect yourself against accidental FORMATs, either eliminate the FORMAT command altogether, or keep it in the safely unusable form with the trick shown above. You'll understand more of what this is about later in the book.

There are times when you may want to transfer a copy of the DOS operating system to a diskette that is already formatted to hold it. The SYS command is intended to solve this problem. There are two reasons why you might need the SYS command. One is if you buy a program diskette that needs to have a copy of DOS on it. This is commonly done with copy-protected programs (which we'll talk more about in Chapters 15, 18, and 19). Disks like that usually have space provided for DOS, but don't actually have DOS on the disk. You have to transfer DOS to them. The second reason why you might need to transfer DOS is when you get a new version of DOS. Like all other good programs, DOS is occasionally updated and upgraded, creating all the versions we've been mentioning. When you have a new version of DOS, you need to transfer the new DOS to your old DOS diskettes.

The SYS command is designed to transfer the two hidden files that are part of DOS from one diskette to another. SYS, however, does not transfer the third file that is part of DOS, the non-hidden file COMMAND.COM. So a complete transfer of the DOS operating system onto a diskette requires that you do two things—a SYS command to transfer the two hidden files and a COPY command to copy the COMMAND.COM file. Whenever you read instructions about transferring DOS to a diskette, the instructions should mention both—SYS and COPY COMMAND.COM. (See more about the COPY command below.)

There is another way to set up a diskette for use besides the FORMAT command, and that is the DISKCOPY command.

DISKCOPY is a command that reads all the formatting and data from one diskette and copies it to another diskette. DISKCOPY is a quick and efficient way to make copies of diskettes. It is so quick and efficient in fact that you will find its use recommended to you over and over again. There are some important problems with DISK-COPY, so I recommend that you be very careful about using it. The preferred way to copy disk data is with the COPY command, which we'll come to later.

The major disadvantage of using DISKCOPY is that it does not allow for bad areas on your diskettes. If either the diskette you are copying from or the one you are copying to have unusable bad areas on them, the sort of bad areas which we mentioned that FORMAT detects, then DISKCOPY will not work properly. On the other hand, the COPY command, the preferred way to copy data, works nicely with bad patches on the diskettes.

Another advantage to COPY over DISKCOPY is that COPY can improve the use of space on a diskette, while DISKCOPY can't. (Again, we'll discuss this improvement of storage space when we cover COPY). Finally, DISKCOPY will wipe out anything that is on the target diskette, while COPY will merge new files with old to put more information on a diskette.

So there are many reasons not to use DISKCOPY, but there are still some good reasons to use it. For one thing, DISKCOPY is faster than COPY if the diskette is full of data. On the other hand, if there is only a little data on a diskette, COPY could be faster because it would copy only the data, while DISKCOPY would also faithfully copy all the unused diskette space.

Another reason for using DISKCOPY is to check a diskette for physical damage or for copy-protection. If you can DISKCOPY a diskette without any error messages, then the diskette is probably not damaged, and not copy-protected. This makes DISKCOPY a quick and easy way to check for these problems.

The final command in our series of four diskette preparation commands is LABEL. We mentioned that the FORMAT command will let you place a label on a disk when you format it (except if you are using the 1-series of DOS, which doesn't support labels). You may want to change a label, or add a label to an unlabeled disk, or remove an existing volume ID label. The LABEL command is designed to do just that for you. Unfortunately, LABEL was introduced with the 3-series of DOS, so 2-series users don't have this command. If you are using the 2-series of DOS, and want to control your disk labels, you aren't out of luck. If you happen to have my Norton Utility program set, it includes a label program that will do the job for you.

5.4 Moving and Removing Files—COPY, DEL, ERASE, REN, and TYPE

In this section we'll learn about changing files around—copying them, removing them, displaying them, and changing their names. All of these commands are internal, which means that you can use them at any time. Let's begin with copying.

The COPY command starts out as something very simple—a tool to make copies of disk files—and then adds enough variations on the theme of copying that it ends up serving three distinct purposes.

The most straightforward kind of copying just duplicates files from one disk to another. For example,

```
COPY A:THISFILE  B:
```

would take a file named "THISFILE" from the disk in drive A and make a copy of it on the disk in drive B. The same thing could be done with wild card file names, so that the copy would copy several files. For example,

```
COPY A:*.*   B:
```

would copy all the files ("*.*") from drive A to drive B. Or we could copy all the files that begin with the letters "XYZ" like this:

```
COPY A:XYZ*.*  B:
```

You can see that we could work many variations on this idea, all of them duplicating files under the same name but onto a different disk.

In the examples so far, we've specified the names of the source or from files, but we've only given the drive specification for the target or to files. In that case, COPY used the same file names. But we can, if we want, specify the names of the target files so that they could have different names than the original copies. For example,

```
COPY   THISFILE   THATFILE
```

will make a copy of a file named "THISFILE", and the copy will be named "THATFILE". Since we didn't specify any drives (like "A:" or "B:"), DOS uses its current default drive for both the source and the target. This means that both copies, "THISFILE" and "THATFILE", will be on the same disk—but that's just fine since the names are different.

If the copy is being made without any change of name, COPY requires that the source and target be in different places. But if the name is being changed on the copy, then the target file can be any-where—where the source is or somewhere else.

For example, if you are copying a file named FILE.1 from the disk in drive A to the disk in drive B, you can do it with the same name like this:

```
COPY    A:FILE.1    B:FILE.1
```

But you can't copy it to the same place that it already is, unless you give it a different name, so that it becomes a distinctly different file (a file that has the same contents, but still a separate file) like this:

```
COPY    A:FILE.1    A:ANOTHER.1
```

So far we've seen two of the three different uses of COPY—to make duplicates on other disks, and to make duplicates under a different name. There is yet another use of copying—combining the contents of several files into one. This combining operation is advanced and tricky—which means you shouldn't try it until you have become more experienced in using DOS. We won't go into all the details here, but will leave that for a more advanced treatment of DOS com-mands. You should know about this feature of COPY so that when you need it, you can study up on it. Here is an example of how it works: suppose we have two files, XX and YY, and we want to com-bine their contents into another file, ZZ. This COPY command could do the trick:

```
COPY   XX+YY   ZZ
```

You should know, however, that there are dangers and pitfalls in doing this kind of copying as well as some special rules. So, when you need it, be careful.

No matter what kind of copying you are doing, the COPY com-mand will proceed whether or not there is already a file with the target name. If there isn't a file with the target name, then a new file will be created. If there is one, it will be replaced—which might destroy some valuable data. There is no warning that an existing file is about to be destroyed, so be careful with all copies—this is one of the ways that you can clobber your valuable data.

On the other hand, COPY does require that the source files be there, naturally enough. How can you make a copy of something that isn't there? COPY will let you know if it can't find the source file you claim you want copied.

If you can duplicate files with COPY, creating new copies, you'd expect that you can destroy files as well. For that there is the DEL/ERASE command. This is one command, but with two different names: DEL, or delete, and ERASE, for erase. Under either name, it will throw a file away. We can ERASE files one at a time, or en masse, using "wild card" file names. DEL/ERASE gives us one small protection against erasing all our files with a slip of the hand: if we give it a wild card name, that means all files, such as "*.*", then DEL/ERASE will pause to ask us if we are sure. For example, if we enter the command

```
DEL   A:*.*
```

DOS will immediately reply

```
Are you sure (Y/N)
```

and won't delete any files unless we type in a reply of Y. But all other file deletion commands proceed without warning. So, this command will proceed automatically:

```
DEL  *.BAK
```

or

```
ERASE *.BAK
```

while this command will pause for confirmation:

```
DEL   *.*
```

or

```
ERASE *.*
```

Although DOS does not give us any way to recover files that have been erased, in fact the data from erased files is still on the disk, and can be recovered by a clever "un-erase" program. If this kind of program is available for your computer, buying it could be one of the best investments you can make; it acts like an insurance policy for your data. When I got my first personal computer, I saw that there wasn't an "un-erase" program available for it, so one of the first things that I did was to write one. That program saved the day for me many times, and I have a stack of testimonial letters from other people who thanked me deeply for creating a tool to rescue their data, too. If you possibly can, get yourself an "un-erase" program.

While erased data can, with luck, be recovered, data that you have lost by formatting cannot be recovered. For more information on the dangers of erasing and formatting, and some tricks to safeguard yourself against these dangers, see Chapters 11 and 14.

Related to both copying and erasing files is a DOS command to change the name of a file. REN, short for rename, will change a file's name as long as the name isn't also in use by another file on the same disk. Renaming is done like this:

```
REN  NAME.OLD   NAME.NEW
```

You'll recall that we got a sneak preview of this REN renaming command when we were discussing how to make the FORMAT command safer.

Like other commands, REN can be given wild card names to rename several files. For example, you could change every file with an extension of XXX to YYY, like this:

```
REN *.XXX  *.YYY
```

or any variation on this idea.

Finally, to finish this section, let's look at the TYPE command. TYPE is a handy way to get a quick look at the contents of a file. TYPE simply writes a copy of a file onto the display screen of your computer. (In fact, TYPE is really just a COPY command with the target of the copy being your display screen instead of another file.) The file you want to see must be something reasonable to look at—it had better consist of display characters, what is called a text file, or else what appears on your screen will be nonsensical. TYPE is done like this:

```
TYPE  SOMEFILE.TXT
```

or

```
TYPE AUTOEXEC.BAT
```

5.5 Odds and Ends—VER, CLS, and MODE

There are three little commands left that we need to cover, two simple ones called VER and CLS, and a more complicated one called MODE.

VER (for version number) and CLS (for clear screen) are both internal commands, which means that they are available at any time; they don't apply to the 1-series of DOS, but all later versions have them. MODE is an external command, and it applies to all versions of DOS (although its use keeps growing).

If you want to know the exact version of DOS that you are using, the VER command will display it. But it only works with versions after the 1-series of DOS, so it can't be used to show exactly which version of the 1-series we might have. If you are whimsically inclined, you might say that there is a VER command in the 1-series, but the version it reports is this:

```
Bad command or filename
```

There is one more nice simple command in DOS, and that is CLS, or clear screen. This command clears the display screen, which can be very useful.

The MODE command is also simple in concept, but much more complicated in detail. MODE is used to control several aspects of the computer's operation that have just one thing in common: we'd use the same English-language word (modes) to describe them.

The computer's display screen can—depending upon which display adapter is being used—operate in several modes. The MODE command can be used to switch between monochrome and color modes, forty- or eighty-column display width, and also test and shift the display screen.

For the computer's printer, the MODE command can shift the mode of the printer spacing (80 columns or 132 columns across, and 6 or 8 lines per inch down).

For the communications line, the MODE command can set various parameters, such as the baud rate and the parity.

Finally, the MODE command can redirect printer output to a communications line, for use with a serial-type printer.

All the features of the MODE command are peculiar to the situations that they serve, and have little to do with learning the basics of working with DOS. The job of the MODE command is to take care of some annoying details, so that the rest of our use of DOS isn't bothered by them.

5.6 Where to Find the Rest of the Commands

This brings to an end our discussion of the simple, necessary, and easy to understand commands. The next chapter gets into most of the more difficult ones—which you might want to read now, or skip over and come back to later when you are ready for them. Not all DOS commands are covered in this chapter and the next. There are several groups of commands that need a special discussion together with related information. You will find more commands discussed in Chapter 8, about "pipes," in the last section of Chapter 9 on paths, and in Chapter 11 on batch file processing. Chapter 22 brings them all back together, with a reference summary of commands.

An Overview of Advanced Commands

In this chapter we'll go over some of the more advanced commands of DOS. This chapter is really just a continuation of the last, but we've put a chapter boundary here as a sort of warning that the material here could be a little harder to follow. If you find information on computers easy to understand, then plunge right ahead; if you think you might just get more confused, skip over this chapter and come back when you are ready.

We won't be covering all the advanced commands here: five groups of commands that need special discussion of related ideas will be covered later in Chapters 8, 9, 11, 16, and 17. This chapter takes care of the advanced commands that can be described pretty much on their own.

6.1 Comparing Copies—COMP and DISKCOMP

When you make copies of files or disks, you may need to confirm that the copy is exact. To be honest, there is little reason to check a copy that you have just made—the copying process is extremely reliable, and it is very unlikely that there will be any errors in copying, unless the copying procedure itself tells you that there were problems.

The main reason for comparing copies of files or disks is to find out if there have been any changes made, although you can also use it to double check a copy that you have made just to confirm that there are no defects in the copy.

There are two comparison commands, one to compare files individually, and one to compare entire diskettes. The file comparison program checks the contents of files, to make sure that they match. On the other hand, the diskette comparison program compares two diskettes, and checks to see if they match exactly; if two diskettes contain the same data so that they are functionally equivalent but differ in some minor way, such as the order the data is stored in, then the diskette comparison program will report them as different.

When should you use either of these comparison programs, and which one should you use (if you have both)? Whenever you are in doubt about whether one copy matches another, you can use these programs. Remember, though, that each file's directory entry holds a time stamp showing when the file was created or last changed; checking the time stamps is one of the most practical ways of checking how up to date files are. But, if you have the slightest worry about whether two copies are identical, then by all means use these comparison programs. Normally the comparison you will want to do is with the file comparison program. A file comparison checks for logical equivalence of two files and doesn't worry about extraneous matters, like where the files are stored on a disk.

The disk comparison is only for use when you want two disks to be identical in every detail, including such things as where the files are stored on the disk, and if there were any files that have been erased. The disk comparison primarily makes sense as a way of checking the disk copy operation, DISKCOPY.

The DISKCOMP command is easy to understand and use. To use it, enter the command name followed by the drive specifications where the two diskettes are. Both diskettes are read from front to back and compared; any differences are reported. Here is a typical example of using disk comparison:

```
DISKCOMP  A:  B:
```

The file comparison command, called COMP, is usually better for you to use than DISKCOMP.

Here is how file comparison is done. You provide the names of two files to be compared. If the two copies have the same name, on different disks, then you needn't specify the name of the second file, but just where it is located with a drive specification. Here are two examples of how you would start a file comparison:

```
COMP    COPY.ONE    COPY.TWO
```

```
COMP  A:FILENAME  B:
```

You can use wildcard filenames to compare a group of files automatically. There are lots of ways that that can be handy; one of the handiest is in comparing the entire contents of two disks. Remember

YOU CAN COMPARE TWO FILES OR TWO DISKS.

that DISKCOMP will compare the full contents of two disks, but it will object to differences that have nothing to do with your data (things such as different disk formats or order of files on the recording media, or a bad area on one disk). Using COMP, you can compare all the data between two disks, and ignore irrelevant differences. You can do it like this:

```
COMP A:*.* B:
```

When we want to compare files, we usually have one of two things in mind: either we want to check that the files exactly match, or else we want to figure out what the differences are. COMP will report any difference between two files, but only in the most exasperatingly technical way. If it finds a difference, it will report both the location of the difference, and the two bytes that differ, in hexadecimal (number base 16). For most people, information in hex is useless and confusing. But at least COMP will tell us if the files it's comparing match exactly.

You ought to also know that if COMP finds that the files it's comparing are of different lengths, it will stop right there without comparing any of the contents. If COMP finds any differences in the content, it won't try to hunt for a place where the files match again. While there are smarter file comparison programs (including the version of COMP that comes with Microsoft's non-IBM versions of DOS), PC-DOS's COMP is rigid and dumb. Our COMP is good for finding out if two files match exactly, but not discovering what the substance of any differences are.

6.2 Editors, Word Processors, and EDLIN

One of the commands that comes with DOS is a program called EDLIN. EDLIN is a simple example of a type of program called an editor. We'll look at EDLIN in more detail in Chapter 20, but this is a good opportunity to learn about editors, word processors, and EDLIN.

Editors are computer programs designed to help us enter and revise written text. This book, naturally enough, was written with an editor program. Any program that you use to enter or revise written text is an editor.

You have almost certainly heard of a kind of program known as a word processor. Word processors are designed to provide the tools needed to work with written text—entering it, changing it, and printing it. As you can see, editors and word processors are closely related. In fact, a word processor is really nothing more than an editor program with rich and useful features. The main thing that sets word processors apart from editors is that word processors include tools to help control the printed format of written material. In short, a word processor is nothing but a fancy editor.

What do editors do for us? They give us the means to enter written text and to make changes in it. Changes might involve adding more text, removing old text, moving parts around, or shifting text from one file to another—in short, all the kinds of things that you might do when you revise a report on a written page.

We need editors for many purposes. We need them when we write letters and reports on our computers, and we need them for writing programs if we do programming. We also need an editor to get the best use of our computers, because an editor is required to create batch processing files, which are one of the best tools for enhancing our use of the computer. (We'll look at batch files, and what we can do with them, in Chapter 11.) In short, an editor is an essential part of our use of the computer.

Because of this, DOS comes complete with an editor, but a rather rudimentary one. Editors are very complex programs, and there are many opinions about what an editor should be like to work with.

Editor programs are considered to be a specialty area, so DOS doesn't include a high-powered editor for the same reason that it doesn't include programs for other specialty areas, such as financial accounting, or VisiCalc-type spreadsheet calculation. The idea is that we will choose our own word processor or editor program, and there is no need for DOS to try to compete with the word processors.

Some kind of editor is all but essential to using DOS so a simple one is included in DOS—the EDLIN editor.

To help you understand the limitations of EDLIN, and to understand why you will probably want to get a strong editor or word processor program, we need to explain the difference between command editing and full-screen editing. EDLIN is a command type of editor, but the best and easiest way to edit written text is with a full-screen editor. In full-screen editing, the written text fills the display screen. The screen acts like a window that can be moved around to show different parts of a document. When changes need to be made, they can be typed directly into the window, a fast and easy task. Command editing is much more laborious. To see parts of the document being edited, or to move around within the document, commands have to be typed in and executed. With a full-screen editor, browsing around within a file is very easy, while with a command editor it can be very tedious.

As an example, suppose that we are looking at part of a document and we want to see the part just a bit earlier in the file. With a full-screen editor this will usually take only a single keystroke, requesting that the editor move the screen's display window back one page or screen. With a command editor like EDLIN, the same operation will require typing in one command to move from the current location in the document to another, and another command to display some lines of the text; each of the two commands will require several keystrokes—a clumsy and laborious process. Changing the text with a command editor can be even more of a nuisance.

If you have a good word processor or editor, use it instead of EDLIN. If you don't have one, I highly recommend that you get one as soon as possible. Use DOS's line editor, EDLIN, only if necessary.

If you are reduced to using EDLIN, see Chapter 20 for some guidance on how to use it.

There is one more thing to mention before we finish the subject of editors. The BASIC programming language is part of your computer's DOS operating system. BASIC has a special-purpose editor built in designed to make it easier to enter and change programs in the BASIC language. You will occasionally find that some large complex programs, like BASIC itself, incorporate special-purpose editors. If you will be writing BASIC programs, you can either write them within BASIC, making use of BASIC's built-in editor, or you can use your main editor, and then pass your programs from the editor to BASIC. Each technique has its advantages and disadvantages, and you can choose which suits you best.

6.3 The Snooping Tool—DEBUG

DOS includes a command tool called DEBUG that can be used for all sorts of snooping around in your system. DEBUG is not an easy tool to use; in fact, it was designed with the needs of advanced programmers in mind, and ordinary folks should steer clear of DEBUG. You should have an idea of what DEBUG can do, so that if you need to do any of the tasks that DEBUG was designed for, you will know where to turn.

Here we'll give you just an overview of DEBUG's features. For more details about how to use them, see Chapter 21, which is devoted to DEBUG.

DEBUG is designed to provide the tools that are needed by some of the most advanced program developers. DEBUG allows you to display any part of your computer's memory so that you can see what is stored there. You can also type in changes to modify the contents of memory. You can also search through memory, looking for the location of some particular information. Also, the contents of two parts of memory can be compared for differences or copied from one area to another.

Beyond the features that we have already mentioned, DEBUG can read a file from disk to memory, and then use its ability to search, display, change, compare, and copy parts of memory to do the same with the copy of the file. If changes are made, they can be written back to the disk, making a permanent change to the file.

Two special parts of the computer's equipment, the registers and the ports, can be read from or written into by DEBUG.

When you display part of a computer program, it will appear in hexadecimal format, which is thoroughly unintelligible. To help make sense out of programs, DEBUG can "unassemble" programs, which means that it translates the hexadecimal into the format of assembly language (which is also called assembler language, or assembly code). Provided that you can make sense of assembly language programs, you can use DEBUG's unassembly feature to help you see what programs are doing. DEBUG also contains an "assemble" feature (available in all versions except the 1-series), which lets you enter assembly code instructions and have them translated into memory data.

YOU CAN SNOOP AROUND WITH DEBUG.

It is also possible to use DEBUG to step through and trace the action of a program. DEBUG has the ability to load a program from a disk and then execute the program, stopping it periodically as needed.

If you have a use for any of these features, DEBUG is the command-tool for you. If not, it is at least interesting to know that they are there.

There are three other advanced DOS commands that are used in connection with program development. We'll take a look at them in the next section.

6.4 Building Programs—LINK, LIB and EXE2BIN

There are three DOS commands that were specially created to be used in creating programs: LINK, LIB, and EXE2BIN. These three commands are only for people who are interested in the subject of program development. If your interest in DOS doesn't include programming—and for some folks that definitely is the case—then you can skip this section without missing anything else.

First, a word about LIB. All three of these programs, LINK, LIB, and EXE2BIN, are considered a part of DOS by Microsoft. For some reason that's mysterious to me, IBM doesn't include LIB in its versions of DOS for the IBM Personal Computers. LIB is supplied, though, as an incidental ingredient that accompanies many of the programming languages IBM sells—for example, IBM Pascal Version 2.00. LIB also comes with most or all of the compilers that Microsoft sells for use on the PC family under its own brand name.

For all practical purposes, LIB is a part of DOS and belongs in any discussion of the two closely-related programs, LINK and EXE2BIN; we'll discuss LIB here, even though you probably won't find it on your DOS disks. You will, though, probably find it on your compiler or assembler disks if you use a compiler or assembler.

When large computer programs are prepared, they are usually built in smaller pieces, and then put together into one working whole. It is similar to the manufacturing idea of combining parts into sub-assemblies, which are combined into finished products.

One of the DOS commands, the LINK program, is designed to do the programming task of combining parts into a whole. LINK combines, or "links together" or "link edits" program parts, and it takes care of the job of making sure that all the right connections are made. If you do programming in any computer language—except for interpretive BASIC, which we'll learn about in Chapter 10—you will be using the LINK program.

Most programming languages make use of a library of handy and standard subprograms, which take care of routine work. A program library is a collection of these useful subprograms, kept in a form that is ready to be used by the LINK program. Most programming languages come with subroutine libraries, and their use is automatic. When we write programs in COBOL or Pascal or FORTRAN, we aren't aware that we are using the accompanying subroutine library; but nevertheless, behind the scenes we are using it. When our programs are link edited, LINK finds the parts that are needed from our program libraries, and automatically incorporates them into our programs.

Programming languages, such as BASIC, C, or Pascal, come with ready-made libraries of subprograms that are an important part of the programming language itself. But we may wish to build our own libraries of subprograms, or even make changes to the standard libraries. The LIB command is designed to do that job.

With LIB we can build libraries from scratch or make changes to existing libraries—adding, replacing, or removing subroutines from the library.

If you have the LIB program, you can use it for program library work. You should understand, though, that library maintenance is a sophisticated chore, and few programmers have much of a need for it. It is unlikely that you, or anyone working with you, will have much need for LIB. But again, it is interesting to know about.

When computer programs are stored on disk in a ready-to-use form, they can be—and must be—in one of two formats that have been specially defined for storing programs. These two formats are known as COM and EXE, after the filename extensions that are used for them.

There are two formats for the simple reason that some programs require more help from DOS in being executed, and others less. The EXE format is used for those programs that need the full range of DOS services in loading them for execution. For programs that do not need as much help, the COM format provides a more compact and efficient way to store them on disk.

Incidentally, since all programs must be stored in files that have filename extensions of either COM or EXE, you can see a complete list of all the programs on a disk by using the DIR command to list the two types of files. For example, these two DIR commands will list the programs on drive B:

```
DIR  B:*.COM

DIR  B:*.EXE
```

(This list will not include interpreter BASIC programs, for reasons that we'll see in Chapters 9 and 10.)

Recall that when we discussed how to make the FORMAT command safer, we suggested that you rename the program file from FORMAT.COM to FORMAT.XXX. Now you know that since all program files must have an extension of COM or EXE in order to be used, you'll know why changing the extension from COM to XXX prevents the FORMAT command from being used. (When we need to use it, we can just change the name back to FORMAT.COM, temporarily.)

Any program can be kept in the richer but less efficient EXE format. But any program that meets the necessary technical rules can be kept in COM format. There is a program provided with DOS to convert programs from the EXE format to the COM format; this DOS command program is called EXE2BIN (a rather cryptic name, unless you know something about the technical details of programs).

Incidentally, the LINK program always produces programs in the EXE format. Eligible programs can then be converted to COM using EXE2BIN. Not every program is eligible for conversion to COM format. As we mentioned, the EXE format provides special kinds of technical aid to programs; if a program doesn't make use of the particular features of the EXE format, then it can be converted to COM format—otherwise, it can't.

For your interest, you can see all of the stages that a program might have to go through to be prepared for use:

- first the program is conceived and designed;
- then the program is written, using an editor;
- then it is compiled or assembled, using a language translator (which we'll discuss in Chapter 10);
- at this point it might be placed in a library, using LIB;
- then it is link-edited, using LINK, and possibly incorporating parts of a library;
- finally, it may be converted to COM format, using EXE2BIN.

That's a summary of the mechanical stages of preparing a program. Of course, lots of thinking, toil, and testing goes into the creation of a program for our PC family of computers. But when it comes to producing a PC program, those are the steps that are used to build it.

This brings us to the end of the advanced DOS commands, except for those that we will discuss in greater detail in Chapters 8, 9, 11, 16, and 17. Next we'll take a look at some special handy features that DOS provides us with, the editing keys.

7

Getting the Most from the DOS Editing Keys

In this chapter we're going to take a look at an interesting feature of DOS that can possibly make your use of the computer quicker and easier: the DOS editing keys.

We can't promise you anything in this chapter. Some people find this part of DOS exasperating, annoying, and useless. Others find it very handy. (I find myself vacillating between the two.) You'll have to judge for yourself if this is something worth learning.

7.1 Setting the Stage for the Editing Keys

When we're using our computer, we're usually giving it instructions by typing away at the keyboard. Sometimes we're entering single keystrokes; for example, when we respond to a program's menu by typing the key that indicates our choice. At other times we're pounding away on the keyboard at length; for example, typing in a document to a word processing or editor program.

But surprisingly often, what we key into the computer is something in the middle between those two extremes. A remarkably large proportion of our interaction with the computer involves typing single lines and then pressing enter. For example, whenever we give DOS a command, like COPY or FORMAT, we are entering a single line of information—a line made up of the command name and whatever parameters it needs.

Since this is done so often, there ought to be ways to make it easier, and that is what the DOS editing keys are about.

The DOS editing keys are a set of operations and functions, all based on the use of some special keys on the keyboard that help us enter or change a line of instructions. For example, one editing key lets you copy the last line you typed in, so that you can repeat something without having to type it in again. Other keys help you make changes to what you have already typed.

All this sounds rather handy—a fast and convenient way to speed your work to reduce the amount of key-pounding that you have to do. But it isn't that simple, and before you spend much time learning how to use them, you ought to know about the drawbacks to the editing keys.

The first problem with the editing keys is that they don't always work, or rather they aren't always made available to us. It goes like this: DOS provides a line editing service that any program, including all parts of DOS, can use to control what is keyed in. This line editing service is where the DOS editing keys take effect. As we key in a line to DOS, the DOS editing keys can be used to help enter and change the line. But only some programs take their input from this DOS service. Many programs do not.

All the commands that are built into DOS naturally make use of the DOS editing keys, but we use plenty of other programs as well. With the other programs, sometimes we can use the DOS editing keys, and sometimes not. Even worse, it isn't well advertised when we can and when we can't use them. This makes it more difficult to set our working style to incorporate the DOS editing keys. If you can't count on being able to use them, then they become an unreliable tool, an untrustworthy friend.

The second problem with the editing keys is simply that you have to learn them. That's the biggest problem in working with a personal computer—there is much too much to learn. To master your computer, you have to learn how the machine works, how diskettes work, how DOS works, how each of your main programs—say a word processor, a VisiCalc-like spreadsheet, perhaps an accounting program—works. It is too much to learn. No one can reasonably learn everything that we all ought to know in order to master our computers.

One of the major tasks that faces us, in dealing with our computers, is to reduce the number of things that must be learned, and to decide what parts, of the thousands of things to learn, are the most important to us.

This brings us back to the DOS editing keys. They are yet another thing to learn about using your computer. They are something handy and productive, but mastering them is hardly essential to using your computer effectively. You might decide that the DOS editing keys aren't important enough to be worth spending your time on. But, on the other hand, they can be useful, particularly the simplest ones (only an enthusiast could benefit from some of the fancier ones). If you learn the most basic of the DOS editing keys at the very beginning of your use of the computer, then they will become part of your general computer skills that you can use all the time with your computer. Learning the editing keys later means that you probably won't be able to integrate them into your comfortable style of computer use.

So, make a quick decision to press on in this chapter and read about the DOS editing keys or skip over it. But don't skip the entire chapter—the last section, section 7.3, explains some special keys that you need to know about, even if you are not going to use the DOS editing keys.

7.2 How the Editing Keys Work

The DOS editing keys work on two simple ideas. The first idea is that you ought to be able to make simple revisions to what you have just typed before you press the enter key, which tells DOS to act on what you have keyed in. The second idea is that DOS has kept track of the last line that you have entered, and you can use all or part of that previous line to make it easier to enter a new line.

In this section, we'll explain how each of the different editing key functions works.

Remember as we go over these DOS editing keys that they apply only in some circumstances. They work whenever we are entering DOS commands, and they work when we are entering information into DOS command programs, and they work with some other programs—but by no means all. Usually they will not work with many of the major programs that you use, such as a word processing program. But where they do work, they can be quite handy.

Let's start out making simple corrections to a line that we have typed, but haven't yet told the computer to act on—we have something typed in, but we haven't yet pressed the enter or return key. If there is something wrong with what we've typed in, how can we correct it? There are two ways.

The first way to make a correction is to cancel, or throw away, the entire line that we've typed in. There is a DOS editing key specially intended to cancel the entire typed line. The escape key (marked "Esc" on our PC keyboards) is used for the cancel operation.

There is also another, completely separate key combination that sometimes has the same effect as the cancel editing key—this is the break operation (which is also sometimes called Control-C). We'll take a look at "break" in section 7.3 at the end of this chapter. Sometimes break works just like the cancel editing key, but it can also terminate, or cancel, any program that you are running. Don't make a habit of using the break key to simply cancel, or discard, a line that you have typed in. If you make a habit of this, at some time you will make one of your programs come to an abrupt end when you didn't mean to.

Again, to cancel or throw away a line of information that you have typed, use Esc, the escape key, which is the DOS editing key that's used for a cancel operation.

If we've typed in something really garbled, then we probably want to use cancel to get rid of it all. But more often, all we want to do is correct some simple typing mistake. Perhaps we typed one letter wrong—say our finger slipped and we typed "FORMA5" instead of "FORMAT"—or we left a letter out—"FOMAT" instead of "FOR-MAT"—and we want to correct that, without retyping the entire line. The way we do this is with the DOS editing keys to back up to where we need to make the correction.

When we use the DOS back-up editing operation, we move one space back in the line we've typed in, and the last character is erased, just as if we had never typed it in. With back-up, we can erase what we have typed in, character by character, until we have erased the part we need to correct.

We actually have a choice of two keys to perform this back-up-one-space operation. We can use either the standard "backspace" key, or the cursor left key. Both of these keys will perform the same operation. The backspace key is located at the top right corner of the part of our keyboard with the letters on it; some keyboards mark this key with the letters B.S. (for backspace), but the IBM PC keyboards mark it with a bold arrow pointing to the left. The cursor left key is located with the other cursor control keys, on the right hand side of the keyboard. It too has a arrow on it pointing to the left; on most PC keyboards, it also has the number 4 on it (on the PC*jr* keyboard, it doesn't).

After we have gotten rid of what we have typed wrong, with the cancel or the backup editing keys, then we can type in the right information, and press enter, so that our computer will act on what we have typed in.

The cancel and backup keys let us make corrections to something that we are typing, but the rest of the DOS editing keys help us reduce the amount of typing that we have to do by letting us reuse what we've entered before.

This reuse only helps when we are doing some repetitive typing—such as entering the same information again and again, with minor changes. Unless we are doing that, repeating ourselves, these other DOS editing key operations don't do a thing for us. So that you have an idea of when this might be useful to us, let's consider an example.

Suppose that we need to copy a number of files from one diskette to another. This is a common operation. We might have a working disk in drive A that has two kinds of files on it—ones that we're changing and ones that stay the same. For the files that change, we ought to make backup copies onto another diskette in drive B, so that we don't lose our latest data. So we have a situation where we want to copy some of the files from a disk, but not all of them. It would be nice to be able to type in once:

```
COPY A: some-file B:
```

copy the one file, and then just change the file name for the others, without having to retype "COPY". This is the sort of thing that the other DOS editing keys let us do.

To do this, DOS keeps track of the last line that we have entered, and uses it as a template that we can copy from. The DOS template combines two ideas. First, DOS keeps track of the last command that we keyed in; this makes it easier to repeat a command. Second, DOS lets us make all kinds of changes to this last command; this is the template idea, which allows us to use an old command line as a model that is copied, adapted, and changed.

The first of the editing keys that works with the template is the copy-all function, which is done with the F3 key on the PC keyboard. This copy-all operation takes the entire template and copies it onto the screen, just as if we had typed in the entire line. If we want to exactly duplicate what we've typed before, copy-all does the job. If we need to make minor changes, particularly at the end of the line, we can use the backup key to erase the part we want to change. Using the example above, we could press the copy-all F3 key to duplicate the command "COPY A: some-file B:", then use backup to erase the "some-file B:" part.

Suppose it isn't convenient to copy all of the template? There are several ways that we can copy just part of it. One is the copy-one operation. Every time we press the copy-one key, one more character from the template is copied onto the display screen. In the example above, if we pressed copy-one seven times, it would duplicate "COPY A:" (including the space), and we could then type in our new file name to be copied followed by "B:"

There are two keys that we can use for the copy-one operation. One of them is the F1 function key; the other is the right cursor arrow key (which on most PC keyboards is marked with both an arrow pointing to the right, and the number 6). Either key can be used when we want this copy-one-character function.

A quicker way to do the same kind of thing is to use the copy-up-to editing key. To do this operation, press the copy-up-to key, which is done with the F2 function key, and then key in one of the characters in our template. The copy-up-to, or F2, operation will duplicate the

DOS CAN COPY FROM A TEMPLATE.

template up to, but not including, the key we pressed. For the above example, we could get "COPY A:" all in two key strokes, by pressing F2 followed by "s", which is the first character that we don't want to copy.

So far, what you have seen of the DOS editing keys may seem somewhat handy, but perhaps trickier, and more elaborate than they are worth. From here, though, it gets even more elaborate—which reinforces my argument that learning the DOS editing keys may be more trouble than it is worth.

If you want to skip over part of the template, and then pick up copying it from some point, you can use the skip-one and skip-up-to keys. They work just like the copy-one and copy-up-to keys, but they skip over the template rather than duplicating it. The skip-one operation is performed by the Del (delete) key, and the skip-up-to operation is performed by the F4 key. From the above example, if we wanted to drop "COPY '" but use "some-file", we would press F4 (skip-up-to), then press "s", then press copy-all to duplicate the remainder of the template. If you are good at this, it's a quick, efficient operation. Otherwise, it's confusing.

If you want to add something in the middle of a template, the Ins (insert) key lets you type in new information while keeping your place in the template. Without using insert, each character you type will also move you along in the template, so that any copying from the template will proceed from the point that is equivalent to how much you have typed. Using insert holds your place in the template, while you type in new information. The way it works is very simple: Say you have copied part of a command from the template, and then you stop and press insert. At this point, the template is put on hold, so to speak, and anything that you type is added to your new command line, without passing over any of the template. After you have finished inserting new material, you could then copy from the remainder of the old template. Naturally, there is an insert-exit editing key to reverse the insert operation. If your computer has an "insert" key, as most do, this key will be used for both insert and insert-exit.

The final DOS editing key lets you set up a new template to work with without actually entering a line for DOS to act on. If you are using the copy-from-a-template idea, you ought to be able to set up a template from scratch and not just use the last line that you entered into DOS. This is what the new-template command is for. F5 is the key used for this new-template operation. When you press F5, whatever shows on the screen as the line you've typed in so far becomes the new template that you can work with.

As you can see, these DOS editing keys are rather elaborate yet they are only good when two circumstances are combined:

- the DOS editing keys are active (not true for many programs); and
- you want to repeat the same or similar lines, several times.

If you don't meet both of these conditions, then the DOS editing keys do nothing for you.

The reason why I suggest that you don't bother learning these editing keys is simple: Why learn the tricky rules for an operation that you can only use sometimes? And when you can use the editing keys, they only save you a little work. But if they appeal to you, use them for all they are worth.

Here is a quick summary of the editing keys again:

Name	Operation	Keys used
cancel	throw the line away	Escape
backup	erase the last character	Back space, left arrow
copy-all	copy the template, in full	F3
copy-one	copy the next template character	F1, right arrow

copy-up-to	copy up to the typed character	F2
skip-one	skip over one template character	Del
skip-up-to	skip up to the typed character	F4
insert	enter new stuff, keep the same place	Insert key
new-template	replace template with this line	F5

7.3 Some More Special Keys

There are some other special keys DOS uses that can be very handy for you, and we'll go over them in this section. They are only loosely related to the DOS editing keys, and you can get good use from them even if you never try the editing keys. There's even one here that some computer makers don't tell their customers they can use.

There are five of these special codes, each of them entered as a control shift of one of the letters of the alphabet. Like all of the control key combinations, they work by holding down the Control key and pressing the other key. Fortunately, when we're doing a control-letter combination, we don't have to worry about whether we're using upper- or lowercase letters; either works just as well.

The most important of these five special control keys, is break, which is also called Control-C. Break, or Control-C, is a special instruction to the operating system to stop, or break out of, what it is doing. This break operation is very important, because it is our best way of stopping the computer from what it is doing, short of turning the power off. If your computer is going wild, or if you just want to interrupt what the computer is doing, break is the best way to do it. The break operation is so important that our IBM PCs mark a special key just for this operation. You can use this "break" key, but the Control-C combination will work just the same. In fact, Control-C is a universal code for small computers meaning Stop. To make it easier to remember this code, you can think of the "C" as standing for Cancel.

When we're working on our computers, the record of what we're doing—what we type in, and what the computer replies—rolls by on the display screen, and soon disappears. Sometimes we would like a permanent written record of what's happening. DOS provides us with a way of doing this—the echo feature. When echo is turned on, everything that is written on the display screen is also sent, or echoed, to the computer's printer. This works in a very straightforward way, so that we can automatically get a printed copy of what appears on the display screen.

Usually we don't want a printed copy of everything that's happening, so echo can be turned on and off, and it is normally off. On our PC keyboards, there is a special key combination for this function. It's done by holding down the Ctrl (control) key, and pressing the PrtSc key (print screen). On the PCjr keyboard, it's done with Fn (function) E (E for echo). Each time we press this key combination, we turn the echo function on or off again. (This is called "toggling," when the same key strokes switch a function back and forth between on and off.)

There are also universal key codes that are used by all personal computers for this echo operation. Since they are universal, we can also use them on our PC-family computers, if we choose to. Control-P is the universal code to turn echo on, and Control-N is the code to turn it off.

You should know that echoing doesn't work with every program. Programs can produce display output in many different ways. Only if the output goes through official DOS channels can it be echoed. Usually it is easy to tell if the output of a program can be echoed, even without experimenting to try it. If a program writes its information to the display screen as if the screen were a typewriter—which means writing everything at the bottom of the screen, and not jumping around to display some information here and some there—then it should be echoable. But if a program works in full-screen mode, using the screen's ability to display information in controlled locations, rather than using the screen like a printer, then the output probably can't be echoed.

You probably won't be able to use echo with your word processing programs, or with most accounting programs, or spreadsheet programs. On the other hand, it will work with the commands that are a part of DOS.

The next interesting and handy special key is the suspend key combination. It's not marked on most PC keyboards, but it's performed by holding down the Ctrl shift key, and pressing the NumLock key; on the PCjr keyboard, the same suspend or pause operation is performed by pressing Fn-Q. When we suspend the computer, it just sits idling, not doing any useful work. This gives us an opportunity to read what's on the screen, or do anything else, without the computer running away. Pressing any ordinary key will end the suspension, and our computer will continue with its work.

Related to the suspend, or pause, function is another universal key code known as Control-S. While the suspend operation stops everything in the computer, Control-S just holds up the display. If the computer is computing or doing anything else, that will continue. But once the computer tries to write to the display screen (through a regular screen-write operation), then it is suspended. The Control-S operation isn't advertised by IBM, but it's there as a feature of DOS.

Remember the distinction: suspend/pause (done with Control-NumLock, or Fn-Q on the PC*jr*) stops the whole computer; Control-S stops the display screen.

The last of the special control codes is Control-Z. As you'll see in more detail in Chapter 9, disk files with written text material include special codes to indicate such things as where one line of text ends and another begins. Among these special formatting codes is a code that marks the end of the file. This end-of-file marker is quite important, and careful attention is paid to it by all programs that work with files of written text. Normally we never have to deliberately enter this Control-Z code at the end of a file—text processing programs take care of that for us. But there are some special circumstances where it must be keyed in, and the Control-Z key combination is used to enter it from the keyboard.

I doubt that you will ever need to use the Control-Z code or function key F6. It is more likely, though, that you will see it mentioned in a book or article on personal computers so you should know what Control-Z is used for.

Here is a summary:

Control key	Function
Control-C	Cancel operation or end program
Control-S	Suspend screen output
Control-P	Start echoing screen output to the printer
Control-N	Stop echoing
Control-Z	Enter an "end-of-file" marker

This ends our discussion of the special key codes used with DOS. Now we'll move on to some DOS topics that are more advanced, more complicated, and more fascinating.

8

The Special Features of Paths and Pipes

The appearance of the 2-series of DOS added amazingly to the usefulness of the way that DOS can serve us and our programs. Much of this enrichment concerns two special concepts: paths and pipes. We'll be covering them in this chapter, along with a few odds and ends that are special to the 2-series and the 3-series of DOS.

8.1 Buzz Words—A Quick Outline of the Ideas and Terms

The subjects we have at hand are a bit technical, and so we'll be using some technical terms, what some people like to call buzz words. Buzz words are useful for the knowledgeable, but can leave beginners confused. What we have to cover here uses plenty of buzz words, many of them colorful, but most of them confusing. To help get you ready, let's run them by for a quick, early look before we go into the details.

We'll be talking about trees and paths through the trees. We'll run a pipeline, and we'll put some filters in the pipeline. We'll work with standard input and standard output, and we'll be redirecting our input and output.

What does all that mean?

When we work with our computer, we "talk" to it and it talks to us. We talk to the computer by typing on the keyboard, while the computer talks to us by writing information on the display screen. So the dialogue with the computer takes place over the keyboard and display. That is, it normally does.

77

There are times when it would be better to have some or all of this conversation take place elsewhere (we'll see why in the sections below). One of the advances in the 2-series of DOS over previous versions lets this conversation be redirected. In the 1-series, when a program writes out some display information it is written specifically onto the display screen. In later versions, programs write out their information to a sort of switchboard called standard output. Normally standard output passes straight onto the screen—but the "switchboard" can redirect the information so that it goes elsewhere. Likewise, where previous versions of DOS read information in directly from the keyboard, the 2-series and later versions of DOS read their information from a thing called standard input, which normally comes from the keyboard—but which can be redirected to come from somewhere else.

Normally, we use programs one at a time, and we can work with them directly, or we can redirect the input or output for these programs. There is another way we can use the idea of redirection: we can hook programs together so that the output of one program becomes the input of the next program. This is done with a pipeline. A pipeline is a series of programs that are connected together so that each one takes its input from the one before and passes its output to the next program.

The idea of a pipeline only works with programs where that kind of operation makes sense. A program that generates data, a generator, could be used as the first part of a pipeline. Along the pipeline should be programs that read and write data while doing something useful with it—for example, sorting the data into the order we want it to be in. This kind of program is called a filter. We'll learn more about how pipelines, generators, and filters work in the following sections.

When we store our data into files on disks, we need to organize the files into separate groups, especially if we have lots of files on a high-capacity hard disk system. To help us do that, DOS lets us create separate directories of files, where the files in each directory are kept quite distinct from the files in other directories. This helps us organize the files. But then we need to organize the directories—which brings us to trees and paths.

A disk has by itself a main, or root, directory. We can add to that root directory new subdirectories, where files can be kept in distinct groups. Each directory, whether a root directory or a subdirectory, can have subdirectories branching off from it. When directories branch off of directories, they form a tree-structure.

With more than one directory on a disk, we need a way to find our way through them, and indicate which we want to use. Paths, or

DOS's SWITCHBOARD CAN REDIRECT OUR INFORMATION.

pathnames, are used to thread our way through the branches of the trees.

That, in a capsule summary, is the subject of this chapter. Now, let's move on to discover the details.

8.2 Telling 'em Where to Go

As we saw in the last section, the standard input and the standard output of a program can be redirected to somewhere other than their normal locations, which is the keyboard for standard input and the display screen for the standard output. There are three different ways that this can be done.

One thing that you have to bear in mind is that redirection only works with standard input and standard output. That means two

DOS FINDS ITS PATH THROUGH THE TREES...

things. First, it only works with those two items—not with any other information that a program may read or write. If a program is designed to use a data file on a disk, then the redirection of input or output will have nothing to do with that. Redirection only works with what programs think of as their keyboard input and display-screen output.

The second thing to remember about redirection only working with standard input and output is that not all programs use them when they talk with the keyboard and display screen. Many programs use methods other than DOS's standard methods for the keyboard and screen. This is particularly true of programs that work in full-screen mode, where information is displayed all over the screen. Most editor and word processor programs, and spreadsheet programs, will not use standard output for their screen displays. There is no sure way to tell which programs do and don't use the standard input and output methods, but there are some simple rules that you can use to guess: if a program is a part of DOS itself, or if a program is very simple and straightforward, then it probably uses standard input and output, which can be redirected. But if a program creates full-screen displays, or in general is complex and interactive, then it probably does not use standard input and output. When you are in doubt, you can check easily enough by just experimenting with redirection of input and output.

As we mentioned before, there are three different ways to specify the redirection of input and output. Here we'll look at the simplest way to tell DOS what we want to do with input and output.

Let's take the directory listing command, DIR, as an example. If we enter the command

```
DIR
```

then we'll get a directory listing on the display screen. What if we would like to save that directory listing information in a data file? Then we can redirect the output into a file, like this:

```
DIR   >FILENAME
```

After the command, we can specify where its output is to go to, or its input is to come from. The greater-than symbol ($>$), is used to redirect the standard output. We can think of this $>$ symbol as an arrow that means "send it to." After the $>$ we indicate where we want it to go to. Usually this will be the name of a file, and the standard output will be written into this file. If the file didn't exist, it is created; if there was a file with that name, then the old information in the file is replaced with the output data.

For commands and programs that need input, the same thing can be done to redirect standard input. For input, the less-than symbol ($<$), is used as an arrow that means "take it from." You'll recall that the FORMAT command expects to get some keyboard input: it needs keyboard input to tell it when a disk is ready to be used, and if more disks are to be formatted. The responses to these questions could be in a file; if the responses were in a file named ANSWERS, then FORMAT could be used like this:

```
FORMAT   <ANSWERS
```

In that example, FORMAT would read its responses from ANSWERS but still write its output information onto the display screen. To redirect both input and output, do this:

```
FORMAT   <ANSWERS   >QUESTION
```

Before we take a look at when and why we would want to redirect input and output, there are two more details to cover.

When we redirect output to a file, it wipes out any information that was in the file. This doesn't have to happen. We can tell DOS to add the standard output to the end of the file, following anything that is already stored in the file. This is done with two > symbols, which means "append it to." As an example, here are two **DIR** commands, whose output would be combined into one file:

```
DIR A:  >INFO

DIR B: >>INFO
```

After these commands, the file INFO will contain the directory listings of the disks in drives A and B.

The one other thing about redirected input and output is that it doesn't have to be done with a file. It can also redirect to the name of one of your computer's devices, such as the printer. LPT1 is a standard device name for your computer's printer, so you can redirect output straight to it, like this:

```
DIR  >LPT1
```

When and how can we make use of this redirection of input and output? The examples that we have used so far give a pretty clear idea of how we can use the redirection of output. The main reason for redirecting output is to keep a record of it—either by sending it to a printer, or saving it in a file, so that we can work with the information later. Saving the data in a file gives us an opportunity to do all sorts of things with the information—like incorporating it into our word processing files, or using it with a batch file (see Chapter 11 for more on this). Sending output to be saved in a file is extremely useful, and it clearly is the most important use you are likely to have for redirection.

While redirecting output to the printer is very handy, you'll recall from the last chapter that the echo feature can be used to have screen output copied to the printer. Either way can work just fine for you, so it is just a question of which one suits you best. Echoing will give you both a screen and a printed copy, while redirection to the printer will keep your screen clear. If you have other devices besides a printer, redirection can be used to send output to them, while echoing only goes to the standard printer.

There is one potential problem with redirecting output—if a program needs keyboard responses that you don't anticipate, you won't be able to see its messages telling you what it needs. This can happen when you don't expect it—a program may run just fine without needing any keyboard responses time after time, and then at some point

REDIRECTION LETS DOS READ AND WRITE FROM FILES.

run into an unusual situation and, to your surprise, call for a response. So be careful in your use of output redirection.

Redirected input is a trickier matter, and one that we generally have less use for. If you are using a program that needs information in a very standard and predictable form, then you might save yourself some repetitive work by putting these responses into a file that you can use by redirecting input. The uses for redirected input, though, are much fewer than those for output. This is partly because often we can't reliably predict the exact input needed, and partly because we usually don't save much work by having an input response file for the program to read from.

Still, there are times when using input redirected to a file can make your use of the computer easier, or faster, or more automatic; for those occasions it is nice to know that the facility is there when we want to take advantage of it.

I warn you again, though, that there are dangers in using input redirection, much greater than the dangers of redirecting output. One person I know managed to lock up his computer, thanks to an error in an input response file that was being read by the FORMAT command; his only way out of the problem was to shut his computer off and start from scratch. So be cautious if you try to use redirected input.

Before we end the subject of redirection, let me tell you about an interesting minor trick. You know that the two commands DATE and TIME will display DOS's current record of the date and time on the display screen. That could be handy in a batch file to just show the current date and time. Unfortunately, DATE and TIME expect us to type in a new value for the date or time so they would ordinarily stop the operation of our computer, waiting for us to type in the new values. However, redirection of input can solve this.

Both commands will accept a simple carriage return (or enter key) in place of the new value; the carriage return means "don't change the value, leave it as it is." If we create a file that contains an empty line, a line with nothing in it (not even blank spaces) but a carriage return (or enter key), then we can use that file as input to the DATE or TIME programs. We might call that file NOTHING, or CR (for carriage return), or whatever. Once we've created that file, we can issue DOS commands like this:

```
DATE <NOTHING
```

```
TIME <NOTHING
```

When we do that, the DATE and TIME commands will show their current values and not pause for a new value. It's not exactly the greatest trick in the world, but it does have its uses. And one of its uses is to give us a simple demonstration of how input redirection works.

For another idea, we can reverse the process and use redirection to avoid seeing what a command would otherwise show us. For example, if we wanted to do a COPY command, like this:

```
COPY *.* B:
```

but we didn't want the list of copied files to clutter up the display screen, we could redirect the screen output into a throwaway called NUL. That would work like this:

```
COPY *.* B: >NUL
```

The operation would work the same, but we wouldn't see the messages that report the details.

8.3 Filling Up the Pipeline—SORT, FIND, and MORE

Programs use data, so it is natural that the output of one program might be needed as the input to another program. DOS provides a handy way of making this automatic. Before we see how DOS does this for us, let's consider how we could accomplish this with what we already have. If we have a program named ONE, which creates data that is needed by another program named TWO, we could use > and < and a working file name to pass the data like this:

```
ONE   >WORK
```

```
TWO   <WORK
```

The first program will write its data into WORK and the second will read back from it.

This is the basic idea that DOS accomplishes with pipelines. A pipeline is just an automatic way of doing what we did with ONE, TWO, and the file WORK. In a pipeline, DOS takes care of creating the work file to pass data through. To create a pipeline, we just write the program names on the same command line, separated by a vertical bar, (¦), which is the signal for a pipeline. Here is how we would pipeline the programs ONE and TWO:

```
ONE ¦ TWO
```

If you want to, you can informally think of the data as passing directly between the two programs, but actually it is stored temporarily in a file that DOS creates especially for this purpose. The first program writes out all of its data and ends operation before the second program begins working and reads the first part of the data. When the whole operation is done, DOS removes the temporary files used to pass pipeline data so that they do not clutter up our disks. The whole process goes on quietly, behind the scenes, without needing any attention from us.

A pipeline can have as many programs in it as you want it to, for example:

```
ONE ¦ TWO ¦ THREE ¦ FOUR ¦ FIVE
```

There is an obvious difference between the programs at the beginning, middle, and end of a pipeline. Unless there is something unusual going on, the first program in a pipeline will generate data. The ones in the middle will do something with the data, but still pass it on; this kind of program is called a filter. The last program in a pipeline could be a consumer of data to balance the generator on the other end. Usually, however, the last program of a pipeline is a filter, just like any of the ones in the middle. If the last program is a filter, then it passes the finished result to standard output, and it will appear on our display screens.

To understand filters better, lets take a look at the ones that DOS provides us with. There are three main ones called SORT, FIND, and MORE.

Each of these three programs is a classic example of a filter—they read from standard input, do something with the data, and pass it on to standard output. SORT is quite obvious—it sorts the data that it is passed. SORT treats each line of data as a separate entity, so it is the order of the lines of data that SORT rearranges. Normally SORT arranges the lines in first to last order, but a switch, "/R", will make the sort work in reverse order. Another switch, "/+n", (where "n" is a number such as "/+12"), will make the sort start on the nth column of each line. A common example of the use of SORT, and of the use of the + switch, is with the DIR directory command.

DIR will list files in more or less arbitrary order. If we combine DIR with SORT, we can get the directory listing in order by filename, or by the filename extension, or by the size of the file. This pipeline will sort the files into order by name:

```
DIR ┊ SORT
```

By using the + switch to shift the sorting over to the column where the file size is displayed, we can get the list in order by size:

```
DIR ┊ SORT /+14
```

When we have information displayed on the screen, there is often more than can fit onto the screen at one time, so some of it may roll off the top of the screen before we get a chance to study it. The MORE filter is designed to display only as many lines of information as will fit onto your computer's screen, and then wait for a keystroke to indicate that you are ready to see more. Naturally MORE is only used at the end of a pipeline—it wouldn't make much sense to use it anywhere else.

The FIND filter is used to identify the lines of data that have, or don't have, some particular data on them. To use FIND, you must specify what you are looking for enclosed in double quotes. FIND filters out the lines that don't contain what we are looking for, and only passes on the lines that do. Here is an example where we use FIND to look for error messages:

```
TEST ┊ FIND "error" ┊ MORE
```

DOS PUMPS DATA THROUGH THE PIPELINE.

This example shows the use of FIND to locate something in the output of another program (the program called TEST). We can also use FIND to locate something in one of our text files. In this case we use redirection to feed the text file into the FIND filter. It's done like this:

```
FIND "Norton" <CHAPTER.8
```

As you might expect, FIND has some switches: the V-switch reverses the search so that lines with the specified information are filtered out and the others are passed through. The N-switch adds in the relative line numbers (which can help you know where the data was found), and the C-switch just gives a count of the lines found without passing any other data on.

While these three filter commands, SORT, MORE, and FIND, are intended to be used inside pipelines, they each can be used by themselves. For example, we can use SORT together with ordinary > <

redirection to sort the contents of one file and place it in another, like this:

```
SORT  <FILE.OLD  >FILE.NEW
```

Similarly, MORE can be used like the TYPE command, but with automatic pauses when the screen fills.

While DOS provides us with three handy filters, SORT, MORE, and FIND, these aren't the only filters we can have. Remember that any program that reads from standard input and writes to standard output can be used as a filter. If you have any ideas for useful filters, you can write programs that carry out your ideas and then make use of them in your pipelines.

8.4 Telling DOS Where to Go

So far we have seen two ways to redirect input and output, with < and > and with pipelines. Each of these two ways causes specific commands to have its input and output redirected. When that command is done, DOS carries on, using the keyboard and screen for input and output.

But there is a way to get DOS to completely change its operation from the keyboard and screen to somewhere else. This is with the change console command—CTTY.

In order to work, CTTY must be given the name of a device that can act as both the keyboard and the display screen—this means that it must be a character type device (which the disks aren't), and it must be a device that can both read and write. Your computer could have something special on it that meets this requirement, but normally the only thing that it will have is a remote communications device, which is usually known to DOS as AUX or COM1. If we enter the command

```
CTTY AUX
```

then DOS will look to the communications line for all of its input and output. In effect, DOS has turned over control of your computer to whatever is on the other end of the communications line. In fact, this is exactly what CTTY is intended for—to allow remote control of a computer. Using the CTTY command, a computer can be told to work with a remote terminal. This opens up all sorts of interesting possibilities—from your home base, you can use and control any number of computers located at remote sites. Or, reversing the situation, you can travel with a portable terminal and still use your com-

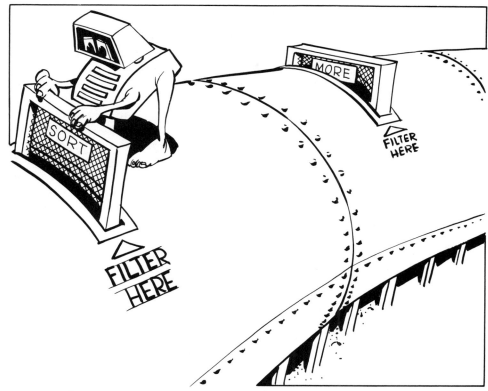

WE CAN PUT FILTERS IN THE PIPELINE.

puter by calling it through the communications line from a
telephone.

8.5 Planting a Tree—MKDIR and RMDIR

As we've mentioned, each of your disks has a main or root directory, and other directories can be added to it. Each new directory
branches out from its parent directory, and each one, in turn, can
have any number of other subdirectories under it.

To create a new directory, the make directory command, **MKDIR**,
or **MD**, is used. When a directory is created, it is empty except for
two reference entries known as "." and "..", which we'll discuss in the
next section.

After a directory has been created, then files (or other directories)
can be placed in it. All of the names in one directory—names of files,

or names of subdirectories—must be unique within that directory, but the same names can be used in other directories.

If we can make directories, we should be able to remove them as well, and this is what the RMDIR, or RD, command is for. To avoid leaving any files or subdirectories without a home, RMDIR will not work, unless the directory is empty.

It is possible to have directories branching out from directories without limit creating a complex "tree structure." You may be tempted to make use of this capability to create a thorough logical structure to your files. The idea is appealing—we create master directories for a major subject area, and subdirectories under it for more details. For example, you might create a directory for all accounting data with subdirectories for each accounting year. Or you might create a master directory for each person who uses the computer, with subject-matter directories under them. There are all sorts of possibilities.

Here are some simple examples. If you want to organize your files by the people who use them, then you might have directories like this:

```
ALICE
JOHN.S
JOHN.W
ROBERT
```

If you're organizing financial accounting data, you might have directories like this:

```
1985\PAYROLL
1985\LEDGER
1986\PAYROLL
1986\LEDGER
```

In this case we organized the categories (payroll and ledger) under the years. If we preferred, we could do it the other way around. The possibilities are endless—our task is to figure out what is sensible and practical for our needs.

In practice, though, complicated tree structures are a terrible idea. The main reason for this is that your computer has to do much more disk work to trace its way through complex directories, and disk access is usually the slowest part of your computer's operation. A secondary reason why complex trees are a bad idea is that the more complicated they are, the harder it is to keep track of them, find necessary data, and, especially important, discard unneeded data. There are nearly a thousand files on the hard disk of the computer system this book was written with, and I often find some neglected file that

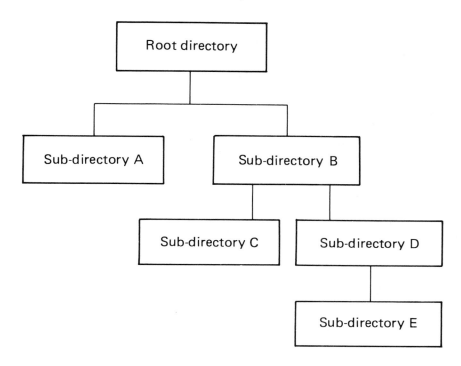

is cluttering up my disk space; if I had a complex tree structure, the problem would be much worse.

Subdirectories are really intended for use with the fast speed and huge capacity of a hard disk system. Unless you have a lot of files on a disk, there is little need for organizing them into isolated groups by putting them in subdirectories.

More important, the extra overhead of work that subdirectories require can cripple the operation of slower, diskette-type storage. Subdirectories are practical only with the fast speed of a hard disk system—which works about five or ten times faster than an ordinary diskette system.

So, as a general rule, you only need subdirectories if you have a multi-million byte capacity hard disk system, and also you can only afford the extra overhead of subdirectories if you have a hard disk. Otherwise, you should not use them.

From my own practical experience, I would recommend that you create as many subdirectories as you find a need for, but make your tree structure the simplest possible: place all your subdirectories onto the disk's root directory. Unless you have a really good reason to do so, don't create branches off any other directory than the root.

To give you a real-world example, here is a list of the directories on the 20 million-byte hard disk of the IBM PC AT model that I am writing these very words with. You'll see that I've followed my own advice and put all my subdirectories under the root directory, so that the directory tree is very simple.

```
(root-directory)
300
300-DOC
300-PROG
COL-PC
COL-PCWK
GL
LIBRARY
MAILING
MASTER
ODD-PROG
ODD-WRIT
PC-TALK
PROGRAMS
SPEED
TOYS
WORK
WP
PC-DOS
TREE
```

Judging when you should create a directory at all is another question. There are advantages and disadvantages to creating lots of small directories. With many directories containing only a few files each, it is easier to keep track of the files that belong in one particular category. But it is more difficult to use files in different directories at the same time, so it can become inconvenient if you have your files split into lots of directories. Also, it becomes harder and harder to manage the totality of your files the more subdirectories you have.

The way you create and use your subdirectories will depend upon your needs and also your taste. Let me recommend what I have found works very well for me. First, as I mentioned, I have only one level of tree. All of my subdirectories branch off my disk's root directory—there are no further subdirectories. When I created my tree, I asked myself what subdirectories would do for me. The answer was to help keep track of my data, but not to keep track of my programs. So I placed all of my programs, including all of the DOS programs and other programs that I have written or bought, in the root directory. There, they serve each of the subdirectories and don't clutter up the directories where I keep data. In the next section we'll learn more about the practical details relating to this.

8.6 Finding Your Pathways—TREE, CHDIR, and PATH

Since a disk can have numerous subdirectories, organized in a tree structure branching out from the root directory, we should have a way of finding out what all the branches of the tree are. The TREE command does this for us. TREE will display a list of all the branches of our directory tree for any disk.

With the potential complexity of a branching tree-structured directory, we need a way to find our way around it. We need ways to find and control where we are, and we need a way to indicate what part of the tree we are interested in: we need a notation, a way of writing down a location in the tree.

How we find our way to a particular subdirectory on a disk is referred to as a path. A path is the route we must follow to trace our way from a disk's main or root directory out to some point in the branching directory tree. The description of the path is called the pathname.

Let's suppose that we have a disk, which of course has a root directory. Then let's suppose that the root directory has a subdirectory named A, and it in turn has a subdirectory named AA, and finally in that subdirectory is the file we want to refer to, which we'll call just FILE. To find our pathway out to the FILE, we need describe the path in a manner like this:

- Starting with the ROOT, find its subdirectory named A;
- then find its subdirectory named AA;
- then find its file named FILE.

Pathnames are written like that, but all the lengthy words are replaced with a short and simple reverse slash (\). So our verbose path description shortens down to this:

    \A\AA\FILE

You'll notice that we didn't say we were starting from the root—the first reverse slash indicates that. If a pathname begins with a reverse slash, that means "start the path from the root."

With this way of writing a pathname, we can tell DOS where in any disk's directory tree we want to work. And vice-versa, DOS can tell us where things are. But if we are going to be working with various files that are under the "\A\AA" directory, it will be a nuisance to have to keep writing "\A\AA" for each file—and we'd be likely to make a typing error at some point. To solve this problem, DOS keeps track of a current directory. If we refer to just a filename, without

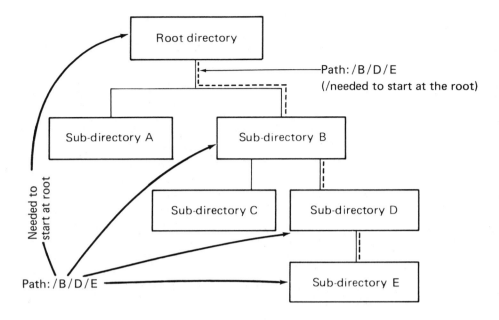

specifying the path to get to it, DOS assumes that it should be in the current directory. We control where the current directory is, with the change-current-directory command, CHDIR (which can be abbreviated CD). For example, to make "\A\AA" our current directory, we would enter the command

```
CHDIR   \A\AA
```

If we wanted to change back to the root directory, we would use this:

```
CHDIR   \
```

To make things even handier, DOS keeps track of a separate current directory for each disk device it has. If you have an A drive and a B drive, we could set the current directories for them, independently, like this:

```
CHDIR   A:\DIR1\DIR2
```

```
CHDIR   B:\OTHER1
```

Then, whenever we referred to the A drive, DOS would look in the "\DIR1\DIR2" directory, while for any use of drive B, DOS would look in its "\OTHER1" directory. If we did a global copy command, like this:

```
COPY   A:*.*   B:
```

then the files from the "\DIR1\DIR2" directory in drive A would be copied to the directory "\OTHER1" in drive B. No other files or directories would be affected.

There are other ways to work our way around directory trees, besides starting from scratch, at the root directory. If we write out a pathname starting with a slash, then we are telling DOS to start tracing the path from the root. If not, then the path finding begins right where we are now, at whatever is the current directory. So this pathname starts with the root:

`\XX\YY\FILENAME`

while this pathname starts wherever the current directory is:

`XX\YY\FILENAME`

There are two special trick names to help us work our way around paths "." and "..". These special names, one period and two periods, are used to refer to the current directory, and to trace back one level to the parent of the current location. As an example of using "." for the current directory, we could have written the last example as

`.\XX\YY\FILENAME`

which is just another way of writing the same thing; the only difference is that it is a little more explicit.

It might seem silly to you at first glance to have a "." entry that just refers to the same directory that you're already in. Why have a directory name that basically means "do-nothing, don't shift to another directory"? The reason emerges when you start thinking about some of the complex ways that you can use directories in batch files, which we'll be covering in Chapter 11. If we can specify a directory name in the middle of a path, like this:

`\DIRECTORY\`

then we also should be able to substitute (in effect) nothing in place of the directory name "DIRECTORY" and that's just what a period, ".", will do for us, like this:

`\.\`

Without the period, we'd have something like this:

`\\`

which would confuse DOS to no end.

The parent name ".." is used if we ever want to trace our way backwards from the current directory. Let's switch back to our first example:

```
CHDIR   \A\AA
```

We're now in the "\A\AA" directory. If we want to find a file named ZZZZ that's in the "\A" directory, which is the parent of the current directory, we can path find our way to it like this:

```
..\ZZZZ
```

This business of using ".." to refer to the parent directory can be used for all kinds of sophisticated tricks—but they would be tricks, and anything that uses them is likely to be tricky and error prone. You'd be well advised to steer clear of the whole business. After all, if you had a complex pathname that traced its way forward and back, like this:

```
..\..\AA\BB\..\CC\FILE
```

then you wouldn't be able to understand it clearly and use it safely.

We mentioned that the CHDIR command is used to change the current directory. There is also a way simply to display the current directory. If you enter the CHDIR command without specifying a new path, CHDIR displays the current directory instead of changing it.

To show you how this works, let's first set the current directory on two drives:

```
CD   A:NOTES
CD   B:LETTERS
```

That sets the current directories on those two drives, which are independent of each other. Of course, those two directories have to exist on the disks in the two drives, or else DOS won't accept the CD commands. Now, if we've forgotten what a current directory is, we can just ask for it like this:

```
CD   B:
```

and DOS will reply like this:

```
B:\LETTERS
```

In all these examples I've explicitly given the drive ID, such as B:, but we can leave that part off and DOS will use whichever drive is the current drive.

There is one more very interesting thing that we have to consider about in finding our way around the paths through the trees, and that is how we find programs and data.

When programs and data are stored on disk, they are no different from one another—they are just disk files that contain one kind of data or another. But DOS uses a different method for finding programs and other data. This seems puzzling at first, but there is a good reason for it and it turns out to be very handy for us.

When we tell DOS to go looking for a data file, DOS looks only in one place: the current directory. (If we specify a pathname with the filename, then DOS looks there rather than in the current directory—but it is still looking in only one place.) This is true whether we specify a particular drive to look on, or use DOS's default disk drive. Each drive has its own current directory (which will be the root directory if it hasn't been sent to some subdirectory with the CHDIR command). This is also true whether we are referring to a data file with a DOS command, like COPY, or whether a program we are using asks DOS to find a data file for it. If DOS is asked to find a data file, then DOS will look in only one directory—the current directory or the directory in the pathname given with the filename.

For programs it is different. When we enter a command to DOS, we are telling DOS to find a program with that name and then to execute the program. The command program might be internal, as we discussed in Chapter 4, or it might be external, which means that the program to carry out that command is located on disk storage. When DOS goes looking for a program file to carry out a command, DOS does not look only in the current directory. Instead, if DOS doesn't find it in the current directory, it will search in as many other places has we have told it to. How do we tell DOS to do this extended search for command program files? With the PATH command.

The PATH command has a slightly misleading name—you might think that it has something to do with paths in general. PATH simply sets the list of paths to be searched for command program files. PATH is a command to set the extended program search paths. Remember that the search always begins in the current directory. If the program file isn't found there, then the search goes on where the PATH command says it should. The PATH command can specify several paths, separated by semicolons, like this:

```
PATH \PROGS;\OTHER\PROGS;\
```

That PATH command would lead the search into four directories, in this order:

- the current directory (automatic—regardless of the PATH)
- the PROGS directory, under the root (from "\PROGS")
- the PROGS directory, under the OTHER directory, under the root (from "\OTHER\PROGS");
- finally, in the root itself (from "\").

One of the most remarkable things about the PATH command is that the search paths can be located on different disks. Even if you don't use subdirectories, you can make good use of the PATH command to have it automatically search from disk to disk looking for the right program, like this, if you had four disk drives, A, B, C, and D:

```
PATH A:;B:;C:;D:
```

The example I show here had just the drive specifications, like this "A:"; you can also add a path specification, like this:

```
PATH A:\B:\
```

or like this:

```
PATH A:\PROGS;B:\PROGS
```

When you just want to get to the root directory of several disk drives (which is what our example above is for) you may or may not want or need to explicitly indicate the root directory. My own experience has been that different DOS versions vary a little bit in the way that they handle something as complex as the PATH command—so you may want to experiment some. Experimenting with the PATH command will teach you more about it, and help you find out what works best for your computer and your version of DOS.

If you want to discontinue the extended program search, this command deactivates it:

```
PATH ;
```

After that, only the current directory will be searched for command programs.

Why would we want to use the PATH command? There are two reasons, one for those who use subdirectories and one for those who don't.

If your computer only has diskettes, and not a large-capacity hard disk system, then you are sure to have more programs than you can fit onto one diskette. You may have two different diskettes loaded into your diskette drives, each with programs on them. If you use the PATH command to search both diskettes, then you don't have to bother indicating which programs are on which diskettes—DOS will automatically go looking for them.

On the other hand, if you have a hard disk system you are probably using subdirectories, and you probably have programs scattered around in various directories. Even if you follow my advice and try to keep all of your programs in the root directory, there will still be times when you need to have some programs in other directories. If you set the PATH command to search through all of the directories where you keep programs, then each and every one of your programs will be on tap for you, regardless of which directory it is buried in.

For example—and this is another real-world example from my own computer—I use this PATH command to search, in order, the three program directories that I use:

```
PATH C:\PROGRAMS;C:\ODD-PROGS;C:\TOYS
```

There is one rather obvious practical note you need to keep in mind about using the PATH search command: the more directories DOS has to search through, the longer it takes to find a command program. It speeds things up to put the most-used program directories at the top of the list.

8.7 Odds and Ends in the 2-Series— ASSIGN, SET, RECOVER, PROMPT, VERIFY, and BREAK

Besides the commands that we have looked at so far, the 2-series and later versions of DOS have a number of other relatively minor commands, each with their uses. We'll take a brief look at them in this section.

The ASSIGN command solves a very special problem that arises when we try to use old-fashioned programs with new computer concepts. Here is the problem: many older programs for personal computers were written in the days when PCs just had small-capacity floppy disks for storage. In those days the standard way of operating a PC was to have two diskette drives, A and B, and to use them in a fixed way: program diskettes were placed in drive A, data diskettes were placed in drive B.

Now, there is nothing wrong with that style of operating. Lots of today's computers have just two floppy drives, A and B, and are used in the way we just described. The problem is that more and more computers have a large-capacity hard disk to work with, usually denoted as drive C. But some programs—far too many—were rigidly written so that they HAD to work only one way: getting programs off drive A and data off drive B (or whatever). This rigidity creates a problem when you try to adapt your programs to a hard disk. The ASSIGN command is designed to help solve the problem.

ASSIGN instructs DOS to reroute requests for one disk drive to another. For example—and this is the most important and useful example—if we assign both drives A and B to our hard disk drive C, then any program that is inflexible enough to insist on asking for drives A and B will have DOS, in a sneaky end-run maneuver, actually refer the requests to the hard disk drive C. That lets DOS outfox some dumb and rigid programs and it helps us a lot.

To do that operation, we issue this command:

```
ASSIGN A=C B=C
```

If we want to undo the assignment, so that program references to A and B go where they were originally intended, we just issue the ASSIGN command with no parameters, like this:

```
ASSIGN
```

There is an important danger in the ASSIGN command that you should be aware of. ASSIGN will redirect destructive operations as well as constructive ones. Commands like DEL *.* or FORMAT can be redirected by ASSIGN so that you could end up erasing or reformatting over data that you didn't mean to.

To avoid this problem, I strongly recommend that you use the ASSIGN command following these rules:

1. Use it when you really need it; don't use it routinely
2. Set it up only in batch files (discussed in more detail in Chapter 11), and have those batch files automatically reset the assignments as soon as you're done with them

Following those rules should avoid most problems with ASSIGN. Next we'll look at an interesting control command called SET.

There can be times when our programs need to have some general instruction that sets some basic ground rules. For example, the PATH command, which we covered in the last section, sets the ground rule for where command programs are to be found. DOS contains a flexible, general-purpose method of doing this, something called DOS's environment. In the environment, DOS keeps little equations, all in the form

```
NAME=VALUE
```

The name indicates the subject matter that the equation concerns, and the value indicates how that subject is to be treated. Any programs that we run on our computers can check the environment to see if there are any equations that concern it.

The SET command is designed to set these environmental equations. We simply enter a command like

```
SET NAME=VALUE
```

and the NAME=VALUE equation is placed in the environment. If there was an old equation with the same name, it is replaced. If there is no value, as in

```
SET NAME=
```

then any old equation with that name is removed from the environment; not replaced with "NAME=" but actually removed.

For some examples, here are the items that are SET in my computer:

```
COMSPEC=C:\COMMAND.COM
PROMPT=$P$G
PATH=PATHC:\PROGRAMS;C:\ODD-PROGS;C:\TOYS
```

This environmental equation scheme can be used for many purposes, and in fact DOS uses it for its own purposes. The search paths, set by the PATH command, are stored in the environment. In fact, the PATH command is just a specialized version of the SET command. If we enter the command

```
PATH  xyz
```

the result is exactly the same as if we had entered this:

```
SET  PATH=xyz
```

If any of your programs are specifically designed to use versions of DOS after the 1-series (and more and more programs are) then they can make use of these environmental equations in any way that they find useful.

Next we come to a powerful but dangerous file recovery program called RECOVER.

There are many ways that your disk data can be lost or damaged, and the whole subject of file recovery is a very important one, which we'll cover in more detail in Chapter 14. DOS does not provide much in the way of file protection and file recovery, but there is one command, RECOVER, which does two limited kinds of file recovery.

If part of a disk has been damaged so that a file can be partly read and partly not, the RECOVER command will remove the unreadable part so that you can use the rest. Depending upon the kind of file that it is, the recovered portion may or may not be usable. Generally this kind of file recovery only works with text files, which contain written material. To use RECOVER in this way, you enter the command followed by the name of the file it is to check for readable and unreadable parts.

Here is an example of the safe version of RECOVER, which checks one single file:

```
RECOVER B:MAZE.BAS
```

The other kind of file recovery done by RECOVER is completely different than the first. Unfortunately, it is easy to confuse the two. In the second kind of file recovery, RECOVER assumes that the entire directory of the disk is damaged and nonsensical. It throws away the entire directory and replaces it with a new one, which contains the data it found on the disk organized into files as well as possible. The new directory contains files with arbitrary names that RECOVER gives them—it is then your job to figure out what is what as best you can.

To use RECOVER in this way, you enter the command without specifying any filename, just a drive ID. Remember that this form of RECOVER wipes out your entire directory with very little warning. Be careful using it. It is EXTREMELY dangerous, as too many sad folks have discovered. You might want to completely avoid the use of the RECOVER command for safety's sake.

Here is an example of the dangerous version of RECOVER, which wipes out the names of all files on the disk:

```
RECOVER B:
```

Next we come to a command that can help enormously in keeping track of where we are on our disks: the PROMPT command.

When DOS is ready for a command, it shows a prompt, which is normally the default drive, followed by a greater-than symbol, like this:

```
A>
```

You can change the prompt to nearly anything, including a display of the current time and date. The PROMPT command allows you to set the prompt as you wish. The format and rules for setting a prompt are complicated, so you should see your computer's DOS manual if you want to use this command.

There are all sorts of fancy things that you can get into with the prompt command (as your DOS manual will show you); in a moment I'll show you one of the more exotic ones. Before we get into that amusement, though, I want to show you the one—and only, in my private opinion—really useful prompt command. This is a variation on the standard system prompt (like "A>"), but instead of just showing you the default drive ("A"), it also shows you the default directory path as well.

If you are making much use of subdirectories on your disks, it's easy to lose track of where you are and what the current directory is. But there is a version of the PROMPT command that will change the

DOS command prompt so it always tells you what the current directory is. It's done like this:

```
PROMPT $P$G
```

That prompt command changes the command prompt to show the current path (that's what "$P" asks for) followed by the familiar greater-than symbol, ">" (which is what the "$G" part of the command asks for). Try this PROMPT command, and you'll find it quite helpful.

Now for the fun part. Try either of these two PROMPT commands, and see what happens:

```
PROMPT $V $T $D $P $G
```

```
PROMPT I await your command, Oh Master $g
```

Now let's get back to some serious business, with the VERIFY and BREAK commands.

When DOS is writing information to disk, it normally accepts the disk drives report that all went well. This is generally OK because disk drives are quite reliable. But if you wish, you can ask DOS to check or verify all data that is written to disk. This is controlled with the VERIFY command, which can set verification on or off. DOS normally does not verify. If you are concerned, you can set verification on but it will add considerably to the time it takes to use the disks. Personally, I don't recommend it.

In the last chapter we mentioned the Control-C or break operation, which will end any program you have operating. The 1-series of DOS only checked for this break command under limited circumstances, while later versions can check for it much more often. The BREAK command lets you instruct DOS to either use the same rules as the 1-series (BREAK OFF), or to check as often as possible (BREAK ON).

That completes the odds and ends that were introduced with the 2-series of DOS (although there are some more special items to come in Chapters 11, 16, and 17). Next we'll look at what was new in the 3-series of DOS.

8.8 New Items in the 3-Series—ATTRIB and SELECT

The 3-series introduced two new miscellaneous commands, ATTRIB and SELECT. We'll begin with the ATTRIB command.

Each file that's stored on our disks can have "file attributes" specified for it, attributes or characteristics that control certain things about the file. There are several important attributes that can apply to any file, called hidden, system, archive, and read-only.

Among these attributes, there is only one that we can deliberately set through DOS commands, and that's the read-only attribute. If a file is marked as read-only, it is protected from being changed or erased by normal DOS operations. If we have important files, and they aren't normally changed, such as programs we have bought, we can add a degree of safety to them by marking them as read-only with the ATTRIB command program. While this doesn't give us an iron-clad guarantee that we won't lose or damage a file, it does make them much safer.

Here is how we use ATTRIB to do this for a file named "X":

```
ATTRIB +R X
```

To remove read-only status, we'd do the same thing with a minus instead of a plus sign:

```
ATTRIB -R X
```

The other 3-series command that we need to mention is SELECT. Personal computers are becoming internationalized, and they must be adapted to the needs of each country using them. For one thing, currency symbols change. In the U.S. and Canada, money is denoted with $, but elsewhere other currency symbols are used. There are also differences in the format that the date and time are displayed, and some differences in what characters are on the keyboard.

SELECT is designed to take some of the effort out of internationalizing DOS. SELECT is a specialized program, which acts in effect very much like the FORMAT /S command (which formats a disk with the DOS system on it). But what SELECT does in particular is to make those adjustments to DOS that are necessary for the country that we want to adapt it to.

We needn't go over the details of the SELECT command, for it's far from an everyday operation for all of us. You should be aware that SELECT exists so that you can use it—or play with it—if you wish to.

9

What You Need to Know About Disks and File Formats

9.1 What's Inside a Disk

A disk is used to hold data that you need to preserve. It is like a filing cabinet—it's a safe place to keep information, and it has a large but limited capacity. Just as a filing cabinet has its contents organized into file folders, a disk has its data organized into files.

The files in a diskette are distinct, and each file contains its own particular data. The files are identified by their filenames, which we'll learn more about in the next section. Within any one disk, each file must have a unique name; but on two separate disks there could be files with the same name. Since files are identified by their filenames, it is a very good idea to make sure that every file on every disk has a completely unique name, except when there is some good reason to reuse the same name. If a file on one disk exists solely to be a safeguarded copy of a file on another disk, that is a very good reason for having a duplicate file name; but even then it is a good idea to give the files different names in order to distinguish the original or master copy.

Most of the space on a disk is devoted to storing our data but some of the space is used by DOS for bookkeeping purposes, such as maintaining a directory of the files on a disk. In the directory, DOS keeps its record of everything that it needs to know about the disk's files, such as how to find their contents. Most of this information is of little use to us, but there are three things about a file that DOS will let us know.

The first is the filename itself. The second is the size of the file. The third is a time stamp that shows when the file was most recently changed. If a file has not been changed since it was created, then the time stamp shows when it was created. These time stamps give both the date and the time (except that the time was not included in the very first release of DOS, version 1.00; if you're using version 1.00, you're a pioneer indeed!).

There are several special things to know about the file time stamps. Although they are displayed to the minute, they are actually calculated to within two seconds of the exact time. When necessary, advanced programming techniques can be used to find the complete time stamp. If a copy is made of a file, the copy gets the same time stamp as the original. There is no way to tell if a time stamp is the original time the file was created, or the time the file was later changed.

These time stamps on files can be very useful in safely controlling your data. Looking at the time stamp can answer questions like:

- Which of these files was I working on yesterday?
- Is my backup copy up to date with my master copy?

Because of this, it is very valuable to make sure that your system always knows the correct date and time. If your personal computer requires you to enter the time when it is turned on, I urge you to never be too lazy to key in the right date and time. The benefits of having the right time stamps on your files can be enormous; sometimes it can be as valuable as an insurance policy. If your particular computer has a clock/calendar feature that automatically keeps track of the time when it is turned off, you are fortunate indeed.

(As we've mentioned elsewhere, clock/calendar hardware is a popular feature in multi-function expansion boards for the PC family, and the IBM AT model comes with a clock/calendar as standard equipment. Since the date and time stamp on files can be quite valuable, it's good to have this feature in your computer.)

There are actually three parts of overhead on a disk, including the directory. Since you may occasionally come across mention of them, it is worth knowing what they are. The first is called the "boot record," and it contains a very short program that is used to help start up the DOS operating system from the disk. Each DOS has a boot record on it whether or not the disk contains the rest of DOS (if a disk has all of DOS on it, it is a system disk, which we'll come to in a moment). After the boot record, the next bit of overhead on the disk is a table that is used to keep track of the available space on the disk.

This table is called the File Allocation Table, or just FAT for short. The FAT records where each file is located so it is sort of an index to the disk. It also keeps a record of the part of the disk's space that isn't in use. When the CHKDSK command reports on how much space is available on a disk, the information comes from the disk's

FAT. The third and last part of the overhead on a disk is the directory, which lists all of the files on the disk. We've already discussed the directory since its contents are so important to us.

All together, the three overhead parts of a disk—the boot-record, the FAT, and the directory—take up very little space on a disk, typically only about two percent of the total. The rest of the space is used to store our data.

The overhead we talked about here is overhead that is intrinsic to the disk itself—the disk's own overhead that uses up about two percent of the disk's space. There is another potential overhead that can also reduce the amount of disk space that is usable to us: the operating system. When DOS is started up, it has to be read into memory from a disk, and naturally this copy of DOS takes up some space on the disk. When we format a disk with the FORMAT command, we have a choice of whether or not we want DOS to be on the disk. With DOS on it, the disk is called a system-formatted disk or, for short, a system disk.

A system disk has the advantage that you can always start your computer system with it. If all of your disks are system formatted,

then any of them can be used to start your computer, which can be a real convenience. On the other hand, having DOS on our disks uses up some of the space we might otherwise have for our own use. The amount of overhead for DOS varies according to the disk capacity and the version of DOS. In might be as low as eight percent or as high as 25 percent. A typical figure is 12 percent. The space devoted to having DOS on your disks may or may not be important to you. I recommend starting out by putting DOS on all your disks, and then later deciding what is best. Chapter 13 covers some of the strategies you might use with your disks.

9.2 All About File Names

Files have file names, and the better you understand how they work the less likely you are to make a mess of them.

First, the simple mechanics of it. File names have two parts, called the filename (itself) and the filename extension. A filename can be up to eight characters long. Here are some examples:

A

LONGNAME

1234

AB_34

The filename extension is just that—an extension to the file name. Extensions can be up to three characters long. While a filename must have at least one character in it, the extension can be nothing at all. When a filename has an extension, the two parts are connected by writing a period between them. Here are some sample filenames with extensions:

JANUARY.85

PROGRAM.BAS

CHAPTER.2-3

1985-12.25

There are some rules about what is a proper filename. The filename and the extension can be made up from any combination of the allowed characters, which consist of the letters of the alphabet A through Z, the digits 0 through 9, and a bunch of punctuation characters:

$ & # @ ! % ' ^ ( ) - _

You can use any of these symbols in any combination. It seems like a terrible idea to use the more exotic symbols, but some of these symbols work very nicely as a form of punctuation in a file name. For example:

JAN_MAY

You'll notice that there are a few common (and some uncommon) symbols that aren't allowed in filenames and extensions:

* and ?	used as "wild cards" (see Section 9.4)
.	used to separate filenames and extensions
:	used to identify drives and devices

/ and \	used for paths and switches
< and >	used for data redirection
, and ;	used to punctuate parameter lists
=	used to punctuate parameter lists (e.g., in SET)
+	used to punctuate parameter lists (e.g., in COPY)
¦	used for piping
[and]	
"	

Only capital letters are actually used in filenames. DOS, in a friendly way, lets us type in filenames in lowercase if we want but it automatically converts lowercase to uppercase. This is why you'll find DOS always listing files with their names all in uppercase letters.

You may discover that there are some trick ways to sneak illegal filenames past DOS. For example, it is possible to create a file that has a blank space in the middle of its name (like "AA BB.CCC") or to create a file that has a lowercase name. Don't play that dangerous game; you are almost certain to regret it.

One of the very nice things that DOS does for us to make life convenient and easy, is that it lets us refer to parts of the computer, such as the printer, with simple names that look like filenames. These are called device names because they refer to devices or parts of the computer such as the printer. In order to be able to do this, DOS has to reserve these names for their special uses so there is a short list of names that you can't use as your own filenames. The exact list may vary from computer to computer. Here is the usual list of names with what they are used for:

NUL —a null or empty file; if a program tries to read from NUL, it finds an empty file; data written to NUL is thrown away. This empty or null device can come in handy at times.

CON —the user console; input data is taken from the keyboard; output data is displayed on the screen.

USER—under some circumstances, this is an alternate version of CON; USER can't always be used as a device name, but CON can. (Unless you know that USER will work, stick with CON.)

AUX —the communications line or asynchronous communications port.

COM1—the first of possibly several communications lines; COM2 and COM3 are used to specify others; COM1 is the same thing as AUX.

PRN —the printer device.

LPT1 —the first of possibly several printers; LPT2 and LPT3 are used to specify others; LPT1 is the same thing as PRN.

With the exception of these special device names, you are free to give your files any names you wish, within the grammatical rules for filenames (one-to-eight characters, and so forth). It is almost the same with filename extensions, but not quite, and we'll cover that in the next section.

There are three more things to know about filenames, which we'll cover in the next few sections and the last part of this chapter: what filename extensions are really about, what wild cards are in filenames, and some special advanced DOS items such as disk labels and paths.

9.3 The Importance of Filename Extensions

You can give your files filename extensions as freely and arbitrarily as you can give them filenames—in fact more freely since there are reserved filenames but there are no reserved filename extensions.

There is a distinct purpose for filename extensions—indicating the category and classification of files. Unfortunately, the importance and usefulness of filename extensions isn't emphasized much so many users of DOS don't fully understand it. In this section we'll explain what filename extensions are all about.

Filename extensions are intended to classify and categorize files so that their purpose can be quickly and simply identified. The assignment of standard filename extensions is rather casual and it is not explained fully anywhere that I know of, which leads to confusion about them.

Here are the standard uses of filename extensions:

- Executable program files have extensions of **EXE** or **COM**; there are two formats for program files (which we'll go into in section 9.5, below) so there are two filename extensions to distinguish them.
- Batch execution files have the extension **BAT**; we'll look into batch execution files in Chapter 11.
- Programming languages make use of several standard filenames, which we'll learn more about in Chapter 10. For source code (the original program), a different extension is used for each language: **ASM** for assembly, **BAS** for BASIC, **COB** (or **CBL**) (the translated program) for COBOL, **C** for C, **FOR** for FORTRAN, and **PAS** for Pascal. For object code in any language, **OBJ** is the extension. For library routines the

extension is LIB. When BASIC uses BLOAD-format files, BLD is the customary extension.

- When a program creates printer-type output but the output is stored in a file, LST is the customary extension. If there is more than one listing file being created at a time, other extensions may be used. Compilers typically use COD for assembly-like object code listings, and the linker uses MAP for the map of the contents of a program. When practical, LST is the best extension to use for printer-type files.

- Editors and word processors use some standard extensions. When the old version of an edited file is preserved for safety reasons, it is given the extension BAK (for BAcKup copy). DOC is very commonly used by word processors for text files. Some word processors prefer to use TXT as the extension for the edited data. FMT may be used to hold the editing format.

- When a program uses a data file in its own format, DAT is often the extension.

- When a program needs a temporary work file, $$$ is most often used as the extension; occasionally TMP is used instead. The program fully intends to delete these temporary work files before finishing. If you ever find a file lying around with an extension of $$$ or TMP, that's a very good sign that something has gone wrong—and you should to take the time to figure out what it was.

- VisiCalc uses VC for storing its worksheets in coded format, and DIF for data in the Data Interchange File format. Other spreadsheet programs may use their own extensions, following a similar pattern; for example, CAL.

To tabulate these most common filename extensions, here is the list in alphabetical order:

ASM —assembly source
BAK —text file backup copy
BAS —BASIC source code
BAT —batch processing files
BLD —BLOAD format for BASIC
C —C source code
CAL —Spreadsheet calculation file
COB —COBOL source code
COD —object code listing from compilers
COM —executable programs in memory-image format
DAT —data files in general
DIF —data interchange files as from VisiCalc
DOC —word processing document

EXE —executable programs in relocation format
FMT —word processor format specifications
FOR —FORTRAN source code
HDR —Data base header
INX —Data base index
LIB —library routines for compilers
LST —printable listing files in general
MAP —program maps from the linker
OBJ —program object code from compilers
PAS —Pascal source file
TMP —temporary work file
TXT —text files for word processors
VC —spreadsheet data, from VisiCalc
$$$ —temporary work file

The more closely you follow the pattern of these extension names, the more easily your files will smoothly fit into the broad use of your computer. This is one of the many ways that you can safeguard the effective operation of your computer.

9.4 Wild Cards and Their Use

Connected with the subject of filenames is the subject of wild cards or generic file names. A wild card is a non-specific part of a file specification that can be used to match more than one particular file.

Every file has a specific, unambiguous filename (and extension), but you can refer to more than one file at a time by using wild cards in a file specification.

There are two forms of wild card—the question mark (?) and the asterisk (*). When a question mark is used in a file specification, for example as

```
THISNAM?
```

then it will match with any letter in that one particular position of the filename. So THISNAM? would match with any of these files:

```
THISNAME
```

```
THISNAM1
```

```
THISNAM$
```

```
THISNAM
```

This works so long as all of the rest of the positions of the filename match exactly. Wild cards, as you might expect, can be used in both the filename and extension parts of the complete name.

The asterisk form of the wild card is just a shorthand for several question marks. While a question mark is wild for the one single character position that it occupies in a filename, an asterisk is wild from that position to the end of the filename or the end of the extension. An asterisk acts as if there were as many question marks as there are positions left in the filename or in the extension. A wild card asterisk in the filename stops at the end of the filename and doesn't extend into the extension part. If you use the question mark form then you can be specific about the following positions in the name; with an asterisk you can't (if you try it anything after the asterisk will be ignored without warning).

A completely wild name would be either of these:

```
*.*
???????.???
```

and they would match any filename and extension. Note that they mean exactly the same thing since an asterisk (*) is just shorthand for a series of question marks.

We can combine the use of both ? and * however we want to. For example,

```
DIR ?.*
```

will show all the files with filenames only one character long and with any extension. This example,

```
DIR ?E*.*
```

shows all files with an E in the second position of the name. You can work out lots of variations on this idea.

These wild card specifications are mainly used with four commands, the DIR directory listing, the DEL/ERASE file erase command, the REN/RENAME file name change command, and the COPY command. It also has a special copy-and-concatenate use with the COPY command (see the complete discussion of the COPY command in Chapter 5 for details). If "concatenate" is a new word to you (it was to me), it means to connect the two files together into one.

Other than the commands mentioned (DIR, DEL/ERASE, REN/RENAME, and COPY), most programs that require a file specification will not successfully use a name with a wild card, even if the wild card specification ends up matching only one single file. There are advanced programming techniques, though, which make it easy for a program to make good use of wild cards. DOS provides some special services to programs for just that purpose. It is a good thing for programs to make use of these services of DOS, so that when we use the programs we can give them filenames with wild card specification. Not all programs do so and we shouldn't be disappointed when they don't.

Beware! Use of wild cards can be very dangerous. Many a DOS user has erased files that weren't supposed to be erased by the accidental misuse of wild cards. Giving a wild card to a program that doesn't expect them can lead to other mishaps.

When you do want to use wild cards—especially when you want to use them with the DEL/ERASE command—it's a good idea to test to see what files will match the wild card specification. You can do this simply with the DIR command, giving it the same wild card name that you're about to use with another command. For example, before doing something potentially dangerous like this:

```
DEL *.BAS
```

test what files it will apply to with this:

```
DIR *.BAS
```

This process of using DIR to get a wild card list before taking action can be automated, with the magic of batch files, as we'll see more in Chapter 11.

9.5 File Formats and What They Mean to You

It helps to understand what your disk data is like—how it is structured, what it looks like, and how it is stored. In this section we'll take a look at disk file formats.

First, how is data stored on disks? The scheme is simple and efficient. As DOS sees it, the storage space for data on a disk is made up of fixed-size chunks of space called sectors. The size of the sectors may vary from one type of disk to another, but within one disk the sectors are all the same size—typically 512 or 1024 bytes.

DOS manages the space on a disk by allocating sectors, or clusters of sectors, to any files that need them. If a disk has too many sectors to conveniently keep track of them one by one, then sectors are combined into logical units called clusters of sectors. Either way, space on a disk is allocated to files in uniform, fixed amounts. As a typical example, a single-sided 5¼-inch diskette might have its space allocated as individual 512-byte sectors, while a double-sided diskette might use two-sector clusters so that its space is allocated two sectors at a time—which would be 1,024 bytes for each cluster.

While this is interesting to learn about, we don't need to know this information at all, and that is one of the beauties of DOS's way of storing data on disks. DOS reads and writes disk data in fixed-size sectors, and allocates that space one or more sectors at a time. We don't see these fixed-size sectors at all. Instead, DOS lets us store our data in any size that is convenient to us. DOS worries about fitting our data into the fixed-size sectors, and does it so efficiently and so quietly that we never have to concern ourselves about the mechanics of how the data is stored.

Shoe-horning our data into fixed-size sectors is work for DOS and not for us or our programs. This is a very good thing because it makes a clean division of labor: DOS worries about where and how to store our data, and all that our programs have to worry about is how to use the data.

There are more or less four file formats that are used to store our data on disks—three special formats and a sort of a catch-all format.

Two of the three special formats are used to store executable programs. The formats are known by their standard filename extensions—COM and EXE. COM files are used to hold programs that are completely ready-to-execute; this is a memory-image format, which means that what's on disk is identical to what is in the computer's memory when the program is executed.

The EXE format is more sophisticated; EXE programs require some last minute fix-up work to be done as they are loaded from disk into memory. This fix-up mostly involves placing the program into the right part of memory, and letting the program know where it has been placed. The EXE format is mostly used for the more complicated type of program that is produced by compilers. Because of the extra overhead EXE format programs are bulkier when they are stored on disk, but inside the computer's memory they can be just as compact as COM-type programs.

There is nothing about these two special program file formats that is of much practical consequence to us. In fact, the main thing worth knowing about COM and EXE program files is just their filename extensions. By looking for COM and EXE files we can see which are the executable programs on a disk.

The BASIC programming language is an exception to many rules, and that's also true when it comes to program files. If you have BASIC programs that are run with the BASIC interpreter, then those programs are stored in files with the extension BAS. You may think of these as executable programs, and from our point of view they are. But from the point of view of DOS, a BASIC program in a BAS file is just data that the BASIC interpreter reads in

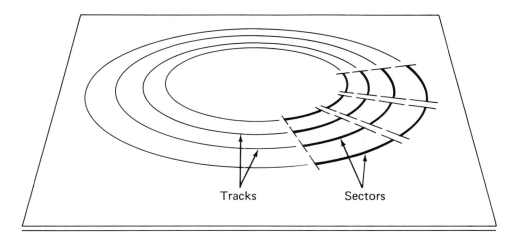

Tracks　　　Sectors

order to find out what to do. This is a technical point, but one that is worth knowing. As DOS and the computer see it, the BASIC interpreter is a true program and a BASIC BAS file is just data; that is why the BASIC interpreter is stored in a COM file—because it's a true program.

That covers the two special program file formats. The other special file format—one that is particularly interesting to us—is the ASCII text file format. This is the format that is used to store our text data such as correspondence, reports, and the source code form of programs.

There are various terms used to talk about this file format—sometimes it is called a text file, or an ASCII file, or a word processing file. We'll usually call it an ASCII text file. ASCII text files use a format that is very flexible and is adapted to serve many purposes. It is probably the most widely used format for computer data; it is certainly universal to small personal computers. (ASCII refers to the code scheme that computers use to recognize the letters of the alphabet, and so forth, that make up a file of written text; ASCII is short for the American Standard Code for Information Interchange—it's the standard code used for computer characters. In layman's terms, ASCII means written material as the computer sees it.)

An ASCII text file consists mostly of a stream of written information—the alphabetic letters, numbers, and punctuation that make up the types of things that we people write. What you are reading in this book is typical of the contents of an ASCII text file; in fact, in my home these very words are stored on a disk in an ASCII text file. Besides the words—or text—an ASCII text file contains some formatting information that helps make the text more useful. At the end of an ASCII text file is an end-of-file format marker (this is the ASCII character number

26, which is also sometimes called Control-Z; Control-Z is discussed along with some other special characters in Section 7.3).

Inside an ASCII text file, the text is marked into lines by having two formatting characters placed at the end of each line; these two characters are known as carriage return (ASCII character 13) and line feed (ASCII 10). This is really all the formatting that is normally placed in an ASCII text file—carriage return and line feed at the end of each line and end-of-file at, naturally, the end of the file. ASCII text files normally don't have any more format punctuation in them—there normally aren't paragraph or page markings. But, in the definition of ASCII there are formatting characters that can be used for this kind of marking, and more besides.

(We've been mentioning some special characters by their ASCII codes. For example, ASCII 13 is the carriage return character. Everything inside a computer works like a number so every character has a numeric code, whether it's a letter of the alphabet, like capital A, which is ASCII 65, or whether it's a special character, like end-of-file, which is ASCII 26. If you know, or will be learning, the BASIC lan-

guage, BASIC refers to these numeric character codes like this:
CHR$(26).)

The kind of programs that we call editors or text editors all work
with ASCII text files. DOS itself comes with a simple but powerful
text editor called EDLIN; we discussed EDLIN a little in Chapter 6
and we go into more detail about it in Chapter 19. Word processors,
too, usually work with ordinary ASCII text files. However, sophisticated word processors, like the popular WordStar, need more complex formatting information than what ordinary ASCII easily
accommodates, so they augment and bend the rules some to get the
kind of data that they need. As a consequence, WordStar text files
are a little different than ordinary vanilla-flavored ASCII text files.
Yet, underneath the trappings of a WordStar file there is a simple
ASCII text file.

What's particularly interesting and important to us about ASCII
text files is that they are the most common and most interchangeable
of all file formats. That means that if we have one program tool that
uses ASCII text files, then we can expect to be able to move data
from it to other programs that use ASCII with a minimum of fuss
and difficulty. This can be a tremendous advantage in flexibility.

Lines as we see them:

Mary had a little lamb,

Its fleece was white as snow.

And everywhere that Mary went,

The lamb was sure to go.

Data as it is in the file:

Mary had a little lamb, <end-line> Its fleece was white as

snow. <end-line> And everywhere that Mary went, <end-line>

The lamb was sure to go. <end-line> <end-file>

Because of this, it can be greatly to our advantage to have as much data in ASCII format as possible.

If you are programming or having programs designed for you, you should consider using the ASCII text file format, even if it is not the most convenient for your programs. In the long run the benefits can be considerable.

After these three special file formats—COM program files, EXE program files, and ASCII text files—we come to the catch-all format of the general data file. Unless a file has a special format, it consists simply of data stored on a disk. Usually data files are made up of fixed length parts called records. The records can be as short as a single byte or as long as you like. To read or write such a data file a program tells DOS the basic information about the file, such as what the record size is, and DOS does the work of finding where each record is, in what part of what disk sector.

There is one special thing worth knowing about files that are made up of fixed-length records. Since the records are all of the same size, a simple arithmetic formula can be used to calculate where each record is stored. This means that it is possible for a fixed-length-record file to be accessed randomly, skipping arbitrarily from one record to another. A fixed-length record file can be processed either sequentially, one record in order after another, or by random skips. This is one tremendous advantage over an ASCII text file, which must be read and written sequentially, from front to back in proper order.

When you think about files, and consider what can be done with them, you should keep in mind the special random access capability that a fixed-length record file has.

9.6 Diskettes and Other Animals

There are more creatures in the forest than you or I might imagine. Just when we think we've seen them all, up pops another furry critter. So it is with disk storage. For whatever computer you have that uses DOS, you probably know the particular options that are available for disk storage. It's worthwhile to know a little about the full range of disk storage formats.

There are three main species in the disk forest, with lots of variations and a few hybrids thrown in for variety. The three main types are floppy diskettes, hard disks, and electronic disks.

Floppy diskettes are the most common form of disk storage for small personal computers, although they are rapidly being supplanted by newer, more advanced storage media.

Floppies get their nickname because they are made of a flexible plastic, and they can be easily and harmlessly bent. A classic floppy comes in a black, square-shaped protective cover. In the cover is a hub opening where the diskette is grabbed and spun, and another slotted opening where the diskette surface is read and written on magnetically.

The original floppies were eight inches in diameter. Later, 5¼ inch mini-floppies were developed, and they have been the most common size used in personal computers. There are lots of variations in diskettes besides their size. They can be recorded on one or both sides, and the recording density can be in what is called single-, double-, or quadruple-density, which are recorded at 24, 48, or 96 tracks-per-inch density. Also, diskettes can be hard- or soft-sectored, depending upon whether or not the formatting of the diskette into sectors is fixed or variable under program control. One of the most common forms of diskette, especially for modern personal computers, is double-density soft-sectored. Every possible variation is used on some computer, somewhere.

Typically a diskette holds somewhere from 100,000 bytes to 500,000 bytes of data or more, but the full range of capacities is much wider than that with all of the formats that are available.

IBM's high-capacity diskettes can hold 1.2 million bytes, and some exotic diskettes can store much more. Hard disks are higher-capacity storage media than floppies. Hard disks are made of a rigid platter coated with magnetic recording material. Usually they make use of a technology that was first code-named Winchester, so hard disks are also called Winchester disks. Their capacity is dramatically higher than floppies. The minimum capacity is around five million bytes, and some can hold as much as 50 million bytes.

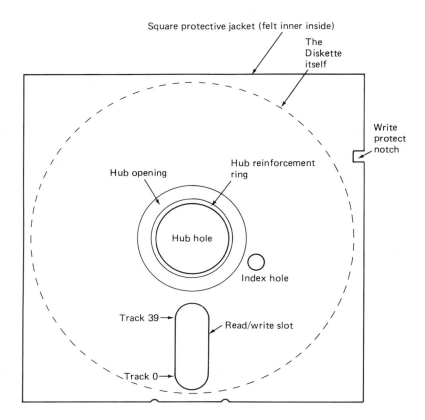

Square protective jacket (felt inner inside)

The
Diskette
itself

Write
protect
notch

Hub reinforcement
ring

Hub opening

Hub hole

Index hole

Track 39 →

Read/write slot

Track 0 →

A true Winchester disk is completely sealed against the outside air and dust so it isn't removable—you don't change these disks like you can swap floppies, but with the high storage capacity there is less need to. There is also a variety of hard disk that has a removable cartridge that can be taken in and out of the disk drive, just like a floppy.

Chapter 16 discusses some of the special needs of hard disk users.

As something of a hybrid between floppies and hard disks, there are micro-disk formats. Micro-disks are about three inches in diameter and are enclosed in a rigid case, like the removable cartridges used in some hard disk systems. The design and the technology of micro-disks combine features of both floppies and hard disks. One unfortunate development in micro-disks is that over half a dozen different incompatible sizes and formats sprang up before any widespread standardization was done. That will probably keep micro-disks from being used as widely as they otherwise might be.

One of the distant cousins in our PC family, the lap-sized DG-1 computer made by Data General, uses this micro-disk format.

The third completely different format of "disk" storage is the electronic disk or RAM disk. An electronic disk isn't disk storage at all but a combination of memory and computer program that produce a simulation of a disk storage device in random access memory (RAM). The point of using an electronic disk is to adapt the speed of electronic memory to the operating standards of disk storage. With an electronic disk, numerous programs and their associated data can be moved from conventional disk to electronic disk, and then used at much higher speed than would be possible on a true disk device. Electronic disk operations are perhaps ten times faster than floppy disks and twice as fast as hard disks, which can be an enormous advantage. There are special problems and considerations in using electronic disks, which are covered in Chapter 16.

9.7 Special Things About Disks

Disks can be used in a rich and complex way in DOS, thanks to the concept of subdirectories and paths that we discussed in Chapter 8. Let's do a quick review and relate it to what we know now about disks.

All disks have a fixed-sized directory of files. This is called the root or main directory. This isn't the only directory that a disk can have, though. The disk's main or root directory can have subdirectories under it, and each of those can also have any mixture of files and subdirectories under it. (If you're working with a 1-series of DOS, the whole topic of subdirectories and related subjects doesn't apply to you).

Where do these subdirectories come from? As they are stored on the disk, subdirectories are just files like any other file that we keep on the disk. Subdirectories are specially marked, however, so that DOS can treat them as part of the directory structure and not as other files are treated. As to how they are stored on the disk, subdirectories are like any other file. This has some interesting and important consequences for us.

First off, a subdirectory can grow in size, just as any file is allowed to grow. There is no arbitrary limit to the number of entries that can be placed in a subdirectory. This is a major advantage over each disk's root directory—because a root directory is fixed in its location and size, and so there is a definite upper limit to the number of files that can be placed in a root directory. Subdirectories can grow without limit (except for the limit of space on the disk).

The second practical consequence of subdirectories being stored like any other file is that it takes longer to get to them, because DOS has to hunt around the disk for them. A disk's root directory is located at the very beginning of the disk, next to a table that keeps track of the available and used space on the disk.

When DOS processes a file that is in the root directory, all of information needed to find it—the directory entry for the file and the information of where the file is stored—is located close together where it can be gotten to quickly. With subdirectories, it is another matter. To work with a file that is kept in a subdirectory, DOS has to hunt through the path of subdirectories that leads to the file; each subdirectory is stored on the disk some distance away from the space table. Tracing through the directory path and going back and forth from the directories to the space table adds a lot of overhead to the work that DOS must do.

If a disk is fast—as most hard disk systems are—and if the path is short—as I recommend that you keep all your paths short—then there isn't much problem. With a slow diskette device or with complicated paths, the extra work can slow your computer down considerably.

There is another feature that was added to DOS disks at the same time that subdirectories were introduced: disk labels. When you format a disk with DOS, you have the option of adding a label. Whenever DOS reports on a disk for you, as with the DIR, CHKDSK and TREE commands, DOS will check for a label and report it to you. This can be handy in helping you keep track of your diskettes so I highly recommend that you label your diskettes, provided you do have something useful to name them. Incidentally, the disk label is stored in the disk's root directory, similar to the entry for a file or for a subdirectory; but the label entry is specially marked and doesn't use any of the disk's working data space.

To get a volume label when we format a disk, we add the /V option to the command, like this:

```
FORMAT /V
```

Then, when the formatting program has finished the regular formatting, it prompts us to type in a volume label, with a message like this:

```
Volume label (11 characters, ENTER for none)?
```

Volume labels can also be added to a disk (or changed or removed) with a variety of programs that were specially written for that purpose. My Norton Utilities program set has a program like that, and—thankfully—DOS also includes one, starting with version 3.0 (but not, unfortunately, earlier versions).

10

What You Need to Know About Programming Languages

Even if you don't do any programming, there are some important and interesting things you should know about programming languages. How programming languages operate affects the way your computer works for you, and the performance of your computer is deeply affected by choices that are made about which language is used and how that language is used. And, of course, if you program or have programming done for you, it is very important for you to understand what programming languages are all about.

If your interest in DOS doesn't include any interest in programming languages, you can safely go to the next chapter: you won't be missing anything fundamental.

On the other hand, if programming is of special interest to you, you'll want to read this chapter closely and also refer back to Section 6.4, where we covered the DOS commands that apply specifically to program development.

10.1 What Are Programming Languages?

Programming languages are the way that people talk to computers in order to tell them what to do. A programming language is used to record, in an exact way, the instructions that the computer is to carry out. There are many programming languages, and even if you are a newcomer to computing you probably know the names of some of the most common ones: BASIC, COBOL, FORTRAN, and assembly language. (Assembly is also called assembler, and sometimes it's called "machine language"; these terms mean roughly the same thing.) Less common ones that you might have heard about are Pascal, FORTH, C, PL/I, and Ada. There are many more.

What sets them apart from each other? Several things. One is whether a programming language is "high level" or "low level." A low-level language, like assembler, is more oriented to the computer than to the people who are programming in it. High-level languages, like BASIC and Pascal, are more people-oriented. What does that mean? It means that in a high-level language our programs say more directly what work we want the computer to accomplish, while in a low-level language our programs say more directly how the details of the work are to be carried out. In a low-level language, much of the program will be occupied with details that have little to do with what we actually want to accomplish. The difference between a high-level and a low-level language is similar to the difference between giving a carpenter a detailed blueprint of what you want built (high-level), and telling him where to put every screw and nail (low-level).

Another difference between languages is their intended purpose: COBOL is for business programming, FORTRAN is for engineering; BASIC and Pascal are for general-purpose use. Finally, there is how "structured" a language is. "Structured" is a technical programming term that refers to some principles and techniques of programming which help make programs more reliable and easier to fix and change. Modern structured languages, like Pascal and C, help produce reliable, easy-to-maintain programs; less structured languages, like BASIC and FORTRAN, resist efforts to write programs of good quality. Later in this chapter we'll take a closer look at why this is important to you.

Computers don't work directly with anything you or I would recognize as civilized speech. They take their marching orders in a form known as machine language or machine code; it is also sometimes called absolute code. Machine language is usually very intricately coded, and is very hard for a human to make sense of—it is designed for the convenience of computer circuitry, not for our convenience.

When machine code is displayed for us to look at—and heaven forbid that we should have to look at much of it—it is normally shown in the numbers and letters of hexadecimal notation. An example:

```
83 06-0AF7 03
```

This particular machine language instruction tells the computer to add (83) the value three (03) to whatever number is stored at a certain memory location (06-0AF7). A typical machine language instruction has three parts—an operation (add in our example), a source operand (three in our example), and a destination operand (the memory specification 06-0AF7).

People don't write programs in machine code even when they want to work on that level. Instead, they use a symbolic equivalent known as assembly language. The key thing to know about assembly language is that it substitutes symbolic names for the detailed numbers of machine language. To write our sample instruction in assembly language, we would write ADD instead of 83; the assembler takes care of the work of substituting the proper operation code for the word ADD. An assembler does a lot of things that make the programmer's work easier, but fundamentally all it is doing is translating meaningful symbols (ADD) into machine codes (83). An assembly language programmer writes out every detailed instruction that the computer will perform.

Assembly language is a low-level programming language—in fact the lowest—because programs in assembly contain all the tedious details necessary to produce a working program. Every instruction that the computer will perform in carrying out the program appears, in symbolic form, in the assembly program.

Fortunately for us all, there are higher level languages that take care of many of the tedious details for us. High-level languages, like

BASIC, are called high level because each command in the BASIC language is translated into many instructions in machine language. But this many-for-one translation isn't the important thing about high-level languages. The important thing about high-level languages is that most of the tedious details of instructing the computer are taken care of for us. In a high-level language we tell the computer what to do, in a broader sense, and the programming language translates our commands into the narrow, detailed instructions.

For example: In BASIC we might write

```
LET TOTAL.PAY = HOURS.WORKED * HOURLY.RATE.OF.PAY
```

while the machine language equivalent might be a dozen—or even several hundred—instructions.

Don't make the mistake of thinking that with a high-level language we can just tell the computer what we intend to have done. We have to tell the computer how to accomplish what we want done. This, in fact, is what programs are—a statement of all of the steps that have to be performed to accomplish some purpose. A program is an "algorithm," a statement of the strategy and tactical details needed to per-

form some work. The difference between high- and low-level languages is in how tediously the details must be spelled out. In either case, the details of the work must be specified in the program and not just the intended result.

There are two main ways that our programs, as we write them, get translated into instructions that the computer can use—compiling and interpreting. Since the very common language BASIC uses both methods, we'll compare them in the next section where we discuss the two kinds of BASIC.

10.2 The Two Kinds of BASIC— Interpreted and Compiled

For a computer to carry out what our programs ask it to do, the programs must be translated into machine language in one way or other. There are two ways that this is done, known as interpreting and compiling. Most programming languages come to us in one form or the other. BASIC is unique because Microsoft provides both interpreted and compiled versions of BASIC for the IBM PC family.

(Assembly language programs are translated by a process called assembling; but that's really just the same thing as compiling. It's traditional in the world of computers to call the translation of assembly language *assembling*, and the translation of high-level languages *compiling*.)

There is a simple way to understand what interpreting and compiling are. An interpreter does its translation on the spot as the program is run, while a compiler does its translation in advance before the translated program is used. There is a simple human analogy to this. An interpreter works like the simultaneous translators at the United Nations, while a compiler works like a scholar who translates Homer from ancient Greek into modern English. Necessarily, the on-the-spot interpretive translation will be rough-and-ready, while the compiled translation can be quite polished.

It wouldn't matter to us whether or not a program is interpreted or compiled, except that it influences how we interact with programs. First there is the matter of speed.

Compiled BASIC—or any compiled language—runs much faster than interpreted BASIC for three reasons. First, an interpreter does its translation work while the program is running, each time the program is run. While you are using an interpreted BASIC program, the translation work is done as you are waiting. With a compiler, however, the translation overhead is done in advance, only once; whether the overhead of compiling is large or small, it has already been done before we use the programs so that compiled programs run faster. Following the analogy of a book translator and a U.N. interpreter, it doesn't matter how long it took to translate a book (compile a program), we can read the book (run the program) as quickly as we wish. When we listen to a U.N. interpreter, we can't listen any faster than the interpreter speaks.

A second reason why compiled programs are faster running than interpreted programs is that programs usually execute certain sections many times. With interpreted BASIC, that means the same part of the program is translated over and over again. If a speaker at the U.N. repeats himself, the simultaneous translators work that much longer. Finally, a compiler gets to look at the whole program before writing up the translated version; this gives the compiler an opportunity to do a polished translation—to optimize the finished result into an excellent translation. But the U.N.'s simultaneous translators don't get to polish their phrasing; what's said now is translated now, even if it leads to a poor choice of words. And that makes interpreted BASIC very slow. How slow? My own tests with the IBM PC's interpreted and compiled BASIC showed speed differences as high as 50 to one—a breathtaking difference—but 10 times faster is more typical and still impressive.

Don't be seduced by dreams of speed though. Many programs spend their time waiting for data to come and go from disks; a faster-running compiled BASIC program won't speed that up. Many BASIC programs run fast enough in interpreted mode. It is only if an interpreted BASIC program is taking too long while it is computing that there would be any speed advantage in having it compiled.

There are other interesting and important differences between interpreted and compiled BASIC. The most important difference is that with an interpreted program, you can change the program while it is running. You can stop a program, make corrections to it, and then tell the interpreter to carry on. When programs are being developed this is a tremendous advantage, because it makes much more efficient use of human time in writing and testing programs.

There is one more important difference between compiled and interpreted BASIC. Due to some technical details in the way that the PC family of computers manage their memories, there are different restrictions on how much memory can be used. For interpreted BASIC, the combined total of the size of the program and the size of the data is limited to 64K, or 65,536 bytes. Compiled BASIC programs can use that entire 64K for data alone, while the program may grow to any size without reducing that space available for data. (What we've said here has to do with designed-in limits on BASIC programs and data; naturally the amount of memory available in your computer puts another practical limit on the size of data and the size of programs.)

10.3 How Compiled Languages Work in DOS

There is a certain conventional way that compiled languages work in DOS, and it's worthwhile to understand the main points even if you will never do any programming.

What we'll be describing here is the customary way that Microsoft's compilers work. Since Microsoft supplied IBM with the official programming languages for the PC family, the Microsoft style has set a standard that many others follow. Compilers from other companies may work in curiously different ways from Microsoft's or they may be the same. Either way, the basic principles that we'll cover here still apply.

Programs as people write them are called source code. Source code programs are ASCII text files, which we covered in Chapter 9 on file formats. There is a convention for the filename extensions used for source code, and it is a good idea to follow it. By this convention, the filename extension indicates the language the program is written in. The names used for the most common languages are these:

BASIC	.BAS
Pascal	.PAS
C	.C
assembly	.ASM
COBOL	.COB
FORTRAN	.FOR

One warning about BAS files. BASIC is often an exception to the rules in computing, and that's true here. While our BASIC source code programs all have filename extensions of BAS, not all BAS files have the same format. BASIC uses three different file formats for source programs. One of them is the standard ASCII text file format, which all compilers use. In addition, BASIC has two special formats

that only interpreter BASIC uses. The first of these is a compressed "tokenized" format, which consists of a BASIC program translated into the format, that interpreter BASIC uses internally. This tokenized format takes up about 23 percent less space than the normal ASCII text format, and interpreter BASIC is able to read and write it faster as well. The other special format is the protected form of BASIC programs. When a BASIC program is protected, it is encoded in a way that resists efforts to reveal the program source code.

Interpreter BASIC can work with any of these three forms of BAS files, but the BASIC compiler, like all other compilers, needs to have its source programs in the standard ASCII text format. Interpreter BASIC can store any of the three formats, and they are selected through an option in the SAVE command. If "SAVE filename,A" is used, then ASCII text format is written. If "SAVE filename,P" is specified, the protected format is written. If neither the A option nor the P option is used, then BASIC uses its tokenized format.

Compiled (or assembled) languages all work the same way in DOS. Preparing a program for execution involves two main steps after the program has been written. These two steps are called compiling (or assembling, for assembly language), and linking.

How a compiler works varies from language to language. In some cases, like the Microsoft BASIC compiler, the compilation is a simple one-step process. In other cases, like the IBM macro assembler—which, once again, was supplied by Microsoft—the translation appears to us as a one-step process, but actually behind the scenes the translation takes two steps, and the source code is read twice by the assembler program. For some of the most advanced compilers, like the IBM Pascal compiler (written by Microsoft), two fully separate steps are performed. In the case of Pascal, the first stage of the compiler reads the source code and translates it into a semi-digested form. The second stage of the compiler then gobbles up the semi-digested program, chews on it for some time (performing numerous internal steps that do different things), and then spits out the compiled result.

The more sophisticated the compiler, the more able it is to produce compact, efficient, fast-running machine code. A really advanced compiler is able to detect all sorts of unnecessary duplication of work and produce highly optimized machine code.

The job of a compiler is to translate source code into machine language in a standard form called an object file, or object code. Object code is the fully translated program in machine language. But object code isn't quite ready to be used—it still needs some work done on it, called linking, or link editing, which we'll get to in a moment. Object code is stored in files with the standard filename extension of OBJ.

Why isn't the object code ready to use? There are two closely related reasons, both having to do with incorporating other programs into the compiled program. These other programs can be subprograms that we have written, or they can be part of the programming language's standard library.

When our programs ask the computer to do something—such as displaying a number on the screen—as often as not what we've asked the computer to do is something quite common, yet laborious to carry out. In the example of displaying a number on the screen, two standard operations need to be carried out—first, convert the number from its internal computational form into a display format that people can read, and, second, to actually place that display format onto the screen. Each of these operations is done a lot, and each requires quite a few machine-language instructions to carry it out.

It would be silly for a compiler to generate all the necessary machine-language instructions each time we did such a common operation. Instead, compilers have a library of subroutines that perform these common tasks. So when the compiler comes to that part of a program, instead of generating the lengthy machine-language

code needed to do the task, it just generates a brief "call" to one of its library routines—and the library routine is prepared to do similar work for any part of our programs.

The task of patching together different programs is done by the link editor, or linker, called LINK. Having a linker makes the whole process of preparing programs much more flexible, since it means that compilers can use libraries of routines, and programmers can write their programs in separate parts and later combine those parts into complete programs. The linker takes in object files (with file name extensions of OBJ), and libraries (with filename extensions of LIB) and combines them to produce a finished working program. For more about the LINK program command see Chapter 6.

A library is nothing more than a collection of object files with a built-in table of contents to tell what's where. Each programming language comes with its own specialized library. When the linker goes to work on a program's object files, it checks which subroutines each file needs from somewhere else, and also which subroutines

each file can supply for others to use. All the cross connections are made, and any library routines that are needed are gathered together. The result is a machine-language program, with all of its parts supplied and converted from object (OBJ) format into the format of a ready-to-run program (EXE).

There is a library maintenance program, called LIB, which allows you to control the modules in a library—adding them, removing them, replacing them, and even building your own libraries from scratch. Although LIB is not a part of IBM's version of DOS, LIB is often included in the DOS that comes with other brands of computers, and when we buy an IBM compiler—such as the IBM Pascal Compiler—we usually get a copy of LIB along with it. For all practical purposes, LIB is an ingredient of DOS as programmers use DOS. LIB is discussed with other programming tools in Chapter 6.

Ready-to-run programs can have two forms in DOS, and they are known by their filename extensions as EXE files and COM files. The difference between the two is technical, and the details aren't of much interest to us. In essence, a COM-file program can be loaded into memory as is, while an EXE-file program has some last-minute preparation work done on it as it is loaded into memory. The linker always produces EXE-type programs but under the right circumstances they can be converted to COM format. There is a DOS utilities to convert from EXE to COM called EXE2BIN. Compiled programs must usually be in EXE format, although some programming languages do permit the use of the COM format.

There is one more important thing that you need to know about compiled programs in DOS—the subject of run-time support. Compiled programs need library routines, as we've already seen. There are two ways that these library routines can be provided. The first way is from a regular library. When they are supplied this way, the resulting link-edited program is self-sufficient and doesn't need anything else to be run on our computers.

The other way to provide library routines is through a run-time module. A run-time module is a separate file of subroutines that are connected to our programs not when the program is linked, but when the program is run. In effect a run-time module is a last minute, help-you-on-the-spot form of library.

Whether or not a run-time module is needed depends on how the compiler for that language was written. One company that sells compilers might produce a COBOL that uses a run-time module, while another compiler company might make a COBOL that doesn't. Among the Microsoft compilers, Pascal and C don't use run-time modules; COBOL and FORTRAN have to use them. And straddling the fence is BASIC, which can be compiled so that BASIC programs are either self-sufficient (getting all their routines from the library) or dependent on the run-time module.

Run-time modules are easily identified by their file names. For example, Microsoft BASIC's is named BASRUN.EXE and COBOL's is named COBRUN.EXE.

There are some practical consequences involved with run-time modules: size, speed, and expense. If you have 20 programs in stand-alone format, then they will contain 20 individual copies of the most common subroutines—which can take up a lot of storage space on your disks. If the same 20 programs used a run-time module, then one copy of the subroutines could service them all for a sizeable saving in disk space. A typical size difference is 10 or 15 thousand bytes for each program.

Run-time modules tend to take longer to use, because some of the work of making connections has to be done over and over again; this makes them partially analogous to interpreted programs. One test that I performed with a compiled BASIC program ran one-third faster in stand-alone form than the form that used BASIC's run-time module. When speed matters, a program that uses a run-time module is at a disadvantage.

OBJECT FILE 2

LIBRARY

OBJECT FILE 1

LINKER

READY-TO-RUN PROGRAM

Stand-alone programs can usually be distributed without any special permission or licensing agreement from IBM or Microsoft (or whoever else produced the compiler). In some cases, though, the run-time modules must be separately purchased for every computer that they are used on. This involves not only extra expense, but a real administrative nuisance as well. If you are selling programs that need the run-time module, you may have to ask each of your customers if they already have the run-time module or if they need to buy it. The alternative is to include the module in the cost of every copy of your programs, forcing some of your customers to unnecessarily buy a duplicate copy of a module that they already have. Even if you aren't selling programs but are just distributing them within your organization, the same problems arise. Programs that require a run-time module can be a real headache.

10.4 Choosing a Programming Language

If you are going to program—or have programming done for you—then it has to be done in some programming language. All too often, the choice of programming language is made casually or by default. It shouldn't happen that way. The choice of a programming language can deeply affect the quality of your programs—how fast they run, how easy they are to update, and even how well they are built. Under some circumstances the programming language should even be a factor in choosing which of several competing programs to buy. This is particularly true for accounting programs.

If you are a user and not a writer of programs, you might be puzzled as to why the choice of programming languages should matter to you. Think of it this way. If you owned a business and were about to have a new factory built, it would matter a lot to you whether that factory was built out of wood or steel and glass—you would have to live with the heating bills and the cost of fire insurance. You probably would leave the decision to a professional engineer, but you'd want to be reassured that the decision was made right—you might even want to have the final say yourself. And you'd make absolutely sure that your factory wasn't being built out of adobe mud. But there are an awful lot of mud-built programs on the market. More than you might imagine possible.

There is no completely simple guide to making a wise choice among programming languages, but here we'll give you an idea of what the main factors are in making an intelligent choice.

Let's start by considering the language level. There are three levels to choose from: low, high and extra-high. The high-level languages are BASIC, Pascal, COBOL, FORTRAN, C, FORTH, and a host of others. These, of course, are the mainstream of programming languages and we'll have quite a bit to say about how to choose among them. Before we go into that, lets consider the alternatives of low-level and extra-high level.

Low level means assembly language. Assembly has the advantages of compact program size and fast running speed, but some enormous disadvantages. It requires highly-skilled programmers to write; it is much more time-consuming to write and to test, and when changes are called for it is enormously more difficult to update. The only people who should use assembly language already know why they need it. If you are reading an introductory book like this, neither you nor anyone who works for you should ever consider assembly language. On the other hand, if you are buying programs the advantages of assembly programs look very attractive—fast speed and compact size. This advantage is a sound one to go for if the product is mature and well tested. If you buy a newly introduced program that was written in assembly, then you are running a higher risk that the program will have errors in it and that the errors won't be easily corrected.

What are extra-high level languages? Some of the most sophisticated programs for computers are, in effect, programmable themselves. How could a program be programmable? By being so flexible that it accepts commands and instructions that take on some of the characteristics of programs, such as logical decisions and controlled repetition.

There are two main categories of these programmable programs. First are the spreadsheet programs, such as Multiplan, Lotus 1-2-3, and the grand-daddy of them all, VisiCalc. Second are data base programs, particularly dBASE II and III. Programs of this type are sophisticated enough to act as their own (specialized) programming languages. Here are two examples of how they can be used: If you are looking for an income tax program, you can find ones that work on their own or ones that are templates—that is, programs—for Visi-Calc. If you want a mailing list program, you can get a stand-alone one or one that works through dBASE II or III.

What are the advantages and disadvantages of using extra-high level programming? There are two main advantages. The first advantage is a magnification of the benefit of using a high-level language: programs are quicker to write and test, easier to adapt, modify, and improve, and the programmer is relieved of more tedious details, particularly the details of data and file management. The second advantage is that the programs and data are even more easily integrated with other programs and data (provided they are developed using the same extra-high level tools; mixing different dBASE II data may work dandy, but mixing dBASE II and Multiplan may be a disaster).

The main disadvantage of using an extra-high level language is that it tends to lock you into the use of one proprietary tool, dBASE III, Multiplan or whatever. This can reduce your future options and the mobility of your data to other systems. A lesser disadvantage is that extra-high level languages tend to be slow, sometimes awfully slow; this problem grows smaller over time as extra-high level tools improve and as computers become faster. Extra-high level languages are generally interpreted rather than compiled.

My personal opinion is that the disadvantages of extra-high level programming languages are slight and that the benefits are enormous. As a general rule, I think you should always choose to use an extra-high level programming language whenever you have the choice.

Most programming is done in ordinary high-level languages; they are the mainstream of programming languages. Let's take a look at the principal high-level languages and see what matters about them.

There are six main languages to be considered: BASIC, C, COBOL, FORTH, FORTRAN, and Pascal. The greybeards in this list are COBOL and FORTRAN so let's consider them first.

Both COBOL and FORTRAN were among the very first programming languages to be developed, and they have been the mainstay of traditional, large-system computing. COBOL was designed for business-oriented programming, while FORTRAN is oriented to engineering-style calculations. The principal advantage that these two languages have for use on the PC family of computers is that there are many programmers available who are fluent in them; this is particularly true for COBOL. At times it has seemed that COBOL programmers were a dime a dozen, and wise programming managers chose COBOL as a language since COBOL programmers were more readily—and cheaply—available.

There are some strong reasons against using COBOL and FORTRAN, even though they have been so widely used in traditional computing. COBOL and FORTRAN programs and programming skills don't necessarily transfer well to the smaller and more interactive environment of personal computers. But there is an even more important reason for avoiding them. Since the days when COBOL and FORTRAN were developed, a great deal has been learned about what makes a good programming language, and what techniques lead to safe, reliable, and easily maintained programs. Most of these techniques sail under the banner of structured programming. Older programming languages are not oriented towards structured programming, and they may resist attempts to use them in a structured way. FORTRAN is particularly bad in this regard.

Because FORTRAN is archaic, because it is difficult to structure, and also because it is relatively easy to translate FORTRAN programs into BASIC, I would recommend against using FORTRAN. (My private opinion is that FORTRAN programming on an IBM personal computer is inexcusable.) While COBOL has many disadvantages as well—again, it is archaic and its implementations are usually inefficient, bulky, and slow-running—there is less reason to avoid COBOL.

There are much better languages than COBOL, yet COBOL is reasonably easy to structure, and it doesn't translate easily into another substitute language. COBOL is not a language of choice, but if you have good reasons to want to use COBOL—existing programs or existing programmers—then by all means use it. Unlike FORTRAN, COBOL isn't a language to avoid, it is just not a language to choose.

For microcomputers, BASIC is the first and foremost language (thanks mostly to Microsoft). BASIC is not a good language for structured programming—in fact it is as bad as they come. Even so, BASIC has some tremendous advantages that have made it the first choice of many program developers for microcomputers. First, it is the most widely available language for microcomputers, which means that programs you write and buy are likely to be more readily transferred to other computers. This should improve the salability of your own programs, and reduce the cost of programs that you buy.

FORTH

PASCAL   C

FORTRAN COBOL   BASIC

This gives BASIC a strong plus. Also, BASIC programming skills are the most widely available among experienced microcomputer programmers, which is another argument in favor of BASIC.

The strongest argument in favor of BASIC is that it is uniquely available in both interpretive and compiled versions. Microsoft provides both for the PC family. Thanks to these dual versions, you can have the best of both worlds by programming in BASIC. You can develop programs in interpretive BASIC getting all the advantages of interactive program development. Then, after a program has been thoroughly tested, it can be compiled for fast running speed. This is a unique advantage that makes BASIC very attractive for program development.

(Two warnings though: if you intend to develop interpreter-BASIC programs, and then later compile them, pay close attention to the subtle differences between what the two versions of the language allow. It is a good idea to start test-compiling early in the process of developing a program to avoid a nasty surprise later. And you shouldn't assume that you will be able to compile interpreter-BASIC programs that you have bought; converting them into compilable form may be a difficult task and the programs may be in protected format, which can't be compiled.)

Among programming languages that facilitate modern structured programming techniques, Pascal and C are highly regarded. These two languages provide all the features needed to write effective, fast, safe, and reliable programs for our computers. Pascal and C are similar. The main difference between them is that Pascal emphasizes safety at some sacrifice of power, and C emphasizes power over safety. Both are very fast. (If you have heard that Pascal is slow, you've heard about the "p-System" Pascal, which is interpreted; DOS uses a fast compiled Pascal.)

Either Pascal or C is an excellent choice for programming personal computers. Between them, Pascal may be the better choice since Pascal emphasizes safe programming, and many computer science college students are well trained in Pascal. In fact, Pascal was developed specifically as a language for teaching good programming practices. My own programming for the IBM PC has been done almost exclusively in Pascal and C—Pascal before and C these days. My preference, by far, is for Pascal, but I am—grudgingly—using C now because it is more closely tailored to my current programming needs.

If you don't understand why I have been emphasizing the terms structured programming, safety, reliability, and ease of maintenance, then you have been lucky to avoid the agonies that many traditional computer users have suffered in recent years. In the past, a great many poorly engineered programs were written with little thought to the importance of sound design principles in programming. Later, this lack of good design and engineering came back to haunt large computer shops.

The ugly task of maintaining poorly written programs has come to eat up the majority of time and money at many computer sites. There is no excuse for this expensive mistake to be repeated in the modern world of personal computing, but unfortunately many people who program microcomputers are taking a very shortsighted and amateurish approach to their computers. A major contributing factor in the production of bad programs has been the use of the BASIC language, regardless of BASIC's many virtues.

There is one odd language left in our list of mainstream languages: FORTH. This curious and quirky language has the unusual distinction of being designed for efficient interpretation. This means that FORTH, like BASIC, gets the benefits of both interpretation and speed—but FORTH gets to have both virtues at the same time (only compiled BASIC is faster). Because FORTH is so unusual in its form and is known by so few programmers, I can't particularly recommend it. If you are drawn to FORTH, for whatever reason, I see no reason to avoid it.

Besides the high-level languages we've gone over here, there are a host of others. I think that it is unwise to even consider any of them. Would you buy a car you can't get parts for? Should you use a language that few programmers know how to maintain? Should you use a language that is unlikely to be updated to match new computer features? Not unless you like to suffer.

There is one more factor to consider. You don't really use a programming language, you use an implementation of that language. If your programs are in Pascal, then they must be compiled by a Pascal compiler, and you may have a choice of more than one compiler. The quality of the compiler should influence your choice between different compilers, and perhaps even between different languages—better to have a well compiled COBOL than a poorly compiled Pascal.

In this regard, Microsoft has a huge advantage that should bias you in favor of using Microsoft compilers. Microsoft started out in the language business—they wrote the first BASIC interpreter for microcomputers—and it has been their specialty. Generally we can expect Microsoft compilers to be of good quality (but check the reputation of any particular one you are considering using).

Microsoft has two other advantages that should make you want to choose one of their compilers. Since they are the authors of DOS, we can expect that their compilers will be well integrated into the operating system, and will be updated more quickly and thoroughly than those of any of their competitors. And as one of the biggest and most successful software producers, you don't have to worry about Microsoft going out of business.

This shouldn't prevent you from considering using other companies' compilers. Often a company that specializes in producing one product—such as one compiler—can do a much better job than a large company with many products. You might find, for example, a COBOL compiler whose reputation is much stronger than Microsoft's COBOL. You must weigh the risks and benefits.

Let's end with one final warning. No matter how standard a programming language is, different compilers usually provide different features when you get down to the details, and programs are often dependent upon these details. This tends to apply more to small microcomputers than to traditional large-scale computers. Just because your programs are written in COBOL don't assume you'll be able to switch from compiler-R to compiler-M if you later want to. The usual experience is that once you begin using one particular compiler you are stuck with it. Migrating to another compiler may not work at all. Beware.

11

Batch File Secrets

Batch processing files are one of the most useful and powerful features of DOS, and we'll take a look at them in this chapter. First, we'll cover the simple idea of what a batch file is, and then get into some of the fancier tricks of using batch files. Finally, we'll finish the chapter with some suggestions and examples to help you get the most out of batch files.

11.1 Introducing Batch Processing—REM and PAUSE

The basic idea of batch processing is simple and ingenious: if you need the computer to perform a standard task, why should you have to key in the details of the task every time you run it? Instead, let the computer be told what it is supposed to do by reading its commands from a file. With a batch file, DOS doesn't perform our commands extemporaneously—instead it reads from a script.

There are some interesting details on what a batch file can do, but first let's see the elemental part. Batch processing is always done with a "batch processing file," which must have the filename extension of ".BAT". The file must be an ASCII text file (which we described in Chapter 9), and you can create it with any ordinary text editor, such as the EDLIN editor that comes with DOS. You can also use a word processing program to create batch files, though you should be sure to check if your word processor needs any special instructions to create an ordinary ASCII text file.

Inside the batch processing file are ordinary DOS commands, just as you might enter them on the keyboard. There can be one or many commands in the file with each command on a separate line.

You put a batch file to work by entering its filename without the BAT extension (although you could key that in if you wanted). This works exactly the same way that you use a program—you type in the name of the program, or the name of the batch file, and DOS goes looking for it. Whenever DOS's command processor encounters a command that isn't internal, it searches the appropriate disk for a file to carry out the command. The file could be a program file (with an extension name of COM or EXE), but if it turns out instead to be a BAT batch processing file, then DOS starts executing the commands held in that file. It then disregards any further commands in the original batch file.

Let's take a look at a very simple batch file to get an idea of how it works. Suppose we've created a file with the name D.BAT. Notice that it has the proper extension of BAT. Since the filename itself is "D", then "D" is all that you would need to type in to invoke this batch processing command. Now the contents of this batch processing file might be something very simple, such as a single line that reads:

```
DIR
```

which, you probably remember, is the name of the directory command that lists the contents of a disk.

With this batch processing file set up, what would happen if we keyed in "D" and pressed enter? DOS would search for this batch file and then start executing it. DOS would find just the one command DIR, so it would just give us a directory listing.

This example is about as silly and as short as you could imagine. You might be thinking that it is a completely artificial example with no practical value. Surprisingly, no. There is a use for batch processing commands like this. What this command does, in effect, is let you use D as an abbreviation for DIR. That may not seem like a big deal, yet it cuts the keystrokes you have to type in half, from four to two (counting the enter key). This is one of the main purposes of batch files—to simplify the typing you have to do to get your computer to do some work for you. One of the best uses of batch files is simply to provide convenient abbreviations of commands.

One of the rather clever things that DOS does is to keep track of where it is working in a batch file. When the file has more than one command, DOS knows how to carry on. When each command is finished, DOS searches for the file, reads past as many command lines as it has processed, and then starts the next command.

Why would you want to have batch processing files? We've already seen one reason—to create an abbreviation for a command name. There are two other good reasons, even before we get into the advanced stuff.

The reason for using batch files that you have probably anticipated is the most important one: grouping several commands into one functional unit. Quite often you need to do several things to carry out one task. For example, to write the very words you are

FOR BATCH FILES, DOS READS FROM A SCRIPT.

reading, I used a batch file that has four steps: the first runs my text
editor program so that I can type in these words; the second checks
what I have written for sspeling erers; the third runs my editor again
so that I can correct the spelling errors; and finally, the fourth makes
a backup copy of what I have written onto another disk.

That batch file looks like this:

```
V     %1        (my editor, Vedit)
WP    %1        (a spelling checker, WordProof)
V     %1        (my editor, Vedit again)
COPY %1  D:
```

I could, if I wished, do each of these four steps separately; however, I chose to run them as a batch file. But putting them all into
one batch processing file has done two very useful things for me.
First, it has saved me the trouble of invoking each step by itself. Second, and more important, it has established a standard operating dis-
cipline: each time I write, I will check my spelling and I will make a

BATCH FILES TURN MANY COMMANDS INTO ONE
COMMAND.

backup copy. Laziness won't keep me from doing those two important tasks.

The most important reason for using batch files is to gather
together, under one name, all the separate steps needed to perform a
unified task. The reason for doing that is as much for uniformity and
completeness as it is for convenience and ease.

Finally, there is one more key reason for using batch files, besides
abbreviation of commands and combinations of commands. That
reason is safety. If you don't know it already, there are some mad-
deningly dangerous commands available to us in DOS. These are the
commands that can wipe out our data in the blink of an eye. There
are three such dangerous commands: DEL/ERASE, which discards
data; COPY, which can overwrite good data with bad; and FORMAT,
which can wipe out the entire contents of a disk beyond all hope of
recovery. Batch files can reduce the danger of using these
commands.

Suppose that we routinely need to ERASE a file called DATA.OLD while preserving the file DATA.NEW. If you have to type in the command

```
ERASE DATA.OLD
```

there is just a little chance that one day, absent-mindedly, you will type in NEW rather than OLD. Wouldn't that put you in a pickle?

If you had a batch file with that ERASE command in it, you wouldn't have to worry about that kind of mistake. In fact, you might have a batch file that safely and reliably ERASEd all sorts of files without a worry—because if you got the batch file built right, then the commands would go right each time. Never a slip. You might even name that batch file something evocative and easy to remember like KILL-OLD. Remember, if KILL-OLD is to be a batch command, then the file that defines what it does must be named KILL-OLD.BAT.

In the rest of this chapter, we'll be looking at special DOS commands that are specially made for use in batch files. Before we get into these special commands for batch files, let's pause to mention a special batch file, the one called AUTOEXEC.BAT.

When DOS starts up its operation, it's prepared to perform any start-up commands that we want it to do. That can be very handy—it can be used to get DOS off to a running start. The mechanics of how this is done is very simple: when DOS starts up, it checks to see if there is a batch file named AUTOEXEC.BAT on the disk that DOS is starting up from. If there is an AUTOEXEC.BAT file available, DOS starts carrying out the commands in this file, just as if we had entered the command AUTOEXEC as our first instruction to DOS.

We can also enter the command AUTOEXEC, just like any other batch command, any time that we want to. The one special thing about the AUTOEXEC.BAT file is that DOS will, if it is there, perform the commands in that file for us quite automatically. That can be very helpful if there are any start-up operations that you want to perform when you fire up your computer.

You can use AUTOEXEC.BAT to perform any beginning commands that you want: for example, to start up the program that you use the most. There are also slightly more exotic uses for the AUTOEXEC command, which we'll discuss in Chapter 17.

We'll show a simple example right here. If you have a system formatted diskette that you want to use to start up a particular program, say WordStar (which is invoked with the command WS), then you might want to have this for your AUTOEXEC.BAT file:

```
DATE
TIME
WS
```

There are some commands built into DOS that are there just to make batch file processing better. Two of these are the REMark and PAUSE commands. REMark, of course, is intended to let you put comments into a batch file, which can be very useful as a reminder of what is going on in the batch file—the REM comments can say, "this is what I'm doing." The PAUSE command is just another form of the REM command, but pauses until a key is struck before continuing with the rest of the batch file.

The PAUSE command is good for two purposes—one is to keep some useful information from rolling off the screen. With a PAUSE command, you have a chance to look at what is on the screen for as long as you want before the computer carries on its work. The other use is for safety. If a batch file is about to do something that might endanger some of your data, then a PAUSE to check that everything is in order is a very good idea. This can be particularly valuable before a command that might ERASE or COPY over your data.

Here's an example that might be used with an accounting program:

```
REM      About to delete monthly data
REM      is that what you want to do?
PAUSE    Press break if not, otherwise ...
DEL   JOURNAL.DAT
DEL   JOURNAL.IDX
```

If you use the PAUSE command in this way and decide that you don't want things to carry on, how do you stop them? The break command, also called Control-C, will stop the operation of the batch file so that it will not carry on to whatever it was going to do. On some computers there is a special key for the break command, while on others it is just entered by holding down the control key and pressing the C key. Either way, Control-C or break is what you use to stop a batch file from carrying on—and the PAUSE command gives you the opportunity to do it at the right moments.

Here is an example of how PAUSE might be used for safety:

```
COPY DATA.NEW   DATA.OLD        make a safe copy of our old data

PROCESS         DATA.NEW        use a program that creates new data

DIR             DATA.NEW        check the directory for info on new data

PAUSE   If all is well, delete old data; otherwise, press BREAK

DEL             DATA.OLD        discard old data
```

This example is, as we said, a little artificial, but the ideas are ones that you will probably want to use. Notice that DIR is used to take a quick look at the new data—it will show us both the size and the time

PAUSE STOPS A BATCH FILE WAITING FOR OUR INSTRUCTIONS.

stamp on the new data file, which ought to be enough to tell us if the PROCESS program was successful in creating the new data. If everything looks good, we proceed from the PAUSE statement to clean things up by deleting the copy of the old data. If things aren't all well, then we break at the PAUSE so that the old data isn't deleted, and we can try to fix whatever went wrong.

What we've seen so far makes batch files look very useful. But what you can do with them is even more useful than you have seen so far, as we'll see in the next section.

11.2 Slightly More Advanced Batch Processing

You'll remember that I mentioned using a batch file to help me write this chapter. The name of the file might be WRITE.BAT, and, simplifying things a bit, the contents of that batch file might be like this:

```
EDIT    CHAPTER.11

SPELL   CHAPTER.11

EDIT    CHAPTER.11

SAVE    CHAPTER.11
```

But there is something drastically wrong with this batch file: it only works for Chapter 11. I would need to change it to work on any other chapter, which would be pretty stupid. The solution? Parameters. When I invoke the batch file, instead of just entering the batch command

```
WRITE
```

I would give a parameter, indicating what chapter I wanted to work on, like this:

```
WRITE 11
```

Meanwhile, inside the batch file WRITE.BAT, everywhere the chapter number was needed, the batch file would have a special symbol, "%1", which would tell DOS to substitute the parameter that I had entered. So our batch file would look something like this:

```
EDIT    CHAPTER.%1

SPELL   CHAPTER.%1

EDIT    CHAPTER.%1

SAVE    CHAPTER.%1
```

There can be more than one parameter, so a digit is used after the percent sign (%) to indicate which parameter is used. %1 is used for the first parameter after the command name, %2 for the second, and so on, for up to nine parameters. (If you need anywhere near that many, you're probably making things much too complicated.) Parameter number zero, %0, is used to get the name of the batch command, but there is rarely much point in that.

There are some more things to know about batch files in general before we go onto the extra features of DOS's batch processing. Inside a batch file are commands that could be program names or other batch file commands. If the command is a program, then when that program is done we can carry on with the batch file. If the command is the name of a batch file, then control never comes back to the original batch file. In technical terms this means that batch files are chained but not nested. If batch file A invokes batch file B, when B is done things stop; they don't carry on where A left off.

There is a way to make that happen, though, if we really need to. It's done with a technical trick that allows us to keep track of where we are in one batch file and return to it when another batch file is finished. This is an advanced and tricky subject and this isn't the place to go into all the details, but we'll show you the essence of how to do it, which has two parts. First, when batch file A needs to invoke batch file B, we don't just put in the name of B like this:

```
B
```

Instead, we do what's called "invoking a secondary command processor", and we tell it to perform batch file B. That's done like this:

```
COMMAND /C B
```

Remember that that line is in batch file A. The part that reads "COMMAND /C" keeps track of where we are in batch file A before starting to perform batch file B. The second step of the trick is to end batch file B with a line that reads

```
EXIT
```

That command tells DOS to peel back to where it was in batch file A.

One of the batch commands that could be in a batch file is the file's own name. A batch file can invoke itself starting an endless repetition of the same work done over and over again. This can be very useful when you have to repeat some operation. The break command, commonly called Control-C, can be used to break out of this endless repetition. Putting a PAUSE command just before the repetition starts can be a good idea.

It is also possible for a program to control its own destiny by writing out the contents of a batch file that will be executed when the program is done. This is a very clever mechanism that makes it possible to use the full, logical capabilities of a programming language to decide what commands are to be carried out next.

It is done is like this: we create a batch file, let's call it A, which runs our program; following the program, our A batch file tells DOS to carry out a batch file named B. But the program that is run by the A batch file itself creates the file B.BAT so the program decides what is to be done when it finishes. The program in the A batch file creates whatever exact instructions are to be performed in the B batch file.

To show you how that is done, we'll create an example that is similar to what several programs do, including IBM's Top View system. We want to run a program, which we'll call XXX, and we want that program to be able to control what happens after it finishes. Instead of running XXX by typing in its name as a command, we set up a batch file that has two steps, like this:

XXX
YYY

The first step of the batch file, as you can see, runs the program XXX itself. The second step of the batch file runs something called YYY—but there isn't actually any program named YYY. Instead, YYY is the command name of a batch file (YYY.BAT), which is created by the program XXX. The contents of that batch file, YYY.BAT, is built by our program XXX, so it gets to determine what happens next.

Our first batch file, the one that ran the program XXX, is chained to the batch file YYY—but what YYY does is determined dynamically by the program XXX.

This trick can be used for endless different purposes, but I can explain one that will give you a concrete idea of how it is used. The program we called XXX might be a word processing program; when we finish using the word processor, it might ask us if we want to pass what we've written through a spelling checker. If we say yes, we do want a spelling check, then XXX will create a YYY.BAT batch file that runs the spelling program; but if we say we don't want it, then XXX will create a YYY.BAT program that does nothing at all—which ends what we're doing.

If you go in for this sort of trick, test your work carefully and beware of certain traps. For example, it is much safer for a program to create the next batch file that will be executed than to try to change the batch file that is currently being performed.

11.3 Even More Advanced Batch Commands—ECHO, SHIFT, GOTO, IF, and FOR

Since the introduction of the 1-series, DOS has added many more advanced features in batch processing. So advanced, in fact, that understanding them pushes a little at the outer edge of what an introductory book like this should cover—but we'll make sure that you have some understanding of their capabilities at the very least.

When DOS is working its way through a batch file, it shows the commands that it is executing on the screen, just as if you had typed them in. This is good and bad—good to show you exactly what is being done; bad to display extraneous information. After all, one of the points of a batch file is to turn several commands into one unified operation.

When you run a program, a listing of the program doesn't appear on your screen, so why should a listing of a batch file get displayed? This little conflict is resolved by the ECHO command. ECHO is used to tell DOS to display, or not display, each batch file command as it is executed. With command ECHO on, each command appears on the screen as DOS processes them; with command ECHO off, the commands aren't shown. The ECHO command itself controls command echoing, like this:

```
ECHO   OFF

ECHO   ON
```

Any commands performed between the OFF and ON will not appear on the screen. That is, the command itself won't; if the command program generates any display output, that will continue to show on the screen.

One of the things that ECHO OFF will suppress is the display of comments from the ordinary batch file commands REM and PAUSE. But we might want some comments to appear on the screen. To make that possible, there is a third option to the ECHO command besides ON and OFF. If the command name ECHO is followed by anything other than ON or OFF, then what follows ECHO is displayed as a comment on the screen. The command is entered like this:

```
ECHO   message
```

It works with any message that doesn't begin with ON or OFF. ECHO's messages appear whether command echoing is on or off, and it has one real advantage over the REM command. When we use the REM command, the REM itself appears on the screen, which doesn't do anything to clarify the message. With the "ECHO message" command only the message appears, which is cleaner and clearer.

One of the enrichments that DOS provides is a logical capability within batch commands. This means that batch command files can react to developing situations in a scaled-down version of the kind of logic that can be used in a computer program. There are four batch commands that are related to this logic capability—SHIFT, GOTO,

ECHO OFF SILENCES DOS.

IF, and FOR. As we mentioned before, the full glory of these commands is really an advanced topic beyond the range of this book, but we'll give you a sketch of what these commands can do.

Let's start with the SHIFT command. If you have a batch file that uses several of the % replacement parameters, the SHIFT command lets you move the parameters over, one by one, to make it easier to process the parameters. When a SHIFT is done, the parameter symbol %1 takes on the value that used to be %2, and %2 gets the value that used to belong to %3. So all the values are shifted over one place. This makes it more practical to have one batch file process a number of files fairly easily. Your batch file can work with one filename, taken from the %1 parameter, and then SHIFT the list over to deal with the next filename. The real use of the SHIFT command comes when we use it with the GOTO and IF commands, which we'll explain in a moment. But to help you understand what SHIFT does, let's create an artificial example.

Suppose we want to create a batch file that will COPY a list of files; let's say, for simplicity, that we want to be able to give it a list of any three filenames, and have it copy them from drive A to drive B. If the name of the batch file is 3COPY, and our file names are X, Y, and Z, we want to copy them by just entering the command

```
3COPY   X   Y   Z
```

Here is what our "3COPY" batch file might look like using the SHIFT command:

```
COPY    A:%1  B:

SHIFT

COPY    A:%1  B:

SHIFT

COPY    A:%1  B:
```

Since each SHIFT command moves the parameters over, the second and third COPY commands find the filenames Y and Z in the first parameter, or %1, location. It should be obvious to you that this example is a little artificial, since we could have just used %2 and %3 in the second and third COPY commands. But we are setting the stage for something more complex, where the SHIFT makes more sense.

The example we showed will copy exactly three files. What if we would like it to copy more files without a limit? In that case, we can set up a program loop, which will SHIFT and COPY forever. To do that we use the GOTO command, which will make the batch command loop around in circles. This time, let's see an example before the explanation:

```
:ONWARD

COPY A:%1  B:

SHIFT

GOTO ONWARD
```

The first line we see here, ":ONWARD", is a label, which is needed so that we can loop around in circles. The label begins with a colon to identify it, and it can have any symbolic name we want to use. I chose ONWARD but we could have used any other short name. The label, by the way, must be on a line by itself just as we show it. Following the ONWARD label are our familiar COPY and SHIFT commands; the COPY does the work and the SHIFT command moves the % parameters over one, ready for the next COPY command. Then comes the GOTO command. The GOTO tells DOS to find the label that follows the GOTO command, and then to pick up processing from there. Since we GOTO ONWARD, DOS will go back up to where the ONWARD label is and continue from there.

What we have here is a loop, something that will make DOS go around in circles. Each time around, another file will be copied and then the parameter list will be shifted over one. As we have it in this example, this could go on forever, but naturally at some point we'll run out of filenames to copy. But the batch processing file will continue looping forever—with the COPY command complaining that we aren't giving it any names to copy.

To keep this batch file loop from going on forever, we can use the IF command. The IF command will test some logical condition, and then if it is true it will carry out one command. One of the things that we can have the IF statement test for is if a file name exists. We might replace our GOTO ONWARD statement, with this:

```
IF EXIST %1  GOTO ONWARD
```

This IF statement will test to see if there is a file with the name that the parameter %1 gives—if there is such a file, it will loop around to the ONWARD label and we'll continue merrily along. But if we've run out of filenames, then the IF won't loop back and the batch file will end.

There is more to GOTO and IF than we have seen so far. Our example of a GOTO skipped to a label that was earlier in the batch file, but it could just as easily have been later after the GOTO statement. Skipping to an earlier point in the file will set up a loop, while skipping forward will bypass some commands. Depending upon our needs, either direction of GOTO will work.

The IF statement can test for things other than the existence of a file. It can also test for two other conditions: one is to check if any program has reported trouble by signalling an error code to DOS. We test for these like this:

```
IF ERRORLEVEL 1 GOTO SOMEWHERE
```

The other kind of condition is a string comparison, which we can use to test for some particular parameter value. For example:

```
IF %1==FINISH  GOTO  SOMEWHERE
```

For all three kinds of IF conditions there is a corresponding IF NOT condition.

There are more complicated details to the IF command that we can go into here—it becomes quite an advanced subject when you look at everything that IF can do. When you are ready for all the complications, check your computer's DOS manual for all the details.

There is one more advanced batch processing command, which gives us another way to repeat commands: the FOR statement.

FOR lets us create a list of, for example, filenames, and then repeat a command with each of the names in the list. It involves a symbolic variable marked with two percent signs, "%%", and that variable is set to each of the items in the list in turn. Here is an example:

```
FOR %%NAME IN (A,B,C,D,E) DO  COPY A:%%NAME  B:
```

In the example, the COPY statement will be repeated with each of the names in the list—A,B,C,D,E—substituted for the symbolic variable %%NAME. In effect, this FOR command is translated into five separate COPY commands:

```
COPY A:A  B:

COPY A:B  B:

COPY A:C  B:

COPY A:D  B:

COPY A:E  B:
```

If you are ingenious, you can create some very clever batch processing files using the FOR command. It is also quite easy to create a mess with it since the whole process is rather tricky.

All of the advanced batch processing commands that we have covered here have their uses, but they certainly aren't for beginners. There is also some question about how useful they might be for advanced users when everything is considered. A lot depends upon how much taste you have for trying complicated tricks. If it suits you, don't let me discourage you at all from trying it—just be careful.

11.4 Suggestions and Examples of Batch File Tricks

In this section we're going to show you some examples and tricks in using batch files. Let me warn you right away that some of the examples are a bit complicated, and it's possible that you might get lost as we go over them. If so, back off from them for a while and keep your own use of batch files simple and straightforward. Later, when you are ready for some of the messier tricks, you can come back to the more complicated examples.

Let's start this discussion of the uses of batch files with some philosophy—the philosophy of the black box. Roughly speaking, there are two ways of using a personal computer: expert and dumb-dumb. Experts know what they are doing (or think they do), and they usually enjoy being involved in the mechanics of how work gets done. Us dumb-dumbs don't really know what's going on, and probably don't care—we want the results and don't care to get involved in the mechanics of how it's done.

For dumb-dumbs, computer operations need to work like what is called a black box; we don't need to see how the box gets its work done, as long as we are confident it is doing the work correctly. While it is very nice to have an expert's technical knowledge, for most users of computers the more the computer is a trustworthy black box, the better.

One of the features of DOS that can help make it work like a friendly black box is batch file commands. My reason for explaining this so elaborately is to instill in you the idea that batch files are more than just a convenient, efficient, and safe way to direct the computer's operations.

Batch files are also a key way of building black boxes to help make the use of your computer less technical. When you understand this idea, it can guide you into making the best possible use of batch files. The key thing in making batch files work like black boxes is to write them in a style that makes them work as smoothly and as unobtrusively as possible.

Several features of DOS help make this unobtrusive operation possible. One is the ECHO command, which lets you suppress the display of the commands that are being carried out. Another is the redirection of output. Sometimes you need to include a command in a batch file, but really don't want to subject the computer user to whatever output it displays. A prime example of this is the CHKDSK command, which can clean up messy file allocation on your disk left over from some programs. If you want to CHKDSK but hide its report from the screen, the output can be redirected like this:

```
CHKDSK >NUL
```

Notice that we sent the output of CHKDSK to the null device so that it is thrown away. This is a handy way to get rid of extraneous display output. On the other hand, it might be better not to throw the information away completely—if something has gone wrong, you might want to come back and look it over. You might use a little catch-all file to store this information in, like this:

```
CHKDSK >CATCH.ALL
```

Two of the most useful things you can put into batch files are remarks and pauses using the REM and PAUSE commands. It is surprisingly easy to lose track of exactly what you are doing. That sounds really dumb, but it's true—especially if you are doing the same thing over and over again. If you are, say, working your way through a list of files, then you might lose your place in the list. That problem can be solved by using the REM command to show you the parameters that your batch file is working with. Example? All my batch files that run my text editor end with this REM:

```
REM  Was editing the file named %1
```

And, of course, the parameter %1 shows me the file name.

The same thing can be done with the PAUSE command, but PAUSE has some extra advantages. If you are running something lengthy and automatic through a batch file, PAUSE can be used to suspend the operation so that you see the current screen display, and also decide whether or not to proceed with the rest of the batch file. If you don't want things to proceed, the break key will shut down the batch file command.

Pausing for approval to continue is a very important part of any batch file that does anything potentially dangerous. For example, you might have a series of programs that deliberately leave their work files on disk so that you can recover the data if anything goes wrong. In a batch file like this, you could have the last step of the batch file ERASE the files and then you could put a PAUSE just before the ERASE, giving you a chance to check that everything was all right before the files were destroyed.

On the subject of the ERASE command, if you use ERASE/DEL in a batch file it's a good idea to put a DIR command right before it so that you see a list of the files that are about to be erased. This is a nice safety feature, since it keeps you in the know.

There are some commands in DOS that are very useful to use that are a nuisance to type in. With batch files, you can use them liberally with no effort at all since the batch file does all the work for you. One of the most important is the check disk command, CHKDSK.

CHKDSK is useful to put in your batch commands for two reasons. First, it lets you know how much working space is left on your disk—and it is useful to see that often so that you get early warning about running out of space. CHKDSK also inspects the disk for some logical damage (meaning scrambled data but not physical damage) on the diskette, and it's a good thing to do that frequently even though the scrambling isn't a common occurrence.

It is also quite handy to add the DIR command to most of your batch files. You can put in a specific command (indicating what files you want to know about) to see things like the file size and the files' date and time stamp. Examples: DIR %1 or DIR *.BAS. You can also use the show-me-everything form of the DIR command just to see what's on the disk you are using. If you usually have a lot of files the /W switch, which is an option of the DIR command, will list them across the screen so that they take up fewer lines. Example:

```
DIR *.*
```

```
DIR *.* /W
```

```
DIR
```

With piping, you can get the listing sorted so that they appear in alphabetic order, which makes for easier reading. This is done with a pipeline, combining DIR, SORT, and MORE:

```
DIR : SORT : MORE
```

There is a very simple, but very handy, batch file that I call BAA because of what it does with the default disk drive. Probably the most common set-up for PC family computers is to have two disk drives, A and B. The most common and efficient way to use those drives is to dedicate drive A to holding programs and drive B to holding data on which the programs work. Since it is usually more convenient for a program to use data from the default disk drive, the BAA batch file is designed to temporarily switch the default to drive B, execute the program (from drive A), and then switch the default back. For a program that we'll call XXX, the batch file would look like this:

```
B:          (switch the default to B)
```

```
A:XXX       (run XXX from drive A but use B as the default data drive)
```

```
A:          (switch the default back to A, ready for the next task)
```

Naturally you would set up one of these batch files for each program that you wanted to use it for. The natural name to give the batch file would be a handy abbreviation of the name of the program. (You can't give the batch file the same name as the program since DOS looks for programs before it looks for batch files. With both a program file and a batch file with the same name—but different filename extensions—when you enter the name as a command, DOS will execute the program and bypass your batch file.)

On the other hand, if you would prefer to use the name of the program as the command name that you use to activate a batch file like the BAA batch file, then you can use the RENAME command to change the program file to an alias name and then use the original name for your batch file.

Before we finish with the BAA batch file, we should note that you can easily set up a generic BAA file that uses a parameter to specify the program name. In this case, the BAA batch file would look like this:

```
B:

A:%1

A:
```

You could do this if you wanted to, but the main point of batch files—and of computers in general—is to make your work simpler and easier. It makes more sense to set up a separate batch file tailored to the needs of each particular program that you run. In fact, it is likely that each program's batch execution file will have more in it than the BAA file shown above; what else will be in there depends upon what you need to help you best use your programs.

Closely related to the BAA batch file is a trick that you can use to make it easier and more convenient to make backup copies of your data. The most common operating style, for computers with two diskette drives, is to use the A drive for diskettes full of programs (and batch files); the B drive is dedicated to data that the programs work on. Now, how do you make backup copies of that data? The only sensible way to do it is to leave the data diskette where it is, in drive B, and change the program diskette in drive A for the diskette you use to back up the data in drive B. Now there are two convenient ways to use batch files to supervise this backup copying: one is under manual control and the other is fully automatic.

The manual way to make backup copies is to place a batch file on the backup diskette. The only task of this batch file is to copy from B to A like this:

```
COPY    B:*.*    A:*.*
```

This is the straightforward backup operation; you might give it a command name of SAVE or just S for short. When the computer is being used by someone who knows when a backup copy of the data is needed, then this simple method is best. But there is a more elaborate method, which adds an element of idiot-proofing to the backup operation.

The automatic method makes use of batch-file chaining so it gives us an opportunity to see how chaining is done. Let's set the stage with a little explanation, seeing what we want to do so that you can better understand the chaining trick. For the backup method mentioned above, the knowledgeable computer user removed a program diskette from drive A, replaced it with a backup diskette, entered the command SAVE, and then switched back to the program diskette. But our user had to know what steps to follow. To idiot-proof the backup operation (as much as we can), we'd like a batch file to lead us by the hand in the steps to be done, and that's what we'll explain here.

The first part of this scheme, the first link in the chain, is the batch file that was already being used on the program diskette in drive A. (Recall that the point of this operation is to backup new data after the end of a program operation—we can assume that our computer user was using a program, and naturally we expect that a batch file was being used to run the program.)

At the end of that batch file, we place a command to switch over to another batch file that is located on the data diskette in drive B, which will be the second link in our chain of batch files. That batch file has to have a command name (which is the filename minus the .BAT extension), so we'll call it AUTOSAVE. The last line in the batch file that was being used on the program diskette will switch control over to AUTOSAVE, like this:

B:AUTOSAVE

Notice the "B:" part, which is important. The current default drive at this point should be drive A, so we have to specifically tell DOS to look to drive B for the AUTOSAVE command.

Now, why are we chaining to another batch file? Why don't we just continue using the batch file in drive A for whatever we need to do? For one simple reason: we're about to remove the program diskette from drive A, and DOS wouldn't be able to find the instructions inside the batch file. So, temporarily, we switch our base of operations, the location of our batch file, over to drive B. This is the heart of our chaining trick.

What will be inside this AUTOSAVE batch file? Two things: one is the working part, a COPY command to copy the data from the master data diskette in drive B to the backup diskette in drive A. The other thing that will be in the AUTOSAVE batch file is the idiot-proofing, in the form of simple instructions to the computer user of what to do; this we do with PAUSE commands. Our AUTOSAVE batch file looks like this:

```
PAUSE Place the data backup diskette in drive A

COPY   B:*.*   A:*.*

PAUSE Replace the program diskette in drive A
```

To match your particular needs, the comments in the two PAUSE statements can be more specific; they can use your terminology for the particular diskettes to be used with drive A. For example, they could say "accounting data back-up" and "accounting programs," or whatever is appropriate.

What happens after the second PAUSE statement in this AUTOSAVE command file? Since the default drive is A, DOS gives the prompt for drive A, and our computer user at the keyboard can enter the next command. On the other hand, we could add a third link to this chain of batch files by putting the name of a batch command as the fourth and last line of AUTOSAVE. Then DOS would take off executing that batch file, and things would be even more automatic. If we wanted to, the name of this command on the last line of AUTOSAVE could be a parameter (like %1), so that the command line that invoked AUTOSAVE would also indicate what was supposed to be done when AUTOSAVE as done.

With this trick of passing the name of the next command as a parameter to AUTOSAVE, you could have one universal form of AUTOSAVE batch file that you could use with every one of your program and data diskettes. If you wanted to, you could write a custom AUTOSAVE batch file for each different use or you could use the universal form with its parameter. Use whichever technique better suits your operation.

This example of chaining batch files for the purpose of backing up data should give you an idea of how command chaining can be used to add more automation to your computer operations. Commands can be chained from diskette to diskette (as we did in setting up AUTOSAVE), or they can work on the same diskette. There is less reason to chain commands when you are not switching diskettes, since any command that you chain on the same diskette could be just included in one command file. But that's a matter of taste and style. Some people might prefer to do lengthy operations as a chain of commands, and others might prefer to use one large command file. The result is the same. Where batch file chaining really pays off is in allowing you to switch diskettes and still keep operating under the automatic control of batch files.

Besides all the handy things that you can put inside of batch files, there are some very useful things you can do outside them—that is, how you name and organize them.

One of the handiest of these is what I call the A-B-C trick. Many of the things we do with our computers have a logical series of steps. For example, if you are writing programs the first step might be to use your text editor to do the writing, while the second and third steps would be compiling the program and then testing it.

Another example is when you are writing a letter or report. There the first step is composing the letter, and the second would be to check its spelling; the third step would be to re-edit it for corrections. For each of these steps you'll set up a batch file to supervise it. You could give each of these steps meaningful names like EDIT, COM-PILE, and TEST. It is a very good idea to give batch files simple meaningful command names. On the other hand, for quick convenience, we could just as easily name these steps A, B, and C or 1, 2, and 3.

There are two advantages to the A-B-C trick: the command names are shorter and quicker to key in, and it is easier to combine them and remember the names of the combinations. There is a logical progression to the steps we go through, and our batch files can simply number the steps 1, 2, 3 or letter them A, B, C. If our edit step is named A, and our compile step is named B, then a batch file to do both edit and compile would be named AB, which is easy to remember and key in.

There is one obvious disadvantage to the A-B-C trick: you have to remember that A means EDIT (or whatever) and so forth. This can be confusing to your co-workers or even to yourself. But when you won't have any trouble keeping track of the meaning of the steps, then A-B-C is a good way to go.

To show you how far this can go and how useful it can become, take a look at what I do when I write Pascal programs. There are actually five separate steps to creating a Pascal program (for your interest, they are edit, first stage compile, second stage compile, link edit, and then test run the completed program). I have separate batch files for each step (which I happen to name 1 through 5 because it suits me), and then lots of different combination batch files. Depending upon the kind of program I'm writing, it makes sense to use different combinations of the five steps. Sometimes I do step 1 by itself, and at other times I combine steps 1 and 2. Other combinations are handy at other times.

By having a batch file for each step by itself, and as many combinations as I find useful, I'm in full control of what is going on when I write these programs—and it's all quick and convenient for me. The same idea can be applied to any multi-step operation that you do.

The more complicated the steps, the greater the advantage in setting up A-B-C type batch files to supervise them.

There is more handy thing you can do with A-B-C, and that is to create parallel batch files for tasks that are similar in general, but different in detail. To use the example of programming again, I happen to write programs in three languages—Pascal, assembly, and BASIC. For each of them, I have the same set-up of batch command names.

For me, editing a program is always done with the command named 1 and the compile or assemble is always begun with the command named 2. What the command "1" actually does is different in each case, but what it means to me is always the same—it means let me use my text editor to write a program. The same thing applies to writing a letter or to writing this chapter. Everywhere, the first step, which I call "1", is to use my editor to compose something—a letter, a program, or a part of this book.

The next step after that is step "2" and it's quite different depending upon what I'm doing—for writing, step "2" is a spelling check, while for programming step "2" runs a compiler or assembler. But as I use them, these numbered batch processing steps make perfect sense, since they follow the natural progression of whatever work I am doing.

Another handy trick with batch files is to have different versions lying around in waiting. Why would you want to do that? Let me use my programming as an example again. Sometimes I do my programming work on ordinary diskettes; other times it is handy for me to move everything onto an electronic disk. And finally, when I work on my biggest programs, I need to use both an electronic disk and ordinary diskettes. So I keep three versions of my main programming batch files. Now there are two ways to handle this, and one of them I think is a really nifty trick.

The first way is to have all three versions active at once, under slightly different names. For example, my step one, named "1", could have its diskette version named "1D" and the electronic disk version named "1E". While this puts them all on tap at once, it means that I have to remember which version I'm using and keep entering that form of the command name. That's clumsy and error prone. The second way uses a foxy trick to solve the problem.

The trick is to keep all three versions around under the same command name but with an alias for a filename extension. So my electronic version of the "1" command would be in a file named 1.ELE. Now, as you know, batch files have to have the extension BAT, so this ELE file can't be used as it is—but it can be moved into place very easily. With a simple COPY command all ELE batch files can be activated, like this:

```
COPY *.ELE  *.BAT
```

which does the trick. Each of my three versions of my batch files is kept with its own distinct extension name. Each set is then activated by an appropriate COPY command, which makes it the current working version and overrides whatever version was working before. And I don't have to use any different command names—the names stay the same but different versions take effect. Naturally I don't type in the COPY commands—another series of batch files does that for me.

Since the real magic of using batch processing files comes from tailoring them to your own needs, our suggestions and examples can only scratch the surface of the possibilities, and can only hint at some of the things that you can accomplish on your own through the creative use of batch files. There is almost nothing in the use of DOS that will reward your efforts like the rewards of speed, convenience, and safety that you can gain by making full use of batch files.

To help make that point even further, we'll close this chapter with several more examples of batch files.

Here's one very useful idea for a batch file. When we set up working diskettes for different purposes, often there are a few standard programs that we want on each of them—for example, the program files for the commands CHKDSK, FORMAT, and EDLIN. Here is a batch file that will format a disk and then copy those three commands onto the disk:

```
FORMAT B:  /S
COPY   CHKDSK.COM  B:
COPY   FORMAT.COM  B:
COPY   EDLIN.COM   B:
```

There's a completely different idea for a batch file that we haven't even mentioned at all—batch files that don't do anything (anything active that is) but which simply show you information. For example, if you tend to forget the names of some DOS commands, you could create a short batch file, called HELP.BAT, with something like this in it:

```
REM   To check a disk use CHKDSK
REM   To format a system disk use FORMAT /S
REM   To reroute disk I/O use ASSIGN A=C
```

... and so forth.

If you want to create this sort of information-only batch file, let me point out some tips. First, if the information is too much to fit on the screen at one time, use the PAUSE command to stop things between screen loads. Second, you should know that there are three distinct ways to have a batch file display information on the screen, and each of them acts a little differently; one is with the REM command; the second is with the ECHO command (which normally is used after an ECHO OFF command), which can act like the REM command, but a more attractive appearance. The third method involves putting the actual information to be displayed into separate files, and then having the batch file use the TYPE command to display the contents of the information files, like this:

```
ECHO OFF
TYPE INFO.1
PAUSE
TYPE INFO.2
PAUSE
```

12

Odds and Ends You Need to Know

In this chapter we'll cover an assortment of useful and interesting things to know. Some of them will be new topics, and some of them will be new perspectives on items that we have already looked at before.

12.1 Finding Out What's at Your Command

It isn't always obvious what your computer can do for you, especially when you are first getting to know it. Here is a quick summary of what commands you can ask your computer to carry out at any given time.

Recall that as DOS sees things there are two kinds of commands that it can be asked to carry out—what DOS knows as internal commands and external commands. The internal are built right into DOS so they are always ready for us to use. The external commands are performed by programs that are kept on disk, so they are only ready for us to use when we have a disk mounted that has a copy of the command program.

While the internal commands are always ready for us to use, there is one very minor disadvantage to them, at least for the beginner—there is no simple, straightforward way to have your computer tell you what their names are. With external commands there's a simple way to learn their names, which we'll come to in a moment—but not for the internal commands.

Here, for reference, is a list of the internal commands that you can expect to have on tap at all times. The exact list varies depending upon which version of DOS you have:

All versions of DOS:

COPY	makes copies of disk files
DATE	displays and sets DOS's record of the date
DEL	deletes (erases) disk files
DIR	lists the files on a disk
ERASE	erases (deletes) disk files
PAUSE	used in batch files to stop and display messages
REM	used in batch files to display messages
REN	renames files; changes their filenames
TIME	displays and sets DOS's record of the time
TYPE	displays the contents of a disk file on the display screen

Versions 2.00 or later:

BREAK	controls how often DOS checks for break, Control-C
CHDIR	changes which directory is the current one on each disk
CLS	clears the display screen
CTTY	puts DOS into remote control by redirecting the "console"
ECHO	turns command echoing on and off and displays messages
FOR	used in advanced batch files to work through a list of files
GOTO	used in advanced batch files for looping and skipping
IF	used in advanced batch files to test for logical conditions
MKDIR	creates a new subdirectory on a disk
PATH	tells DOS where to search for external command programs
RMDIR	removes a subdirectory from a disk
SET	sets environmental equations that can control programs
SHIFT	used in advanced batch files to work through the parameters
VER	displays which version of DOS is being used
VERIFY	makes DOS double check all data written to disks
VOL	displays the volume identification label from a disk

In a sense we have to memorize the list of internal commands that are available, because DOS doesn't have a simple way of displaying their names for us. Of course this isn't much of a problem, since we have the use of this book and our computer's manuals to give us a

INTERNAL COMMANDS

EXTERNAL COMMANDS

REMEMBER THE DIFFERENCE BETWEEN EXTERNAL AND INTERNAL COMMANDS.

list of the internal commands. Also, any commands that we'll be using much, we learn quickly. But it is nice to be able to display a list of what commands are available, and we can do this with the external commands.

You'll recall that the external commands, which reside on our disks, are either true programs or else they are batch file commands, which are files that list a series of commands that we want carried out together. We can identify programs and batch files on our disks by their filename extensions. (For a review of filename extensions, see Chapter 9.) Programs are stored on disks in two forms, known by their extension names as COM and EXE. Batch files always have an extension of BAT. Together, these three extensions cover all the ground of the commands that can be on a disk.

If we have a disk in one of our computer's drives, for example drive B, we can find out the commands on that disk by doing three DIR-directory listings. We need to do the DIR command three times if we want to see all of the commands that might possibly be on that disk. Here is how to do it:

```
DIR   B:*.BAT

DIR   B:*.COM

DIR   B:*.EXE
```

In our example we looked at the B drive but we could have specified any of the computer's drives; or we could have used DOS's current default drive. In each of the DIR commands we used an asterisk (*) for the filename part, because we wanted to see any and all names that matched the extension we were specifying.

If you have a diskette—one you have made up or one which you have been given—and you are not sure how you can use it, these three DIR commands are very good to give you a quick peek at what commands are set up on the diskette. In the next chapter we'll go over some advice on what you should do about setting up commands on your diskettes.

There is one special case that you will run across when you get a listing of the COM program files. There is a special COM file, named COMMAND.COM, which is actually part of DOS itself and not a separate command that you can execute. If you list the COM files on a disk and see COMMAND.COM among the program command files, don't try to enter COMMAND as a command—you may throw DOS into a tizzy. Incidentally, COMMAND.COM is a program file that contains all the internal commands, such as COPY and DIR. In Chapter 13 we'll learn some practical things about COMMAND.COM.

It is actually allowed to enter COMMAND as a command—we snuck an example of this in the last chapter when we showed you how to "next" batch files by invoking a secondary command processor, like this:

```
COMAND  /C  B
```

If we want to get into doing that we have to tread carefully. It's a complicated and tricky area. I'm not saying you can't do it—I'm just saying that it's tricky and if you want to try it, go carefully.

Before we finish with this section, there is one loose end we should take care of. You know that external commands are invoked by using their filename. But there are three different filename extensions that could be used with a command file: BAT, COM, and EXE. With the different extensions, you could possibly have three different command files, each with the same filename and so the same command name.

Of course we shouldn't have two or three command files with the same command name, that would be a rather confusing thing to do. If you do, though, DOS will only find and carry out one of them. You might expect that DOS would simply use the first one it finds, with any of the three extensions, but as far as I know DOS sets a priority among the three—first COM, then EXE, then BAT.

12.2 Throwing Things Away and Other Information on Devices

We've mentioned a few times earlier in this book the devices that DOS works with other than your disk drives. Devices are parts of the computer that can be talked to—that is, which can send data, or receive data, or both. In this section we'll look a little more at devices and what you can reasonably do with them.

The easiest way to understand what devices are on your computer is to consider the computer's keyboard and its display screen. If you think of them separately, the keyboard is something that the computer can take information from; DOS can "read" what we type on the keyboard, so from the computer's viewpoint the keyboard is an input device. The display screen is just the opposite. The computer can "write" information onto the display screen but it can't read from it. The keyboard is a model example of an input device; the display screen is an example of an output device. If we put the two together and think of them as two halves of one device, we have a model of a two-way input and output device.

The disks in your computer are quite different. While the computer can both read and write information on the disk, the disk isn't really one single place to read or write information—a disk can have any number of files stored on it, each of which can be read or written. So a disk is quite different from our keyboard or our display screen. A disk is something with many independent sources of input and output, but all of them connected in one logical way—they are all accessed through one or another disk drive.

This short explanation gives us a working idea of what devices are, and can be, to DOS. A device is some part of the computer that can be read from or written to. If it is like a disk drive, with potentially many data paths in it, then DOS calls it a block device. Block device is a technical term that really doesn't concern us here. All other devices are called character devices, because DOS can read or write characters to and from them in the name of the device itself. For a disk, a block device, DOS has to find a file on that device to do any reading or writing of information. But with a character device, DOS can talk directly to it.

According to the way that DOS works, all disk-like block devices are identified by a letter of the alphabet followed by a colon, such as

"A:" and "B:". This is the way we refer to our computer's one or more disk devices.

Usually our computers have a real disk drive for every block device that our DOS uses, but it doesn't have to be that way. As we saw in Chapter 4, if your computer has only one disk drive, the A drive, then DOS will create an imaginary B drive, mostly so that you can copy files from one diskette to another and keep the two diskettes distinct. When DOS does this, your one real diskette drive is treated as the A drive and then the B drive alternately. Every time DOS makes the switch from one to the other, it tells us to change the diskettes so that they are kept distinct.

There are other ways that we can have more working disks than there are real disk drives on our computer. One way is for the computer to use part of its memory as a simulated disk drive; this is usually called an electronic disk, or a RAM disk (meaning a memory disk). The point of an electronic disk is that it works as fast as the memory in our computer, which will be five or ten times faster than an ordinary diskette. We'll cover some of the interesting and practical points about electronic disks in Chapter 16.

Besides the disk-type block devices, DOS has a number of character devices that we can use. Some of them are really there, just as our disk drives are really there, and some of them are valuable trickery like the B drive on a computer that has only one real disk drive. Let's see what some of these character devices are and what we can do with them.

One of the most interesting character devices is a fake one called NUL. NUL is a dead-end, or black hole device, that is used to swallow up data that we want to throw away. Why would we want to throw information away? Well, a program may be generating some information that we just don't need, and we don't want it cluttering up our display screen or our computer's printer. If we wrote the program ourselves, we could make the program just not generate the information in the first place; but most of the programs that we use we didn't write—someone else set the rules for when data is generated and when it is not.

If a program generates data, and if the program gives us a choice of where to send the data, we can tell the program to send the data to the black hole called NUL. DOS creates this phantom device called NUL just for this purpose—as an easy way to discard information. So whenever you need to discard data that a program is generating send it to NUL.

You'll recall from Chapter 8 that standard output from a program, which normally goes to the display screen, can be redirected using the ">" symbol (provided you're not using an older 1-series version of DOS). If you want to make this information just disappear, you can send it to the NUL device by specifying ">NUL". It will disappear without a trace.

We mentioned before that character devices can be read from for input, or written to for output, or they may have both input and output ability. The phantom NUL device is actually an input/output device. If a program must read data from somewhere, and you want to give it no data at all, then you can tell it to read its information from NUL.

When a program reads information from any character device, the program is prepared to get an end-of-data or end-of-file signal at some point. We discussed the end-of-file marker on disk files in Chapter 9, and we discussed how it can be signaled from the keyboard in Chapter 7. When any program tries to read data from the NUL device, all it gets is an end-of-file signal.

As you can see, the NUL device can be very useful for discarding output information or creating a dummy and empty set of input data. You are likely to find times when you want to use NUL as a destination for your output data. Don't be surprised if you rarely have any occasion to use NUL as an input device—even if you don't need it, you should know that it is there. You'll see a similarity with the use of redirection; redirecting output is fairly common, and redirecting input is much rarer. But both ways of working are there for us to use if we need them.

NUL is a dummy or phantom device, but our computers have real character devices as well. The most important one is called the console, or CON. The CON device is the man-machine interface—it's the combination of our keyboard (for input) and our display screen (for output). The CON device is the one that DOS uses all the time to talk to us. Many programs take their input from the CON keyboard and write out their output to the CON display screen, and they do this without asking us for permission. Sometimes programs let us choose where data is to come from or go to. These are the occasions when we can direct it to the NUL device, as mentioned above, or direct it to the CON console.

If we tell a program to send its output to CON (instead of to our printer or a disk file), then it will appear on the display screen. Likewise, if we tell a program to read its data from CON, then it will take in whatever we type on the keyboard. Remember that programs usually expect an end-of-file signal to tell them that there is no more data to be read. If we are entering data on the keyboard, we can key in an end-of-file signal by entering the Control-Z code—we hold down the control shift key and press the Z letter key. This gives the program an end-of-file indicator.

You may sometimes see examples of CON being used as a way of creating short text files, particularly batch files, without having to use

DATA DISAPPEARS INTO THE BLACK HOLE OF NUL.

an editing program (like DOS's editing program, EDLIN). This actually isn't a very good idea, because it's clumsy to do, and hard to correct mistakes. Still, it's interesting to know how to do it. The following example shows how to do it (with <Control-Z> standing for the Control-Z shift key combination). The first line tells DOS to copy from the console (meaning the keyboard) into a file called TEST; the last line has DOS display what we put into the TEST file; what's in between is the contents we typed from the console into the file. Here's how it goes:

```
COPY CON: TEST
This is the first line
This is the second line
This is boring so far <Control-Z>
TYPE TEST
```

While CON is the character device that we use the most, it isn't the only one. If we have a communications adapter on our computer it

YOUR PRINTER IS PRN OR LPT1; YOUR TELEPHONE IS AUX OR COM1.

will have a device name. Several different names are used for this: AUX (short for auxiliary device) is most often used; another device name for the communications line is COM1 (for communications line number 1). If our computer can have more than one communications line, they would be referred to as COM1, COM2, and so forth. Usually there is only one line but there could be more. Like the console, the communications lines, AUX, COM1, and so forth can be used for both input and output.

Computers commonly have printers attached to them to make a permanent written copy of any information we need. Like the communications line, the printer has several names. The universal name is PRN (short for printer), while LPT1, LPT2, and so forth are used when you have more than one printer line; LPT is short for line printer, which means the same thing as a printer. Naturally the printer is a one-way output device and can't be used as an input device, unlike the CON console and the AUX communications line.

There are two common ways to connect a small computer and a printer. These two ways are known as serial and parallel. The difference is technical and has to do with whether data is sent to the printer one bit at a time (serial), or with the several bits that make up a character all sent out at once (parallel).

The difference concerns us for only two reasons. One is when we buy a computer and a printer, we have to make sure that we get the right compatible combination. The other is that serial printer connections usually talk to the computer's communications device, whose name is AUX or COM1.

The practical significance is that you may have to refer to your printer as the AUX device, not as the PRN device. It will work just the same but you may have to use another name for it. If you don't know which way your printer is hooked up, you can probably find out by simply experimenting—copy a file to PRN and to AUX and see which appears on your printer.

12.3 The Importance of Where You Are

Sometimes you need to know where you are and sometimes you don't. On your computer, where you are really means the current disk location that DOS is working with. There are two different senses to this, one that applies to all versions of DOS and one that applies only to versions after the 1-series.

In all versions of DOS, DOS keeps track of the current disk or default disk drive. The current default disk drive is where DOS goes looking for disk files, unless it is specifically told to look elsewhere. If we enter a command like this:

```
EDLIN
```

DOS will look on the current disk drive for the command program file to carry out that command. On the other hand, if we specifically want it to look somewhere else for the command, we can tell DOS this way:

```
B:EDLIN
```

This rule, that DOS goes looking on the current disk drive unless told otherwise, applies to both programs that we invoke by entering their names as commands and also to the data files that those programs use.

The practical significance of this is that many programs will or won't work, depending upon whether you have the default drive set to where the program's data is located. Once you have worked with a program for a while, you will learn what it needs and whether it follows the direction of the current default drive, or whether it demands that its data be on certain specific disk drives.

Incidentally, programs that specify which drives their data must be on can be a real nuisance because they reduce the flexibility of your computer operations. (We'll see more about this in Chapters 16, 18, and 21.) If you have the source code for a program, then you may be able to remove any references to specific disk drives. Often this is possible with programs written for the BASIC interpreter since their source code is usually available. Even for other programs you may be able to remove the use of specific disk drives, as we'll see in Chapter 21 on the DEBUG command.

For versions of DOS after the 1-series, the same idea applies except that it is enriched by the idea of a current directory. You'll recall from Chapter 8 that when DOS goes looking for data files, it not only looks on the current disk it also looks just in the current directory on that disk. For many practical purposes each subdirectory on a disk acts very much like a completely separate disk. If a data file isn't in that directory it won't be found, even though it is somewhere on the same disk.

The main thing we have to say here is that it can matter to your programs where the current disk location is, so it should matter to you. To help you keep track of where the current default disk is, the prompt that DOS displays gives the drive letter. For example:

A> or **B>**

As you'll recall, you change the default drive by entering a drive letter (and the colon that goes with it) as a command by itself. DOS will acknowledge the change by responding with a prompt that has the new drive letter in it.

We aren't automatically told the current directory over and over again, as we are told the current drive. To find out the current directory, we use the CHDIR command. CHDIR really serves two functions: one is to change the current directory if we specify a new one. The other is to display the current directory name. To use CHDIR to display the current directory, rather than change it, we enter the CHDIR command with no directory parameter.

You will find that the current disk location is significant with more programs than you might expect. If you have something like an accounting program, you naturally expect that it will be using data files, so it may make use of the current directory. But many complex programs also use data files to hold supplements to the program, such as help screens and a kind of program fragment called an overlay. So even if a program doesn't use data files that you know of, it may be looking to the current disk for some of these supplementary files.

When you start using a program that is new to you, you should expect that there will be a learning period during which you not only find out how to work with the program, but you also learn how to make the program work effectively with your computer.

Integrating a new program into your computer operations really involves a two-way fit—fitting yourself and the program together and fitting your computer and the program together. Part of this process of fitting new programs into your computer's operations involves things like where the programs expect to find their data (and where you would prefer it to be). Be prepared for this adjustment period; if you don't expect it, or if you try to take shortcuts around it, you may make things worse for yourself. We'll see some more about this in the next few chapters.

DO YOU KNOW WHERE YOUR DOS IS ?

12.4 Programs You Should Have

You probably have a pretty good idea about the main programs that you need for your computer. These are the application programs that take care of the tasks that you want to perform on your computer. You don't need me to tell you to get those programs—you already know about them. There are other programs, however, that you might not know about but that you almost certainly need for your system.

One is a selective copy program. This kind of program is like the COPY command that comes with DOS, but with an interesting difference—it can select what it copies. One of the main reasons for using a program like this is to copy only the files that have been changed. The heaviest use that we are likely to make of the COPY command is in backing up our data from a master disk to a backup disk. With a lot of data, this operation can be more time-consuming than necessary, particularly when only some of the data has been changed.

A good selective copy program can check the time stamp on each file, and only bother to copy the files that have been changed. For my work I use the JET program from Tall Trees Systems. Similar programs should be available for your computer. You should look for a selective copy program that operates on your particular DOS computer.

Another important kind of program that you need to get is a file recovery program. This type of program that restores disk files that you have lost due to erasure (a horrifyingly common problem) or damage to the diskette. Versions of DOS after the 1-series include a RECOVER program that will reconstruct a garbled disk directory, which is quite a bit of help for damaged diskettes, but RECOVER is not all that you need. Since erasing files is the biggest problem you should be sure to get a program to recover erased files. For my work I use my own program, called UnErase.

You may be puzzled at the idea that an erased file can be recovered, but it can be. The reason is simple—when a file is erased the data isn't destroyed or overwritten, it is simply "thrown away." This is analogous to taking a file folder out of your filing cabinet and tossing the pages in the waste basket. If the waste basket hasn't been emptied, you could dig through it to find the pages from the file folder.

It works the same way with disk data. When a file is erased from disk, the disk space where the data is stored is taken away from the erased file and placed in the pool of available space on the disk. If no other file has used that space, then the data is still there and it can be recovered. If you use an "un-erase" program right after an inadvertent erasure, you should be able to completely recover all of your data.

The first line of defense for your data is to make backup copies. The second line of defense is to be very careful about operations that can destroy your data (erasing, formatting, copying). An essential third line of defense is file recovery programs, such as an un-erase program, and other file recovery tools. Look for this kind of program and be sure to get it before you need it. File recovery programs are like insurance policies—you have to get them before you need them, not after.

In general, you shouldn't be stingy in acquiring programs. Besides the programs that you know you will need, there are probably plenty of handy auxiliary programs that can make your work easier or more efficient or, as in the case of file recovery programs, safer.

It is probably a worthwhile investment to buy any auxiliary programs that you think might be useful to you, provided you can afford them. After all, you have invested a significant amount of money in a computer to augment your work, and you would be foolish to pinch pennies on programs that can help with that work. Some of the pennies you spend on auxiliary programs will be wasted, but the real value to you of the programs that turn out to be useful will make up for it.

13

Handy Tricks

In this chapter we're going to look at some things you can do to help make your use of the computer easier and smoother. Tricks of the trade, if you will.

13.1 Setting Up Your Disks and DOS

One of the most important things you will do in learning how to make effective use of your computer is to figure out how to get your disks organized. If you do it right, your work will be smooth and the operation easy and sensible. If you do it wrong, it will add a large measure of clumsiness to how your computer works for you. In this section and the next we're going to look at the main tricks of being effectively organized in your disks. There are two main parts to the business of organizing your disks—how you fit DOS into them and how you organize the rest of your files.

Whenever we mentioned the FORMAT command in Chapter 3 on getting started, and in Chapter 5 on elementary DOS commands, we noted that there are two ways you can FORMAT a disk—with DOS or without. Our general advice was to always include DOS in the formatting. Now it's time to get down to the details of what that means.

DOS breaks down into two parts: all the commands that DOS gives us (like the FORMAT command) and DOS itself. The core of DOS, or DOS itself, is loaded into memory from disk when we start up, or "boot" the system. On disk, DOS itself is kept in not one but three distinct files.

These three files make the difference between a system-formatted disk and an ordinary disk. We can start up DOS with a system-formatted disk but we can't with an ordinary disk. When we use the FORMAT command to prepare a disk, we use the S-switch, written "-S" or "/S", to indicate that we want system formatting, that we want the three files of DOS itself on the disk.

What are these three files? They are two hidden system files and one ordinary, visible file named COMMAND.COM. The two hidden system files have special names (which differ from computer to computer), which we really don't need to know since we can't even see the names because they are hidden from us.

Why there are two hidden files and not just one isn't of any practical importance to us, but the reason is interesting. There are parts of DOS that are universal, which apply to every computer that uses DOS; there are other parts that have to be tailored to the exact specifics of each particular computer. To make it easier to create and maintain DOS, the two parts are separated into distinct program files. In technical terms, the universal part provides the DOS services, and the computer-specific part provides the BIOS services.

There is one reason why we need to know that there are two different hidden files: when we use the CHKDSK command to report on a disk's condition, it will report the two hidden files if the disk is a system disk. CHKDSK is an easy way to see if a disk is system-formatted; if there are two hidden files the disk is a system disk, and if not, it's not.

If you have DOS 2.00 or a later version, you have an opportunity to create a third hidden file, if you use the V-switch to put a volume label on the disk when it is formatted. If you have DOS 3.00 or later, you can use the LABEL command to put a volume label onto disks at any time, or change or even remove old labels.

Whether a disk is a system disk and whether it has a label on it will be reflected in the number of hidden files that CHKDSK will report:

Number of hidden files	Labeled?	System disk?
0	unlabeled	non-system
1	labeled	non-system
2	unlabeled	system
3	labeled	system

The third of the files that make up DOS itself is COMMAND.COM, which is the command processor. The command processor has the smarts to interpret the command lines that we enter on the keyboard, or that are read from a batch file. The command processor also contains the programs that actually carry out each of the internal commands. (The external commands, you recall, are carried out by programs that have to be loaded from disk each time they are used.)

There is a very special reason why the command processor COM-MAND.COM is an ordinary file and not a hidden file like the two other parts of DOS itself. To understand why, we need some background information. When all three parts of DOS are loaded into memory, they take up quite a bit of memory space. For computers that have plenty of memory, this isn't very important, but for computers which are short on memory this can be a significant problem—it might leave too little room for some of our larger programs.

The solution to this problem is to make part of DOS only provisionally resident in memory. The command processor is needed when we are entering commands, but it is not needed after DOS has loaded a program and the program is running. The command processor is made provisionally resident in memory to free some memory space while the rest of DOS stays permanently resident. What does "provisionally resident" mean? It means that if the space is needed, the command processor is erased from memory and the space is used for other programs. If the space isn't needed, then the command processor is left in memory ready to be used again.

But what happens when the command processor is kicked out of memory? The command processor is needed again after the end of the program that took up its space. This means that DOS has to get a fresh copy of the command processor back into memory—so it goes looking to its disks, to find the COMMAND.COM file in order to reload the command processor.

This all boils down to one practical significance—we may have to have a copy of COMMAND.COM on many of our disks, even if those disks aren't system formatted disks.

Does all this sound confusing? Let's step through it again and then we'll get down to the practical recommendations.

First, to start DOS you have to use a system-formatted disk. That system-formatted disk will have copies of the two hidden system files and also a copy of COMMAND.COM. After DOS is running, we won't need a system-formatted disk again. How do we identify a system-formatted disk? If CHKDSK reports that a disk has two (or more) hidden files, then it is system-formatted.

Second, when we run our programs we may or may not have plenty of room for them and all of DOS as well. If we do have enough room, then we'll never need anything special on our working disks. If we don't have enough room, the command processor, COM-MAND.COM, will be kicked out of memory. When the program that swept COMMAND.COM out of memory is done, DOS will have to load the command processor again—that means that we'll need to

USE CHKDSK TO SEE HOW YOUR DISKETTES ARE FORMATTED.

have COMMAND.COM on our disks, whether or not the disks are also system-formatted.

With this information at our command, we can work out what the practical details of maintaining our disks are. The handiest thing, if it is otherwise practical, is to have every disk system-formatted. If every disk is system-formatted, then any disk can be used to start DOS and every disk will have COMMAND.COM on it, whenever DOS might need it.

There is a reason why it may not be practical to make every disk system-formatted. Having DOS on a disk can take up a sizable fraction of the disk space—even as much as 25 percent. Usually it's a smaller proportion, perhaps 10 percent, but it's still a good chunk of disk space. When we load up our disks with what we want on them—and we'll come to advice on that in the next section—we may run out of room. Not having the disk system-formatted may provide just enough extra space to make room for what we want.

Here is our advice so far: start out with every disk system-formatted. Later, as your experience grows, decide on which ones you can afford the space. If you have some disks that are system-formatted and some that are not, then you will probably be better off doing one of two things: either have one single "master boot" disk, which you use only for starting up DOS, or try to have every working disk be a system-formatted disk and then specially mark the ones that aren't so you won't try to "boot" DOS from them.

If you create disks that aren't system-formatted, put a copy of COMMAND.COM on each of them unless you know that you have enough memory to not need it. How much memory is enough? Here is a simple rule of thumb: 64K is not enough; 512K is enough and 256K is very likely enough; 128K or 196K may, or may not be enough, depending upon the size of the programs that you use. Experience will show you if you actually have enough memory or if you need COMMAND.COM on your disks.

If DOS goes looking for COMMAND.COM and doesn't find it, then DOS will complain to you with a message such as "Insert COMMAND.COM disk." This message will tell you two things: that you don't have enough memory to keep the command processor resident and that your disks don't have COMMAND.COM on them. The way to tell if DOS looks for COMMAND.COM when it is there (and there will not be an error message) is if the disk is used briefly between the end of a program and the appearance of DOS's command prompt.

After that comes our practical advice on what to put on our disks, and how to treat data differently from programs, which we'll cover in the next section.

13.2 More on Setting Up Your Disks

The next thing we want to look at is what to put on your disks. This raises two special issues: how many disk drives you have and the distinction between programs and data.

When we're doing something on our computers, we want to have everything that we need right at hand. This means all the programs that relate to what we are doing, and all of the data as well. That much is clear enough, but how do we organize the programs and data? That depends upon how many disk drives we have.

If our computer has only one disk drive, then we need to squeeze all the necessary programs and data onto one disk in order to have it all accessible to the computer. It is very unwise to have only one disk drive on a computer for many reasons, and it is likely that yours has two or more. (If it doesn't, I hope that you will dash out and get another disk drive—you'll be glad you did.) If you do have only one disk drive, here is the special approach you need to take: a real shortage of disk space will be your greatest problem.

To help alleviate this problem, you should make the subject matter of each disk as small as possible. Give each disk some functional identity, a subject matter, and gather together the programs and data needed to cover that use. Since it is likely that you will be cramped on each disk (and since you need some growth room on each disk), you should try hard to keep the requirements small. If you can, keep about a third of each disk's space open for the growth of the data you use with the disk. On the other hand, if it is not possible for you to squeeze both programs and data together on one disk, then you will have to work as though you had two disk drives, which will mean that you will have to switch your disks back and forth.

When you have two disk drives, it is best to distinctly divide your disks into program disks and data disks. The program disks are placed in your computer's A drive and the data disks are placed in the B drive. In fact, you will find that most programs are oriented to working in this pattern so they will fit in nicely with this way of organizing the disks, and they will tend to fight back if you use them any other way.

Among the many practical reasons why it is best to keep programs and data files on separate, distinct disks is that your program disks are fairly stable—once you work out the right combinations of programs, you seldom make changes to the program disks. However, the information on the data disks will be changed as often as you update your information. Since you should keep duplicate, backup copies of your data, it will be cleaner and simpler with the data completely isolated from other files.

Many computers have no more than two disk drives, but if your computer has three or more then you have a more complex choice of how to get the best use of those drives. If you tend to have more programs than data (which is a common experience), then you should probably devote all but one of the drives to holding program disks and just one to holding a data disk. On the other hand, if you ever use more data than will fit onto one disk at a time, then you will want to spread the data onto several disks mounted in different disk drives. One strategy that you can use in this situation, to simplify your backup procedures, is to place the stable files on one disk and the volatile ones on another.

When you have disks that are devoted purely to holding data and not programs, then the general advice that we gave of having each disk system-formatted does not apply. Pure data disks have no use for a copy of the DOS system files so you should format those disks without the system.

PROGRAM DISKS AND DATA DISKS : KEEP THEM APART.

Now the question comes up, which programs and what data to place on your disks? The answer, basically, is to organize the disks by usage—by the subject matter that you use them for. If you write programs, then you will have a disk with your program development tools on it. You will probably have a word processing program disk with your writing tools and several data disks to use with it—perhaps one data disk just with correspondence and another one for less casual writing. The key thing is to gather together all of the program tools that are used in connection with one kind of working task. Then your use of the computer's disks becomes much simpler and better organized.

What about the external DOS commands? What disks should you put them on? You can decide about them on a program-by-program basis; which ones you need where—just as you will with all other programs. As a general piece of advice, you don't need many of the DOS commands on most of your program disks. I would advise that you keep a special DOS command program disk, which has everything on it that DOS provides. When you need to use FORMAT or

DEBUG, then you can switch to that disk. But for your ordinary program disks, there isn't much among the DOS commands that you are likely to need often. The main one, which should be on all of your program disks, is CHKDSK, which checks your disks for available space and logical damage. Since it is wise to use the CHKDSK command often, it should be on every program disk.

There are three special command programs that you should also consider including on all of your program disks—the filter commands SORT, MORE, and FIND. Since these three are used in pipelines you should have them at your command at all times, if you make any use of them. (These three commands don't apply to the 1-series of DOS.)

There is one other thing that is a candidate for every one of your program disks, and that is an editor program such as DOS's editor, EDLIN. The reason for this is simple. Even if what we are doing isn't writing, we often need to use an editor program in connection with our work. For example, you need an editor program to set up batch processing files—if you are good at making effective use of your computer, you will be creating and changing your batch execution files often, probably several times a day.

Having EDLIN or another editor on each program disk is very handy. If you have a compact, easy-to-use editor, put it on your disks. If your only editor, besides EDLIN, is a bulky word processor, then just put EDLIN on your disks and learn to use EDLIN just enough to be able to build batch files.

Beyond what we've said here, you should often think about how your main working disks are organized, and whenever you have a better idea about them take the time to reorganize. This effort will pay off handsomely, especially in the early months of your use of the computer.

13.3 Making Commands More Convenient

Most of the commands and programs that we use have names to describe what they do: COPY, FORMAT, TIME. These names are nice and their straightforward quality makes it easier to remember them and use the right command name.

If you are using a command over and over again, it can be tiresome to keep typing the name in. You might want to consider giving your commands some aliases or other names. You might want to change the names entirely, but the most common and reasonable thing to want to do is to shorten the name of the command, perhaps to a single letter so that the keystrokes you have to press are as few as possible.

There are three ways that we can give programs aliases. One is simply to create a batch file under the alias name, which turns around and performs the proper command.

For example, if you'd like to be able to abbreviate the DIR command to the single letter D, or the COPY command to the letter C, you can do it be creating these two batch files. First, one named D.BAT, which has this inside it:

```
DIR     %1 %2 %3 %4 %5
```

and a second one named C.BAT, which has this for its contents:

```
COPY    %1 %2 %3 %4 %5
```

In both cases, the "%1" items are batch file symbols to pass any parameters on to the actual DIR or COPY command.

This is the slowest and least elegant way of creating an alias, but it will work with any command, internal or external. The other two ways of creating an alias only work with external commands.

For external commands, we can make copies of the command program file with a different name. This is quick and easy with the COPY command. For example, if we want to give the FORMAT command an alias of F, we can make a copy with the new name, like this:

```
COPY  FORMAT.COM  F.COM
```

The only disadvantage of making an alias this way is that the command program now takes up twice as much space on our disk. If you're working with a large-capacity hard disk system, that's probably not a problem at all.

Another way to give an external command a new name is to rename the program file with the RENAME command. For example,

```
RENAME  FORMAT.COM  F.COM
```

This has one great disadvantage, though. After renaming a command, it can only be used under its new name and not the old name as well. For our convenience the new short name may be terrific, but it means that the command can't be used in standard operations, or by other people, under the standard name. I don't recommend using this method for giving commands aliases except when your purpose is safety, which we'll discuss in Chapter 14 on danger areas.

13.4 Some Tricks For Advanced Use of DOS

In the line of handy tricks there is one exceptionally useful one that versions of DOS after the 1-series provide. Often we need a list of some of our files because we are going to copy them, or erase them, or just print them out.

Using the regular DOS features, whenever we want to do something with a list of files, we have to key in the filenames, which is a laborious and error-prone process. With the redirection feature that comes with DOS versions 2.00 and later, we can have the DIR command store a list of files into a data file. For example, to get a file that contains a list of all of the BAT, COM, and EXE files on a disk, we can do this:

```
DIR  *.BAT  >LIST

DIR  *.COM  >>LIST

DIR  *.EXE  >>LIST
```

You'll recall that ">", used in the first command here, sends its output to a file, replacing whatever was in the file before; and ">>", used in the last two commands, adds onto an existing file. These three DIR commands together create one list file, which contains all three lists.

After we have used output redirection, we can use our editor, such as EDLIN, to do whatever we want with the list. The most common thing is to turn it into a functional batch processing file. With our editor we would first remove any extraneous information, then change the list to be just the files we want (our purpose, for example, might be to erase just some of the files on a disk), and then finally add onto each file in the list the name of the command we want to perform on the file—erasing it, copying it, or whatever. Finally, after we have used our editor to turn the list into a usable batch file, we can execute the file, and the commands, acting on the list of files, will be carried out.

While this operation may seem a little elaborate, it is much easier and more accurate than typing in an entire batch file with a list of files in it. Output redirection has made the work simpler, more accurate, and safer.

You will probably have more use for this trick than you might imagine. It is quite common to need to copy, erase, or print out a list of files.

14

Danger Areas

In this chapter we're going to look at some of the ways you can make a dangerous mess of things, and lose a lot of your data. These are danger areas, where just the wrong moves could wipe out a lot of valuable information. We'll show you the sources of these dangers and what you can do to avoid them.

14.1 Mixing Your DOS's

One subtle and insidious danger to your data is through mixing up your versions of DOS. There are more versions of DOS than you might imagine. For example, I have four different official versions of DOS and another three unofficial versions. Because the parts of DOS work very intimately together, it is important to not get them mixed up. If you do get them mixed up, then it is very unpredictable what will happen—but one thing that can happen is the loss of an entire disk's worth of data. I've helped rescue two Hollywood writers who lost their data this way.

To avoid this danger, you need to know how it can happen to you and what you need to do to prevent any damage.

Periodically changes are made to DOS, to revise it, extend it, improve it. As we've been seeing in this book, there are several major series of DOS, which we've been calling the 1-, 2-, 3-, and 4-series. In addition, there are minor revisions within each series. Even if your computer currently has only one single version of DOS, it is almost certain that there will be new ones in the future.

You might encounter different versions of DOS three ways. One is simply that you receive a new improved version; this is the safest situation since you are aware that you have two versions. Another way that you can encounter a second version of DOS is by exchanging disks with colleagues—they might be using a different version than you are, and in exchanging disks you might unintentionally be mixing your DOS program files together. The third way can happen when you buy a copy-protected program.

The customary situation when you receive a copy-protected program is that you must use it from the disk it is distributed on, and the disk is prepared to accept a copy of DOS onto it. Copy-protected disks like that are supposed to be formatted as if they have the DOS system on them, but they are not supposed to actually have it on them (we're supposed to transfer DOS onto a reserved blank space on the disk). Sometimes it isn't done this way and the disk already contains a copy of DOS—a copy that might not match yours.

In both of these last two situations, exchanging disks with friends and receiving copy-protected disks, you can encounter another version of DOS that you are unaware of, and you can accidentally start mixing it up with your own version. The problem is insidious since you don't really know that it is happening. Things might work just fine for you for a while, until you get just the wrong combination of programs and operations and—bang—you've lost a disk's worth of data.

How can you prevent this from happening? First, be aware that there are three different parts to DOS—the two hidden system files, the command processor (COMMAND.COM), and the various DOS command programs such as FORMAT. (For more on the hidden system files, see Chapter 13.) For DOS to work properly, all three parts must match—all must be from exactly the same version of DOS.

For COMMAND.COM and the various DOS command programs, it is relatively easy to check to see that you have a matched set, thanks to the date and time stamp that is placed in each disk's directory. To find out the date-and-time marking of your DOS, take your original master disk of DOS (or an unaltered copy of that disk), and do this DIR command:

```
DIR  *.COM
```

You should see COMMAND.COM, FORMAT.COM, and numerous other program files listed. The dates and times on all of them should match, and this gives you the official reference point for checking any other disk.

With that in hand, you can check any other disk to see if the visible DOS program files match that version. With DIR commands to list all of the COM and EXE files (since some DOS programs are the EXE type), you can see all the DOS files on your disks and check their dates. When you do this, you should only be checking the DOS files, which will be COMMAND.COM and COM and EXE files that have the names of DOS commands. Any other program files, which aren't an integral part of DOS, can safely have any date and time on them.

MORE THAN ONE DOS CAN CONFUSE YOUR COMPUTER.

If you find that there is any mismatch of dates and times, you should copy a coordinated set of program files onto the disk so that there is no question of a mix-up.

So far, we've shown you how to check for, and fix up, a mismatch in the visible DOS files. But there are also two hidden system files that are used when DOS starts up, and we have no ordinary way to check to see that they match the rest of our DOS. While we can't check them, we can force them to match our master DOS version. Here is how it is done.

First, we have to see if a disk even has the two hidden files. We do this, as explained in Chapter 13, by using the CHKDSK command. If it reports two (or three) hidden files, then the disk has these two DOS hidden files. We don't know which DOS version they are from, but we can make sure that they match our version of DOS. This is done with the SYS command discussed in Chapter 5.

The SYS command is designed to transfer these two hidden files from one disk to another; the COPY command can't be used because hidden files are invisible to the copy operation—but SYS has a special x-ray vision, that gives it the ability to copy these two files. To make sure that a disk with the two files has the version you want it to have, use SYS to transfer the files from a disk you are sure of (such as a copy of your master DOS disk) to the questionable disk.

With this as background, we see what we need to do when we change to a new version of DOS, or when we receive a new disk that we want to match our version of DOS. For each disk that you need to update or confirm:

- First, check for the hidden files with CHKDSK;
- Second, transfer the hidden files, as needed, with SYS;
- Third, check for the presence of COMMAND.COM and other DOS files, with DIR;
- Fourth, if any DOS programs have the wrong dates, COPY the right version to the disk.

This operation involves enough looking and deciding that you must do it more or less by hand; but it is still possible to reduce the work involved by setting up repetitive batch files.

What if you want to have two different versions of DOS? This is all right, as long as you take care to not mix them up. If you do set up two versions of DOS, for any reason, you should carefully mark your disks as to which version they contain (or if they don't contain any part of DOS). Then you should keep the use of those disks distinct. Remember, as we discussed in Chapter 13, DOS will sometimes reload COMMAND.COM from a disk. If you have started DOS from one disk version, and then insert a disk that has another version of DOS, there is some danger that the wrong COMMAND.COM will be loaded. Fortunately, this is one error that all versions of DOS are good at checking for, so the worst that will happen is that DOS will complain that you have the wrong COMMAND.COM on the disk.

Fortunately for anyone using DOS after the 1-series, these newer versions of DOS contain internal checks to avoid a mismatch in any of the parts of DOS. This provides us with some partial protection against a mix-up, but it is far from completely solving the problem. You cannot, and should not, rely on DOS to protect you from the dangers of mixed versions.

14.2 Disastrous Interruptions

One of the things that can destroy your data is to interrupt the writing of disk information when it is incomplete. There are several ways that this can happen.

One way is if the power goes off on your computer while something is being written. A similar result can happen if you remove a disk while it is being written to, or if you use the break command, Control-C, to tell DOS to interrupt the operation. If your computer has been interrupted in mid-operation, there might be some harm to the disk data; on the other hand, just because your disks were spinning doesn't mean that the computer was writing—it might have been reading from the disk when it was interrupted and that can't do us any harm. Only if we were writing, could any damage be done; even then we might get off scott free.

In general terms, any of the interruptions that we have mentioned run the risk of damaging one file, but there is less risk that everything on the disk is messed up. Sometimes no harm is done and we are lucky. Occasionally one file, the file that was being written, will be messed up. Very rarely will there be more harm.

How do you tell if there has been harm to a disk? The first and best way is with the CHKDSK command. CHKDSK will tell you if there is any logical scrambling of the disk for one file or any others. If CHKDSK gives no error messages, then you know that the disk as a whole is OK, and also that the one file that was being written might be all right but we don't know yet. The next check is to use the DIR command to look at the file's directory entry. If you know which file was being written, ask for it; if you don't, then ask for the full directory listing (DIR *.*).

When you see the directory listing, the main thing to check for is a reasonable size for the file (or for all files). If a file size is given as zero, then the creation of the file was cut off in midstream, and the data that was being written (or any old data that the file had before) has been lost. Sometimes files are created under a temporary working name, and then only given their official name when the creation process is finished. If you suspect that a file was cut off as it was being created, you should check for unusual file names; common possibilities are names with extensions of $$$ or TMP.

There is another kind of interruption of the computer's writing to disk that can do much more harm. This happens if you switch disks in the middle of an operation. The problem relates to the disk's record of its used and unused space, which we discussed in Chapter 9. After a file is written, a record of the space the file occupies is written to the disk—but this record applies to every file, not just one. If this space table, called the File Allocation Table or FAT, is lost or damaged, then every file will be damaged or permanently lost.

This problem can occur in quite an innocent way, and I know of many people who have had it happen to them. You think that you are just beginning to write out a file, and DOS reports that something is wrong with the disk—so you substitute another disk. DOS finishes writing out the file and the File Allocation Table. However, DOS doesn't know you switched disks, so it writes the FAT that was read from the first disk onto the second disk. Every file that was stored on the second disk is now lost. Ugh.

DOS versions 2.00 and later have more protection against this problem built into it, but the danger still exists. The way to protect against this danger is simple—whenever DOS tells you that there is trouble with a disk, never switch to a disk with good data on it. Either fix the one disk, switch to a blank disk, or abort the operation. Don't put in a good disk with existing files because they may all be lost.

14.3 Ordinary Ways to Lose Your Data

So far we've talked about the more interesting and exotic ways that you can lose your data. Now we'll get down to the dull, prosaic, and common dangers.

There are exactly three ordinary ways to lose your disk data: by copying over it, by erasing it, and by—gulp—reformatting a disk.

Of these three dangers, the least frequent is to copy old or bad data onto new, good data. Although there are a million ways we could do this without meaning to, the most common is when we intend to make a backup copy of our data, but we copy in the wrong direction—instead of copying from our newly updated original to the backup disk we copy from an old backup, overwriting our latest data. Oh, my!

There are several ways that you can protect against this problem. One is to follow a strict physical pattern in the way that you copy data—for example, the original always in drive **B**, the backup copy always in drive A. Another is to keep using the same disk as your original, instead of rotating between the original and the backup. Another is to keep more than one backup and rotate them (perhaps one backup disk for odd numbered days another for even). Another is to never make the copies manually, but instead use a batch execution file to make sure that the copy is made correctly. Among the advantages of a batch file is that you can have it display the file dates before any copying is done as a precaution—if the dates don't look right, you can stop and check why.

The next problem, and probably the most common destroyer of data, is the DEL/ERASE command. It is incredibly easy to accidentally erase files that you didn't mean to erase. This happens most often through the unintended or misguided use of the asterisk wild

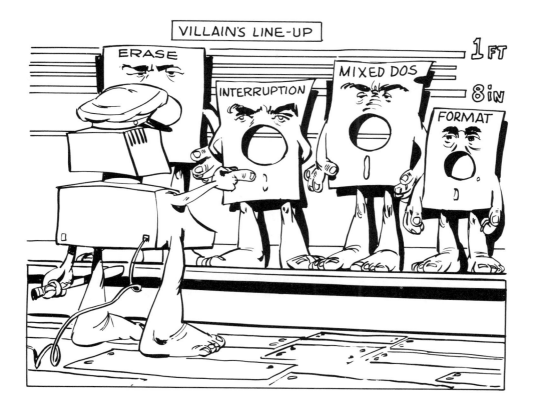

card, which will match any filename or any extension. DOS does contain one small precaution against this: if we enter the complete wild card name, "*.*", then DOS will pause to ask us for confirmation. That's not a lot of safety.

There are two things that you can do to protect against losing files through erasure. One, as we mentioned in Chapter 12, is to get an "un-erase" program if one is available for your computer. The other is to avoid using the DEL or ERASE command manually. If you have any routine need to erase files, don't do it by entering the command by hand; instead, build a batch execution file that will then have the names of the files being erased specified correctly. If you use a batch file, instead of manually entering the erasure command directly, you guard against an accidental mistyping of the names to be erased (provided you get it right in the batch file).

There is another way that batch files can make the DEL / ERASE command safer—by setting up a batch file that precedes the DEL command with a DIR command that shows what's about to be erased. You could call this batch command something like KILL.BAT, and it would look like this:

```
REM Here's a list of the files to be erased

DIR %1

PAUSE If that's not OK, press BREAK, otherwise

DEL %1
```

The last of the dangers we are going to cover is the danger of reformatting a disk that has valuable data on it. This is the goriest of all the dangers to your data because it is completely unrecoverable. If you erase your data, you may be able to unerase it. If you copy over your data some of it may still be left on the disk. But when you format a disk, everything that was on that disk is gone. Every part of every file is gone, beyond any hope of recovery. You can't unformat a disk the way you might be able to unerase a file. It's tough.

The best way to protect against formatting over your data is to only use the FORMAT command through a batch file—and have that batch file first check the disk for any files that are there. Here is an example of what such a batch file might be like:

```
REM        About to format a disk-check for files

CHKDSK  B:

DIR     B:

PAUSE      Are there any valuable files?  If so, BREAK, don't continue

FORMAT  B:
```

By doing all of your formatting with something like this batch file, you add a measure of protection to your data.

Beyond all these things, the best protection for your data is simply meticulous care. Be careful to always label your disks, indicating what is on them. Be careful not to do physical damage to your disks. Be careful about the specifically dangerous operations of copying, erasing, and formatting.

15

Coping with Copy Protection

One of the most exasperating things in the job of effectively organizing the use of your computer is coping with the special troubles of copy protection. It is a messy and annoying area, and we can't make it much better for you. In this chapter we'll give you as much help as possible.

15.1 Tricks of the Trade

Copy protection is intended to prevent copies of computer programs—or other computer data—from being copied. Copy protection became necessary because it is so easy to "steal" valuable software: one legitimately purchased copy could be passed around to dozens or even hundreds of people, and each could easily keep a working copy of the program. This problem arose long before the days of DOS, before small personal computers started being used by serious professionals and businesses. In the old hobby-oriented world of personal computing, stealing software became a game.

To protect themselves, software developers began to copy protect their programs. As soon as that started, pirate programmers began to develop copy busters, which would copy anything. Well, almost anything. The protectors developed more sophisticated protection schemes and the busters tried to match them. The battle was on, and it's a battle that continues.

In the war between the protectors and the copy busters, the busters usually win because whatever schemes the protectors can think of the busters can figure out as well. The busters have the advantage because a copy-protected diskette is full of clues about how it is protected. The only advantage the protectors have is that they get to invent the new protection schemes, and they are safe for a short while until it is decoded by the copy busters.

As with most wars, it's the innocent bystander who gets hurt the most. All of the honest software users have to put up with the problems of using copy-protected programs.

For your interest, you might want to have a little idea of how copy protection is done to better understand your computer and what is going on with it. Part of the story of how copy protection is done is very important to us, as you will see in a minute.

Before diskettes can be used they have to be formatted. Formatting a blank diskette is analogous to drawing lines on a blank piece of paper—it provides a framework on which information will be written. The hardware of the diskette drives can do this formatting in many ways, but for simplicity the operating system software (that's DOS) uses only some of the possible formats.

If a program creates a nonstandard format, then DOS usually cannot read that part of the diskette. Nonstandard formatting is one of the most common ways of doing copy protection. By having at least some of the diskette formatted in a way that DOS can't work with, the disk can't be copied by the ordinary tools that DOS gives us, COPY and DISKCOPY.

There are two completely different ways that this nonstandard formatting can be done to accomplish copy protection, and there is a tremendous practical difference between them. In one style of protection, the programs are not directly protected—and so DOS can read and load them into memory. Then, when the program begins running, it checks its diskette for copy protection, usually by reading from the unconventionally formatted part of the diskette. If all is well, the program continues; but if anything is wrong with the protection, then the program refuses to work. This kind of copy protection doesn't interfere with DOS, which is nice for us. The other kind is not so nice.

In the other style of copy protection, DOS can't load the protected program—the program has to load itself, which normally means restarting, or rebooting your system before and after using the program. This, of course, is a real disruption to the work flow in your computer.

There are basically three problems with copy protection—three ways that copy-protected programs make it harder for us to use our computers effectively. The first problem is copying copy-protected diskettes for backup and safety purposes. This is the problem that people talk about most when they complain about copy protection; frankly, this is the least of our worries. Getting backup copies of a protected diskette is not very much trouble; the program's develop-

ers normally make them readily available and you can always turn to a copy busting program to make your own backup copies.

After you are experienced with personal computers, you learn that damaged diskettes are a rare occurrence. All the worry and hullaba-loo about losing your only copy of an expensive copy-protected disk-ette is mostly nonsense. For an example from my own experience, in 18 months of very heavy continuous use of two, and sometimes three, computers, my office has never damaged even one diskette. This is not to say it can't happen, only that it is rather rare. Diskettes are seldom damaged and backup copies are available, so this isn't such a big problem. An inconvenience, but not a problem.

The real problems come from two other areas. One is the transfer problem. Hard-disk systems—and also electronic disks—are being used more and more and for good reason. For the serious use of a computer system, high-speed and high-capacity disk systems are essential. The history of traditional computing makes it clear that users of small DOS computers will find their dependence upon their computers always growing. This makes it very important that pro-grams can be transferred from diskette media to other media, such as hard disks and electronic disks. Unless some special trick is used, copy-protected programs can't be transferred, and that is the problem.

The last of the three problems with copy-protected programs concerns the ones that don't run under the DOS operating system but load themselves instead. When your use of the computer is casual and sporadic, it hardly matters that you have to shut it down and start it up just to use some program. When your use of the computer becomes regular, you just can't afford the disruption—and the annoying effort—to switch your system back and forth between DOS and programs that won't run under DOS.

If you think that this is small potatoes, think again. Imagine if the telephone company announced that from now on all telephones would be outdoor pay phones, so that every time you needed to make a call you had to run outside with a handful of change. You couldn't fit the use of the telephone into your work or your social life very well, could you? It would be more than an inconvenience—for most businesses it would be an impossible difficulty. So it is with copy-protected programs that don't run under DOS.

It seems likely that copy-protection mechanisms will emerge that serve the needs of both program sellers and program users—for example, the use of hardware serial numbers that make it possible for a program to be freely copied, but only run on the one computer with the right serial number. When we talk about copy protection here we're not talking about any such nice schemes—we're talking about the traditional copy protection schemes, the ones that cause the problems we covered above.

What can you do to cope with copy protection? The snappy answer is don't buy copy-protected programs. In fact, we can expect to suffer less from the nuisance of copy protection in the future for the simple reason that copy-protected programs are less useful to serious professional computer users, and competitive forces will give non-protected programs an advantage in the marketplace. But just saying don't buy copy-protected programs doesn't do you much good. Sometimes you don't have a choice. Sometimes you are stuck using a copy-protected program.

What you can do is four-fold. First, don't make the problem worse by being a villain; if almost no one made illicit copies of programs, we wouldn't have copy protection on so many programs. Second, vote with your pocket book by avoiding copy protected programs as much as you can. Third, vote with your pen—by complaining to the producers of programs that interfere with the smooth use of your computer. Finally, there are some things that you can do to make copy-protected programs fit into your system more easily.

The key to the easy use of copy-protected programs is batch execution files. Even if you have to use a copy-protected program, you can make it easier with the right batch files. What sort of batch files you'll need depends so much on the program, and the way your computer is organized, that we can only give you some suggestions.

One of the main things to consider is which drive is the most convenient one to place your copy-protected diskette in; another is where you want any working data to go—sometimes it's convenient, or even necessary, for the data drive to be the current default drive. Finally, determine if it is practical or safe to place your own batch execution files onto the copy-protected diskette (usually it is, but sometimes not).

Here are some examples. If your computer has two diskette drives and nothing more—which is one of the most common setups—then you are probably using your A drive exclusively for programs and your B drive exclusively for data. In this situation, the best thing to do is to treat the copy-protected diskette like any of your other program diskettes. This means putting any necessary batch files on it, plus the DOS file COMMAND.COM and any other program tools that you might need.

Candidates for inclusion on the diskette are FORMAT, CHKDSK, and the editor you use, which might be DOS's EDLIN. You can only do this, of course, if the copy-protected diskette is in a format that allows you to transfer files to it and if there is enough room on the diskette.

One batch execution file that will make it easier to work this way is the BAA file mentioned in Chapter 11. To conveniently use a program, which we'll call XXX, on drive A, and work with data on drive B, the BAA batch file temporarily switches the default drive. BAA is like this:

```
B:

A:XXX

A:
```

The first line switches the default to drive B and the third switches it back to A. In the second line, the program named XXX is executed (from the A drive), but any data files that it uses will be found on the B drive since B is the current default drive. The natural name to give a batch file like this is some abbreviation of the program name. Or, on the other hand, you could use the RENAME command to give XXX some alias and then XXX can be the name of the batch file. (If the batch file has the same name as the program file, then you type in the name as a command, DOS will execute the program directly and not use your batch file.)

If you have a hard-disk system that imitates a number of diskettes (some hard disks work this way even though DOS discourages it) then the kinds of batch files you need are similar, but they are built a little differently. For example, your main programs and batch files might be on disk partition A, while D might be your customary data work space. B might have your permanent data and F might be your only diskette drive, which is where the copy-protected diskette would have to be loaded. In a case like this you might want to use a batch execution file that is similar to this outline:

```
COPY      B:*.XXX  D:*.DAT      (move your data to the work drive)

D:                              (change the default to the work drive)

F:XXX                           (run the program)

COPY      D:*.DAT  B:*.XXX      (move the data back to permanent space)

DEL       D:*.DAT               (clear it off the work drive)

A:CHKDSK D:                     (clean up any mess)

A:                              (switch the default back to normal)
```

If you can understand the thinking that went into that batch execution file, then you should be able to custom tailor your own batch files to suit your particular needs.

15.2 Something Worse Than Copy Protection

What could be worse than copy protection? Another operating system.

DOS isn't the only operating system around. There are many others, and two are in widespread use that are likely to be available for your computer. One is known as CP/M-86 and the other is the UCSD p-System (often just called the p-System).

Whatever the virtues of any other operating system are, it is very, very inadvisable to be using more than one operating system on your computer. Why? It would be like trying to run an office where half the workers spoke French and the other half spoke English. A mess. As a general rule, each operating system is totally incompatible with each other one—neither programs nor data can be shared. Even

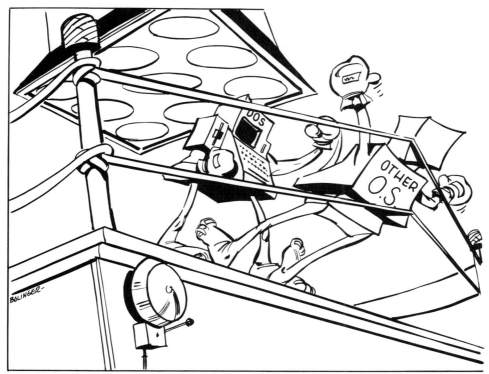

DIFFERENT OPERATING SYSTEMS DON'T GET ALONG VERY WELL WITH EACH OTHER.

worse, from our point of view, the skills and familiarity that we gain using one system won't work on another.

Due to these problems, you will probably not choose to use any other operating system than DOS. But one may sneak up on you. Some programs are sold with a working copy of their operating system; this is particularly true with the p-System, although it can happen with CP/M-86.

If you buy such a program, it is no different than if you had bought the kind of copy-protected program that requires restarting your computer. To use a p-System program, you will have to shut down DOS to use the program. In some ways using one of these programs is worse than a copy-protected program, because a p-System or a CP/M-86 program will probably force you to deal with at least some part of its operating system.

If you are considering buying a large expensive program, be sure to check to see if it is one of those that comes with its own operating system. If it is, then you need to consider if the advantages of the program outweigh the disadvantages of its not working under DOS.

You may wonder just what are the right questions to ask about a program to see if it will fit into your working environment. If you are not a technical expert on computers, you may be concerned that you won't know the right questions to ask. To be sure that you don't encounter the kind of difficulties that this chapter has been discussing, here are some of the right questions to ask about a program you are considering buying:

- Is it copy protected?
- If it is and you use another medium such as a hard disk, can it be transferred to the other media even though it is copy protected?
- Does it run under DOS?
- To ask the same question another way, does it require "rebooting" your system?
- What are the program's hardware and software requirements? (If it doesn't require DOS, it doesn't run under DOS.)

16

Special Tricks for Hard Disks and Electronic Disks

Personal computers are usually based upon floppy diskettes for their storage needs—storage that is relatively slow and small. But many small computer systems take advantage of the special capabilities of hard disks and electronic disks. In this chapter we'll consider their special needs. Before we get into the details, though, we need a little background information.

16.1 A Little Background

The practical use of a computer centers around its storage. That may not seem sensible—after all, the computing power of a computer is what you use a computer for. Beyond that, the features of your computer that you are probably most interested in are likely to be the quality of the display screen—can it do graphics? is it easy to look at?—or of the printer. While we may think the most about our machine's computing speed, or its display formats and printing quality, storage is the element that the entire use of the computer centers around.

The widespread use of personal computers and their operating systems, such as DOS, was based upon the floppy diskette—and for good reason. Diskettes are cheap, reliable, and flexible in more ways than one. Their technical flexibility made it easy to design them into all sorts of computers. Their flexibility of use—easy to put in and take out, easy to store, easy to mail —greatly enhanced how practical it was to get things done with a small computer.

But floppy diskettes have two severe disadvantages—slow speed and small storage capacity. Let's explain a little about each.

A computer consists of a collection of components, all working together. Each part has an effective speed of how quickly it accomplishes its own task. In a rough sort of way, the separate speeds of the different parts can be compared so that we can get an idea of whether they are appropriately balanced. If the parts of the computer are well matched, all is well.

Let's consider what happens if one part is made much faster or much slower. Suppose that the working of one part of our computer takes up exactly 10 percent of the total time needed to get some work done. If we replace that part with one that is 10 times faster, then it will get its job done in only one percent of the old total time—and our whole computer will run nine percent faster. One part is improved ten times, but the whole is improved less than ten percent. If we replace that part with one ten times slower than the original, it now takes 100 percent of the original time just to do that one part of the work. The whole computer now runs 90 percent slower, almost halving its effective speed thanks to just one slow component.

The moral here is that there is little advantage in having one part of the computer disproportionately fast, but there is a huge disadvantage in having one part disproportionately slow. The question is one of balance, and of bottlenecks. If one part is slow relative to the rest of the computer, it is a bottleneck that can cripple the entire computer.

In most personal computers, the greatest bottleneck is floppy diskettes. This statement is not absolutely true, just generally true. How true it might be for you depends upon two things—first, the relative balance of speed in the parts of your own computer, and, second, the relative balance of how your work utilizes your computer's parts. If you and I had identical computers, but you rarely used your disks, they couldn't be a bottleneck for you: If I use mine heavily, mine are certain to be a bottleneck. There are no absolutes here. For most users of most personal computers, the disks are clearly the bottleneck, the limiting factor in the entire computer's working speed.

Let's look at some representative numbers so that you can see what we are talking about. The computer that this book was written on has all three kinds of storage—floppy diskettes, a hard disk, and an electronic disk. In my own practical speed trials, I found the hard disk was roughly five times faster than the floppy diskettes, and the electronic disk twice as fast as the hard disk or ten times faster than the diskettes. But these speed tests were for purely disk operations, not for the whole computer. What did they mean in practice? Is there a bottleneck?

I tested one of the most time-consuming things I do with my computer—checking something that I have written for spelling errors. I knew that my spelling checker did lots of computing, and a fair amount of disk work, but I didn't know about balance. I didn't know where the bottlenecks were for that particular computer task. I tested a large chunk of spelling to check, using each of the three storage media.

Using the floppy diskette, the operation took about three minutes. Then I tried the hard disk, which, for disk work alone, is five times faster. When I used the hard disk for spelling checking, the time was down to about two minutes. Aha! A dramatic improvement—a full third off the time. Was disk access still a bottleneck or was it now in balance with the rest of the computer? A test with the electronic disk answered that—only six seconds came off the time. So even though the electronic disk was twice as fast—in pure disk operations—as the hard disk, the total benefit was very little.

My own speed trials rather dramatically demonstrated both sides of the speed question. Up to a certain point, a faster disk can help you, but beyond that disk speed is not the problem. Your own speed needs or problems are uniquely yours, but typically they will be similar to mine: for most personal computers, ordinary floppy diskettes are somewhat of a bottleneck, and anything that promises to be several times faster will eliminate that bottleneck.

Now let's look at the other side of storage: capacity. There are many formats of disk storage so there are many different capacities. The diskettes used in the PC family range in capacity from a low of 160 thousand bytes (160KB)—for the PC's "lowest common denominator" the single-sided 8-sector diskette—to a high of 1.2 million bytes (1.2MB)—for the AT's special high-capacity diskettes.

There are three problems with using diskettes that won't hold all of our data. First, there is the nuisance of shuffling diskettes around, putting in one set for one kind of work and another set for other work. Not only is this inconvenient, but the physical handling of the diskettes greatly increases the danger of damage to our data. The second problem is that we may want to have more data on tap than will fit into our diskette drives at one time. It is hard to correlate the information on three diskettes when you have only two diskette drives. The third problem is that diskettes set a low limit on how large our biggest single file can be since no file can be bigger than the disk that holds it.

While electronic disks do nothing for our storage capacity problems, hard disk systems do, and they solve all three problems with the limits of diskette capacity. They eliminate diskette shuffling, they allow the simultaneous use of large amounts of data, and they allow single files to grow very large.

You may be wondering how much you might need a hard disk system, or what size will do for you (after all, if you get one that is too small you have the problems of the diskette world). If you can estimate your data storage needs, fine. If not, here is my suggested rule of thumb. For a computer in personal use or professional use

DISKETTE

HARD DISK

ELECTRONIC DISK

BOLINGER

THERE ARE THREE DISK SPEEDS.

without large amounts of data, a hard disk with five million bytes capacity is likely to be enough.

For a professional user or for a business with moderate amounts of records, ten millions bytes (MB) might be right (ten is what I have, and for me it's just barely enough). For extensive business records, a large research data base, or anything similar, twenty (MB) and up might be needed. If you are choosing a hard disk, it is safer to get larger rather than smaller. If you know that you can add more later, then you can safely start small.

With this general information about the needs for and uses of hard disks and electronic disks, let's now move on to the special things you need to know about each.

16.2 The Special Uses of Electronic Disks

To know how to use electronic disks, we have to understand a little of what they are about. Our programs, including DOS itself, expect to read and write information that it keeps in files on a storage medium called disks. That is really all that our programs need to know—that they can read or write files from storage.

Clever folks in the world of computing noticed, though, that an enormous increase in speed could be obtained by not actually reading and writing files from a disk, but instead holding the data in the computer's memory. The program that used that data would not know that the data was being held in memory and wouldn't use it directly in its memory copy. Instead, our programs would request that data be "read" or "written," presumably from disk. Actually, the data would be transferred in memory from the simulated disk to the program that is using it. The working result would be the same, but the speed would be much faster—in the neighborhood of fully ten times faster. This little trick is what is known as an electronic disk, or a memory disk, or a RAM (Random Access Memory) disk; other exotic terms are used, such as flash disk—it all refers to the same thing.

To create an electronic disk, two things are needed: the spare memory to hold the data and an appropriate program to do the work of simulating disk operations in memory. There are several strategies for providing them, and you may find that your computer has several kinds of electronic disk available for it. One kind might use dedicated memory, which is only intended to be used as an electronic disk. Another might share part of your computer's main memory, giving you a useful flexibility about how much memory is used for the electronic disk, and how much is used for ordinary memory. (Mine happens to be of this adjustable kind, which I sometimes find very handy).

Whatever the case, to create an electronic disk on your computer, you will need some special software—which does the disk simulation—and plenty of memory.

As DOS has evolved, so has the use of electronic disks. The 1-series of DOS was not designed to accommodate electronic disks, so they had to be created by modifying DOS—a nasty process. Beginning with the 2-series, DOS could accommodate extra device drivers (which we'll discuss in Chapter 17), so electronic disks became much more civilized. Still, they were foreign to DOS and we had to get them from some independent source (fortunately, they were widely available).

Starting with the 3-series, DOS includes its own electronic disk, called VDISK, which we'll learn more about in Chapter 17. The appearance of VDISK has two advantages for us: it's an official part of DOS (so we don't have to get it separately) and, if we are lucky enough to be using the super-hot AT model of PC, we can have millions of bytes of electronic disk at our command.

When you have an electronic disk, you have a fragile and vulnerable storage medium. If something goes wrong with your computer, or if the power goes off, the data stored in your electronic disk will be lost. A diskette is a pretty safe place to store your data because it is unlikely that it will be damaged. But data stored on an electronic disk is dependent upon the continuing operation of your computer to preserve it; if the computer goes out, the data is lost. Even if an electronic disk has some protection against a power outage, the danger still exists.

An electronic disk is not a place to actually store data—it is a place simply to use it. The normal way of working with an electronic disk is very temporary. At the beginning of a working session, your data can be transferred from its permanent storage location, probably a diskette, to the electronic disk. There it is worked with by your programs. Afterwards, any new or updated data can be transferred back to the permanent, safe, disk storage. When you work with an electronic disk this way, your only danger is that you might lose one session's work.

You will have to judge for yourself how great the dangers are for you with an electronic disk. It will depend upon how reliable your computer is, how steady your power supply is, and how great the loss would be if some work was destroyed. My own experience, even with constant exposure to corrosive salt sea air, and a power supply that jumps with every passing storm, has been good. In fact, the only work I have lost in my electronic disk has been through my own stupidity, not through the fault of the disk.

When you set up to use an electronic disk, you should create batch files that will easily and reliably transfer your data into and out of the electronic disk. If you are concerned about the reliability of your disk, take break points often to copy your new data back to diskette.

To give you an example, here is a batch file that will transfer the entire contents of a diskette to an electronic disk, and switch your operation to the electronic drive. For this example, our batch file takes D as the drive identifier of the electronic drive and assumes that the A drive holds the diskette we want to copy from:

```
REM    Copy to ram-disk

COPY  A:*.*  D:*.*

D:
```

You can have a similar batch file to return the data when you are done. The pair of batch files might be called UP.BAT and DOWN.BAT, or whatever you thought were good names. This example is very simple—you can add your own elaborations to transfer only the files needed.

One aid that can make an important difference in the speed, convenience, and safety of the use of an electronic disk is a fast selective copy program like I mentioned in Chapter 12. A common way of using an electronic disk is to copy quite a few files into the disk but only change a few of them. It is good to have a copy program that is smart enough to save back to real disk storage only the ones that have changed (which can be told by the files' time stamp).

When you set up to use an electronic disk, you will probably not have enough room on the disk for all of the program and data files that you will be using. You must decide which files to place on the fast disk. Under most circumstances that means your data files, but not always. Sometimes you run one program and it reads or writes large amounts of data—in this case, the data should be in the fast electronic disk.

In other situations it is the programs themselves that are being read all the time. Most accounting programs and most large programs written in BASIC repeatedly read parts of themselves into memory from disk. This is also true of many word processing programs, spreadsheet programs, and especially multi-function programs (which we'll discuss in Chapter 18). If you know that your programs use overlays, or load help-screens from disk, then it is likely that they would operate much faster if the programs themselves were loaded into your electronic disk.

If you can fit everything you need onto your electronic disk, fine. If not, you should decide which files to load and that usually means deciding between data files and program files. There are two reasons for choosing to put the program files into electronic memory. One, mentioned above, is that sometimes the program's files are the ones used the most so they are the most deserving of a speed advantage. But there is another reason: if you put your programs but not your data into the electronic disk, then your data is not exposed to the dangers of being lost that an electronic disk creates. If something goes wrong with the electronic disk, you have lost nothing but a copy of your programs—no data and no work is lost.

In general, you want to put the files used most into electronic disk; after that you want to use the electronic disk for files that don't change—program files, or data that is only read, not written. You don't always have a free choice of which files can be placed where, though. This is a problem that electronic disks share with hard disks, so we'll discuss it in a separate section at the end of this chapter.

That covers the special things that we need to know about using electronic disks. Shortly we'll consider the same kinds of things for hard disks. Before we do that we need to pause and look at three

AN ELECTRONIC DISK MIGHT VANISH INTO THIN AIR.

DOS commands that we haven't covered so far, which are special to the use of hard disks.

16.3 Hard Disk Commands: FDISK, BACKUP, and RESTORE

Having a large-capacity hard disk system on your computer adds extra power and capabilities to your system. It also calls for some special servicing, and to meet that need DOS provides three special programs tailored for hard disks. The programs are FDISK, BACKUP, and RESTORE.

FDISK is oriented to one simple matter: sharing your hard disk between several operating systems. DOS isn't the only operating system that can be used with our personal computers, although it's by far the dominant one. When we work with floppy disks, we can switch from one operating system to another simply by switching diskettes. With a hard disk, things aren't so simple.

Different operating systems can't share the same disk space, but they can share an entire hard disk if the disk is divided up into sections for each—this is called partitioning. Separate sections, or partitions, of the disk are set aside for use by different operating systems.

FDISK's job is to create and manage partitions on a hard disk. If you know you'll be using an operating system other than DOS, you can set aside some part of your hard disk with FDISK. Most PC users won't. Very sensibly, most of us are using DOS exclusively for our computing work.

Even if you only use DOS on your hard disk, you'll need to use FDISK when the hard disk is first set up simply to mark the disk as being entirely devoted to DOS.

It's important to know that when you first set up a hard disk on your personal computer, you'll need to use FDISK to establish the DOS partition on that disk.

The use of FDISK is remarkably simple so we don't need to go over it in detail here. What we will do is summarize the most common operation: setting up a hard disk the first time.

When you first set up your hard disk, you need to start your computer with a diskette copy of DOS then invoke the FDISK program. FDISK will present you with a menu of options. Choose the "display partition data" option and see what you have. If it reports that there is already a DOS partition, then you probably want to let it be.

If there is no DOS partition, go back to the menu and choose the "create DOS partition" option. You'll be asked if you want to devote the entire disk to DOS; normally you will. After you create your DOS partition, you'll need to reboot your computer, and then use the FORMAT command to format the DOS partition and place a copy of the DOS system there (using the /S option of FORMAT, i.e., FORMAT C:/S). Once all that is done—which seems like more steps than it should be, but that's the way it is—your hard disk will be ready to use and you'll be able to startup DOS from the hard disk without having to use a floppy diskette copy of DOS.

One word of caution before we finish discussing FDISK. Once you've created a DOS partition and started using it, you should be careful to not destroy it with FDISK. If you tell FDISK to change the partition data, you'll probably lose everything that's stored on the disk. That could be a disaster if you don't mean to do it. Be careful using FDISK.

Once you start using a hard disk system, you're sure to load it up with lots and lots of data. That's what a hard disk is for. Now, how do you safeguard that data? For one thing, you should make periodic backup copies of the data on your hard disk and that's where the commands BACKUP and RESTORE come in.

BACKUP is designed to copy your data from a hard disk to as many floppies as are needed to hold it. Starting with the 3-series of DOS, you can also use the same techniques that BACKUP provides to copy from any type of disk to any other—you can even backup your floppies onto a hard disk. While it's nice to be able to transfer data in any direction, the main use for the BACKUP command is to make safe-keeping copies of your hard disk data onto floppy diskettes.

BACKUP provides us with several options that make it easier to control how we copy our data. If we want to copy the entire contents of a hard disk (which we'll assume is drive C) onto floppy disks (which we'll assume are placed in drive A), we use the BACKUP command, like this:

```
BACKUP C:\ A: /S
```

Here are the key ingredients of that command: the parameter "C:\" instructs BACKUP to start from the root directory of drive C. The "/S" switch tells BACKUP to copy all the subdirectories as well as what's in the root directory. By starting at the root directory, and by including any subdirectories, we've told BACKUP to copy everything that's on the disk.

If we wanted to, we could backup just the contents of a particular directory by specifying the particular directory pathname (instead of the root directory). Using or not using the "/S" option would include or exclude any subdirectories of the particular directory we've chosen.

Here are some examples of the various ways to use BACKUP. For all these examples, we'll assume that we're backing up from a hard disk that is in drive C to floppies in drive A. First, this will backup the entire hard disk:

```
BACKUP   C:\ /S
```

Next, this will backup just the contents of a directory called LETTERS:

```
BACKUP   C:\LETTERS
```

This will do the same, and also include any subdirectories under the LETTERS directory:

```
BACKUP   C:\LETTERS /S
```

Finally, this will backup just the files with the extension name of ".DOC":

```
BACKUP   C:\LETTERS\*.DOC
```

BACKUP is clever enough to work with as many floppy diskettes as are needed to copy the files we've asked it to, and even to spread files across more than one diskette when it's necessary.

You'll find when you backup the contents of a hard disk that it's a time-consuming process that takes lots of diskettes—typically 20 or more. Fortunately there are some shortcuts that can reduce the process.

Once you've backed up all of a disk, you really don't need to copy it all for a while. Just copying any files that you've added or changed should be enough. DOS keeps a record of which files have been changed and not backed up, and BACKUP is smart enough to recognize them if we ask it to. This is done with the "/M" option. That tells BACKUP to only copy the files that we've changed.

What I do with my hard disk, and what I recommend that you do, is to periodically make a complete copy of your hard disk, however often you think is wise. (I think once a month is wise but it's usually several months till I get around to the chore.) Then, much more often, make "incremental" backups copying only the files that have been changed. You might do that daily or at the very least weekly.

If you follow that suggestion, you'll find that your backing up procedures will be very practical.

As a reminder, here are the two commands to use:

(for a full backup)	**BACKUP C:\ A:**
(for an incremental backup)	**BACKUP C:\ A: /M**

There are two more aspects of BACKUP that you should know about. One is the date option. Like the M-modified option, the date option lets you select which files will be backed up, but selecting them on the basis of the date (which indicates when they were last changed) being on or after a date that we give to BACKUP. This lets us choose to backup recent materials, without regard to whether they have been backed up before or not (which the /M option uses.) That's a handy alternative.

The other thing that you need to know about BACKUP is that it will completely take over a diskette and wipe out any existing files on the target diskette, unless we tell BACKUP to be more civilized. This is done with the /A option, which tells BACKUP to add its files to whatever is on the target diskette. Without the /A option, BACKUP will clear out whatever is already on the target disk.

Naturally there is a RESTORE command to match BACKUP. RESTORE reverses the backup operation with the same sort of features. There is one practical inconvenience that you should be aware of. More often than you might think, an occasion arises when we want to restore a copy of a file that's been backed up, but we want to place it in another directory—basically so that we can work on it separately from the original copy. Unfortunately, RESTORE will only restore files to exactly the same directories where they were backed up from. Keep this in mind when you selectively restore files.

16.4 The Special Uses of Hard Disks

In this section we'll cover what's particular to the use of high-capacity hard disk systems.

The heart of the successful use of a hard disk system with DOS is the intelligent use of the directory tree, which we described in Chapter 8.

The main problem with using a tree-structured directory is figuring out when to separate files into distinct subdirectories, and when to keep them together in one main directory.

There are probably as many strategies for the effective use of directory trees as there are people using DOS, and I certainly can't claim to offer definitive advice about the best way to use them. But some things seem clear to me, and that is what I will try to explain here.

The main reason for creating any subdirectory is to keep track of the files in it. If you don't have a strong reason for needing to keep track of some files as a distinct group, then you shouldn't have them in their own directory. What are good reasons why you would want to keep track of files as a group? One reason is for "parallel" or "generation" backup.

If you have some data that is changed regularly, for example your accounting files, you might want to keep some old versions or generations of the files in case you make a mess of the current version. With accounting data, that might be the end-of-the-month data for each of the last few months. The reason for using a separate directory for this kind of data is mainly so that the file names can be kept the same.

If there is an easy and sensible way to use alternate names for previous generations of your data, then there is no strong need to use a subdirectory, although it still might be a real convenience. Any time you need to keep more than one version of the same data under the same name, you have a good reason for using a subdirectory.

Another reason why you might need to keep track of files in a distinct subdirectory is simply so that you can keep track of them. DOS may do a very good job of keeping track of hundreds of files in one

SO, LET'S DISCUSS THIS COMPULSIVE NEED YOU HAVE...

A HARD DISK NEEDS A DIRECTORY TREE.

directory but we usually can't. To manage our files well, we need to be dealing with a reasonable number of them at a time—which means that we should group them into subdirectories in ways that make sense to us, and that are small enough for us to comprehend the entire list of files. If there are a hundred files in a subdirectory, you aren't going to know what they are all about, and you won't readily be able to identify anything wrong with a list that big. If a file is missing, damaged, extraneous, or out of date, how would you know if it was buried in a list of a hundred other files? One of the strongest reasons for creating subdirectories is simply to keep the file lists in a manageable size.

On the other hand, the files that we don't need to keep track of we might as well place in one main holding area—either one catch-all subdirectory or the disk's root directory. The main candidate for these files is all of our programs: the DOS command programs and our other programs as well. Also, there is little reason not to have all of our batch execution files in the same main directory. So, unless you have a reason to do otherwise, place every program file, every file with an extension of BAT, COM, or EXE, in your main directory.

If you literally have all of your executable files, and all of the BAT, COM, and EXE files in one place, then you can have DOS always look there for its programs. As you'll remember from Chapter 8, the PATH command is used to tell DOS where to look for command files. If all of our command files are in the root directory, then the PATH command to tell DOS where to look would be like this:

```
PATH   \
```

where the reverse slash tells DOS to look in the root directory. If our command files are not in the root directory, but in a subdirectory, say with the name "COMMAND.DIR", then our PATH command would look like this:

```
PATH   \COMMAND.DIR
```

To make effective use of the subdirectories that you create, you should create batch files that switch your operation to them. As an example, if we have a subdirectory to hold our correspondence, which me might call LETTERS, then we could create a batch file that would switch the current directory to the LETTERS subdirectory. This batch file might be named LETTERS.BAT so that its command name was LETTERS, or we might just make it L.BAT to give us a short, one-key command name.

The working contents of this batch file might be very simple:

```
REM                 Switch to correspondence directory

CHDIR \LETTERS

PATH   \LETTERS;\
```

This batch file does three things: it has a remark that tells us what it is doing (a very good idea in all batch files), a change of the current directory, and a change of the path. Now if my advice on command files was followed strictly, the PATH command would be unnecessary—all the commands would be in the main command directory. But, most likely for one reason or another, you will have some command files located in each of the subdirectories. If you do, then you need to use a PATH command like the one shown to tell DOS to look to that directory for commands and then to the main directory.

If you have the commands you'll be using scattered among several directories, then the PATH command should refer to them all in the order that you want them to be used. (I say that it is a bad idea to have your commands scattered around but you may have your own reasons. Wherever your commands are, be sure that you get access to them with a PATH command which goes looking for them all.)

Each of our main operations should have a batch execution file for it, similar to the example shown here. The batch file should set the context of operation by performing a CHDIR command and a PATH command, first and foremost. Second, it should show you anything you need to know like the message relayed by the REM command, which just reminds us of what we are doing. Another useful bit of information would be a listing of the files, using the DIR command, so that we can see the names, size, and time-stamps on our files. A third thing that these commands might do is to begin the necessary operation—by executing a program, by copying files to a backup directory, or whatever. Anything you need done when you switch to a new subject matter could be performed by the batch file that takes you to the subdirectory.

Here's an example of that sort of batch file, which switches to a working directory, and also sets the program search path:

```
REM   Switch to new Pascal programming
CD    C:\NEW-PROGS
PATH C:\PASCAL
```

If you have a batch file to take you into each subdirectory area, you should have one to take you out again. For example, I have a batch file named ROOT.BAT, that returns me to my root directory no matter which subdirectory I have gone to.

Here's what ROOT.BAT looks like:

```
REM   Return to hard disk root
CD   C:\ (to set the current directory)
C:       (to make sure C is the current drive)
```

There are reasons why you might put your command files into various subdirectories, besides doing it because you feel like it (which is reason enough). One reason is that you may have several versions of a batch file or even of a program (some programs can be "patched" to custom tailor them, and you might keep several different tailorings around for different purposes). You should make sure that your PATH commands take this into account.

As we've mentioned before, some programs read parts of themselves into memory after they have started operation. This is done with complex programs that have "overlays," and it is also done with interpretive BASIC programs.

Generally these program parts are treated as data and not as programs, which means in practical terms that DOS will go looking for them only in the current directory (set by the CHDIR command),

and not through all the defined program paths (set by the PATH command). This means that the subsidiary parts of a program must be located in the current directory. If you use a program like this on data that is located in several different subdirectories, then you will need copies of the program's subsidiary parts in each directory.

There are two ways that you can deal with this problem. One is to simply keep separate copies of the parts in each directory in which they are used. This will waste some disk space (since there will be multiple copies of the files), but it makes for fast and convenient use. The other approach is to keep one master copy of the parts and then copy them into a subdirectory as needed. A batch file that executes the program can copy the program parts into the right directory before the program starts, and delete the parts after it is done. For an example of how this is done, we'll say that we are working with WordStar (which uses overlays) in our LETTERS correspondence file:

```
REM        Switch to writing LETTERS using WORDSTAR

CHDIR  \LETTERS

PATH   \LETTERS;\

COPY   \WS*.OVR  \LETTERS\WS*.OVR

WS     %1

DEL    \LETTERS\WS*.OVR

CHDIR  \

PATH   \
```

This example has more elements than might be necessary and, just to be clear, it makes some things explicit that could be left to default, but it shows the kind of things we want to do. Step by step, this example

1. tells us what we are going to do
2. switches the current directory to LETTERS
3. sets the program path to LETTERS and the root directory together
4. copies WordStar's overlays from the root to LETTERS
5. finally, runs WordStar using the parameter to give the file name
6. afterwards, deletes the overlays

7. changes the directory back to the root
8. and also changes the path back to the root.

This is the sort of thing that we should do in setting up our own working batch files.

16.5 Common Problems and Tricks

There are some problems that are common to the use of hard disks and electronic disks. Most of these problems come from shortsighted program developers who make their programs rather inflexible in the way they use disks. It is appallingly common for programs to be written with the built-in assumption that the only disk drives that will be used are the A drive and the B drive.

Your computer system might have other drives. It could have a third and fourth diskette drive, which would be drives C and D. If you have either a hard disk or an electronic disk, it is likely to be referred to as the C drive. Unfortunately, all too many programs don't allow for this possibility. (By the way, when you encounter programs like this, you should complain loud and long to the programs' authors.)

If your programs are completely flexible about the drives they can use, fine. If not, there are some steps you can take. It may be possible to change the programs either in their source code or by patching them. In Chapter 21 we'll get into patching a bit. If a program is written in interpretive BASIC, then you are likely to have access to the source code; in other programming languages, you may have the source code as well. Whether we work with a program's source code or try to "patch" the program, our goal will be the same: to change the program's references to specific disk drives.

Usually when a program works only with a specific disk drive to access a file, it refers to the filename with a drive prefix, like this:

```
A:FILENAME.EXT
```

The culprit here is the "A:" part, which instructs DOS to look specifically to the A drive (or some other drive). If we can change items like this in a program, we should change them either to another specific drive that we want to use, or else remove the drive specification entirely so that DOS is being told to use the current drive rather than a specific drive.

If it is possible to find and change these elements in a program, then you will be able to get the program to use the disk drives that you want. If you make any changes like this, you should be very careful, and you should also test the changes thoroughly before

SOME PROGRAMS ARE VERY INFLEXIBLE.

trusting them to work correctly. Generally this is a very simple and safe change to make to a program. Doing it will give you much more flexibility in the use of your programs.

The ASSIGN command will solve much of this problem by temporarily rerouting a program's requests from one drive to another. For example, if you have a program that expects to work with drives A and B, but you have all of the data on a single hard disk, which is the C drive, then you could assign all references to A or B to C instead. This will accomplish your goal and save you the trouble of tampering with the program. Naturally the best way to use an ASSIGN command like this is in a batch file, which reassigns the drives before using a program, and then sets them back when you are done.

For example:

```
REM  switch to accounting programs
ASSIGN A=C B=C
BASIC  ACCNTING
ASSIGN
```

17

Set Up: Customizing DOS

In this chapter we're going to cover one of the most complex and intriguing aspects of DOS—the ways that DOS can be customized or tailored to our needs.

What we'll be talking about here are some ideas and some software parts that are not completely related to each other, but they do have one thing in common: one way or another, they modify, revise, or customize the operation of DOS for us.

There are a number of ways that we can set up, customize, or initialize the operation of our DOS. They fall roughly into three categories, which we'll cover in the next three sections concerning configuration files, the AUTOEXEC batch file, and resident programs.

17.1 The Configuration File

When DOS first begins operation, when it "boots up," it does some start-up work, or initialization, that sets the stage for how DOS will work and what things it can work with. Beginning with the 2-series of DOS, we can participate in this initialization through something called the configuration file.

In the last stages of its initialization, DOS looks on the disk it is booting up from for a text file with the name of CONFIG.SYS. This file is used to let us specify some of the ways that the system will be configured.

In this section, we'll look at what kind of control we can exercise over DOS through this CONFIG.SYS file.

In format, the CONFIG.SYS file is like a batch processing file: it's a text file full of commands, each on a separate line. While a batch file contains regular DOS commands that we could have typed in at the keyboard, the CONFIG.SYS file contains special commands that only apply to DOS's initialization.

There are eight different commands that we can give DOS in the CONFIG.SYS file. We'll start with the most important and useful one, the DEVICE command.

There are certain things that DOS automatically knows about your computer and the devices (such as printers and disk drives) that are attached to it. These are the default devices that DOS knows about because IBM designed them into DOS. Of course, we can attach all sorts of other devices to our computers. How does DOS learn about them and any special commands that they might require? The answer is through the DEVICE command of the CONFIG.SYS file.

Unusual devices (and we'll mention some shortly) call for special support programs that are called device drivers. DOS is able to incorporate device drivers into itself, using this DEVICE command. For any device driver that we might want to incorporate into DOS, we have to have the program code of the driver stored in a file on our DOS disk. If the name of the file that holds this device driver is named X, then our CONFIG.SYS file would contain a command like this:

```
DEVICE=X
```

When DOS encounters that command in the CONFIG.SYS file, it reads the device driver, X, into memory, and attaches it to the rest of DOS—in effect absorbing the device driver as a native part of DOS.

As you might imagine, writing a device driver is a highly technical subject for expert programmers only. Any device driver has to follow strict DOS rules so that it cooperates with the rest of DOS. Normally folks like you and me don't write device drivers; instead, we get them with any exotic equipment that we're attaching to our computers that happens to require a special device driver. That might be an unusual type of disk drive, a mouse, or whatever.

There are also two special device drivers that are included with DOS. One, which comes with the 2-series and later, is called ANSI.SYS; the other, which comes with the 3-series and later, is called VDISK.SYS.

VDISK is used to create a memory disk, or electronic disk, or RAM disk, using part of our computer's memory to simulate an ultra-high speed disk drive. We'll be discussing these RAM disks more in Chapter 18. There are many different electronic disk programs available, but this one, VDISK.SYS, is provided by IBM as a part of DOS.

ANSI.SYS is a very special kind of device driver that can do some wonders for us. ANSI provides two special facilities to modify the routine keyboard input and screen output that goes on in our computer. The full details are complicated and surprisingly hard to explain, but the essence of it is this: if we have ANSI.SYS installed as a device inside our DOS, we can give it commands that will make it perform two special kinds of magic. One kind is keyboard translation, which can turn one keystroke that we press into something quite different, including a long series of (ANSI.SYS generated) keystrokes. For example, we could instruct ANSI.SYS so that every time we pressed the "!" key, it would be changed into all the keystrokes that make up this phrase: "Now isn't that magic!" The other trick that ANSI.SYS can perform is that it will accept special commands that will fully control the information that appears on the display screen—including such things as where the cursor is located or what color is being written on the screen. Some programming languages, such as BASIC, include features like that themselves. ANSI.SYS gives this kind of screen control features to any program that wishes to use them.

So far we've mentioned device drivers. There are other commands that we can place inside a CONFIG.SYS file. These other commands, unlike the DEVICE command, don't incorporate other programs into DOS. Instead, all these other programs control various switches and settings in DOS. Here is what they are.

The BREAK command, which we can set as either BREAK = ON or BREAK = OFF, controls the default setting of the control-break switch, which we discussed in Chapter 8. The regular DOS command BREAK can change the setting of the break switch; this CONFIG.SYS command controls the default setting that's in effect if we don't enter a regular BREAK command.

The SHELL command indicates the name and location of the command interpreter that DOS will be using. DOS's own command interpreter is called COMMAND.COM, and it's a normal part of any disk that is system formatted to contain a copy of DOS. We aren't stuck with DOS's own command interpreter, though. We can, if we know how, create our own. This SHELL command lets us instruct DOS to use another command interpreter if we want to.

There are four other commands that control the setting of some numerical values and the sizes of some working tables inside of DOS. The BUFFERS = command determines how many disk data buffers DOS creates inside itself. When DOS reads any data from disk it tries to hold it in a buffer (a temporary holding area), hoping that the next time the same data is needed, it will be available in a memory buffer (so that DOS won't have to take the time to reread it from disk). Having more buffers uses up some of your computer's memory, but can—under the right circumstances—speed up the computer's operation.

The FCBS = command controls how many File Control Blocks can be in use at one time by your programs. The FILES = command controls how many "file handles" can be in use at one time by your programs. FCBs and file handles are two different ways that programs can work with disk data, and DOS lets us manage them separately if we wish to. Finally, the LASTDRIVE= command let's us control how many disks or disk-like devices DOS appears to have.

All the control factors that we've briefly mentioned are complex and technical to manage and most people leave them alone, letting DOS use its standard default settings for them. The one item among them that you might want to tinker with is the BUFFERS= command. If you want to test the operation of this command, find some computer activity that you do which uses the disk a lot. Then see how the speed of that operation is affected by first letting DOS set its default number of buffers (usually 2 or 3), and then by setting it to a larger number such as 16 or 32. You may find little difference, or you may find a dramatic improvement.

To do this experiment, you'll have to set up a CONFIG.SYS file, with the BUFFERS=32 (or whatever) command in it. Each time you change the CONFIG.SYS file, you'll have to reboot your computer to put the new CONFIG.SYS file into effect. If you experiment with different numbers of buffers, you'll also want to use the CHKDSK command to see how much memory is being used up by the buffers.

The last of the CONFIG.SYS commands is the COUNTRY= command. This is used to set the format of the date and time to the standard used by different countries.

To give you a practical example of a real-world configuration file, here is the one that's in my computer. It includes two device drivers and some of the special commands that we've mentioned:

```
DEVICE=ANSI.SYS
DEVICE=VDISK.SYS 128 256 16
BUFFERS=64
FILES=20
BREAK=ON
LASTDRIVE=E
COUNTRY=001
```

17.2 Getting Going with a Batch File

As we saw in Chapter 11, batch files are one of the most useful and powerful tools that DOS puts into our hands. Also, we know that DOS will automatically execute a default start-up batch file, named AUTOEXEC.BAT, if we have one present on our start-up disk.

There is nothing that we can do with an AUTOEXEC file that we can't do by manually invoking any other batch file. An AUTOEXEC file is particularly useful because it takes place automatically, without any intervention from us.

What an AUTOEXEC file is particularly useful for is in acting as part of the whole concept of customizing and tailoring the operation of DOS. That's what we're going to take a look at here—how we can use an AUTOEXEC file as part of the process to customize DOS.

One of the first things that we need to know about AUTOEXEC files is that they short-circuit one of DOS's standard operations. When you start up DOS in the ordinary way, DOS will ask you to enter the date and time, and then show you its starting message. We talked about that in Chapter 3. What we didn't mention there is that if we start up DOS using an AUTOEXEC file, those three steps just don't happen at all. This allows our AUTOEXEC file to have complete control over the starting process. If we want to ask for the date and time, then we can put the DATE and TIME commands in our AUTOEXEC file. If don't want 'em, then we can avoid 'em—thanks to the power of AUTOEXEC.

There are certain key commands that we really should execute every time we start up our computer, and the AUTOEXEC file is the perfect place to perform them. What you want and need on your computer will be determined by your particular circumstances, but I can tell you about some start-up commands that nearly everybody needs to do.

Two of the most important are the PROMPT and PATH commands, which we discussed in Chapter 8. PROMPT sets the DOS command prompt that is displayed; PATH tells DOS which directories to search for our command files (our programs and our batch files).

You'll recall that I recommend that you set the prompt showing the current directory, which is done with the command

```
PROMPT $P$G
```

I also recommend that the path be set to combine whatever directories you use for any of your program files.

Whatever prompt and whatever paths you use for your computer, the AUTOEXEC file is the natural place to set them. Putting these two commands in our AUTOEXEC file means that you'll always have them set without having to bother about it.

Similar to the PROMPT and PATH commands is the CHDIR or CD command. You'll recall that this command tells DOS which directory we're working with inside any disk. If you have a large-capacity hard disk system in your computer, you probably do most of your work in a subdirectory rather than in the disk's root directory. If that's the case for you, then the AUTOEXEC file is the natural place to issue the CHDIR command that will place you at your working directory.

There is another natural candidate for inclusion in your AUTOEXEC file, and that's resident programs. In the next section we'll be discussing what resident programs are and what some of them are used for. If you make use of any of these resident programs, then the AUTOEXEC file is a very good place to automatically start them up to perform their unusual magic.

17.3 Resident Programs: PRINT, SHARE, GRAPHICS, GRAFTABL, KEYBxx, and More

Resident programs are one of the most mysterious elements in the world of DOS.

When DOS runs a program, it finds space in the computer's memory for the program, copies it from disk to memory, and then, temporarily, turns control of the computer over to the program.

Normally when a program is finished working, it turns control of the computer back over to DOS, and DOS reuses the memory area where the program was loaded for the next program that we use. With resident programs things work differently.

When a resident program finishes its initial operation, it hands control of the computer back to DOS, but it instructs DOS to not reuse the memory area where the program is loaded. The program asks DOS to leave it resident. DOS in effect puts a barrier in place where the resident program ends, and loads the next program that we use ABOVE the resident program. In effect, the resident program incorporates itself into the small part of DOS that stays in the lower end of the computer's memory. All subsequent programs that we use operate at higher memory locations, leaving our resident program and DOS undisturbed in lower memory locations. So the resident program stays semi-permanent in the computer's memory until we turn the computer off.

What is the point of these resident programs? Unlike most other programs, a resident program stays active after it seems to have finished. The program stays in memory and, through some technical tricks, manages to continue getting work done, even though we are running other programs after it.

There are many uses for resident programs, and you will get an idea of some of the things that they can do when we look at a few of them. DOS includes five different resident programs, which we'll discuss, and there are others—that aren't an integral part of DOS—which we ought to know about.

The first of the DOS resident programs that we'll consider is called PRINT.

To assist in the printing of data, DOS contains a PRINT command that acts as a variety of print spooler. The job of a print spooler is to print information on your computer's printer, without tying up the use of the computer while the printing is going on.

If you've used your computer's printer, you've probably noticed that it's relatively slow compared to the computer's ability to get work done. When we print information on the computer, almost all of the computer's working power is being wasted while the printer is laboriously printing away.

The resident program PRINT solves this problem by taking over the job of feeding data to the printer, while leaving the majority of the computer's power available for other programs to use. It's a bit like reading a book while you're stirring soup that's cooking. It doesn't take all your attention to stir soup, and it doesn't take the computer's full power to print out information. What the PRINT resident program does is get just enough of the computer's working power to keep a printer busy working, and turn the rest of the computer's thinking power over to any other programs we want to run.

PRINT is what is known as a "background" program. Once we start up the PRINT command, it sits in the computer and gets the use of the computer's power just enough to print out what we've asked it to do (just as stirring soup while we're reading a book gets just a fraction of our attention). If PRINT finishes its work, it remains in memory ready for more work (but not taking up any computing power). When we ask PRINT to print something, it occupies a fraction of the computing power to keep the printer busy and leaves the rest of the computing power for our other programs. That's how a "background" program works.

The first time that we invoke the PRINT command, it loads itself into memory and stays there (until the computer is turned off or reset). From then on, any time we invoke the PRINT command we're just telling it to print out a copy of a file (or cancel something that it's in the middle of printing). PRINT has the ability to hold a list of work to be done in what is called the "print queue." As long as there is work to be done in the print queue, PRINT will work away, passing information to our printer. When all work is done, PRINT goes to sleep until we wake it up with a request to print some more information.

We tell PRINT to print information by giving it the name of a file that we want to be printed. PRINT only works off disk files—if we want to use PRINT to print the output of one of our programs, we first have to get that program to store its print-style information into a disk file. Many programs, particularly word processing programs, are prepared to do exactly that for our convenience.

The next command we'll look at is GRAPHICS. When you learned about the things your computer will do, you no doubt learned about the print-screen function, which will copy the contents of the display screen to your printer. The standard print screen operation, though, is only intended to print out normal character data—not any graphics pictures that might be on the screen. While most of use don't use graphics much, graphics screen displays can be quite important, and it's useful to be able to print out a full picture of a graphics display on the screen. If you have the right kind of printer, like the IBM Graphics Printer, then this GRAPHICS program can copy the screen image to the printer.

GRAPHICS is a slightly different kind of resident program from PRINT. While PRINT will work away simultaneously with our other programs (operating, as they say, "in the background"), GRAPHICS is a program that replaces a standard operation that we already have in the computer to improve it. Our IBM personal computers already have the ability to do the print-screen operation, copying character information from the screen to our printer. The GRAPHICS program just augments that by adding the ability to copy not just character text but any graphics image as well.

When we invoke the GRAPHICS program, it loads itself into memory (and tells DOS to leave it resident), and then it does nothing. Nothing, that is, until we press the "print-screen" key. Then the resident GRAPHICS program goes to work, working just like the regular print-screen program (that is built into the computer), but doing it for graphics images as well.

The GRAFTABL program is yet another variation on the idea of resident programs. GRAFTABL leaves itself resident in memory, but what it leaves there isn't a working program but some data. As it turns out, the IBM personal computers have a rich character set known as the extended ASCII characters. We can use all these characters when the program is working in text mode, but ordinarily we can't when we have the computer in graphics mode.

The GRAFTABL program leaves in the computer's memory a definition of what the extended ASCII character set looks like when the computer is in graphics mode. Without the GRAFTABL program, we can't use the extended ASCII characters in graphics mode. With GRAFTABL, we have those characters available—all through the magic of resident programs.

Another use for resident programs is to provide international interpretations of our keyboards. This is what the KEYBxx programs are for. There are actually five of these programs, each identified by two letters:

UK (KEYBUK) for the United Kingdom (England)
GR (KEYBGR) for German use
FR (KEYBFR) for French use
IT (KEYBIT) for Italian use
SP (KEYBSP) for Spanish use

Each of these resident programs loads itself into memory and then stays to reinterpret the meaning of our keystrokes. The changes vary, depending upon the needs of each country and language. As an example, when we load the KEYBUK version and type in the "#" symbol that appears on the American keyboard (it's just above the "3" key, typed in as a shifted-3), what appears on the computer's screen in the British Pound currency symbol. Whatever changes are needed for each country is provided, as a keyboard translator, by these KEYBxx resident programs.

The next of the resident programs that DOS provides for is the SHARE program. SHARE is used to control the use and sharing of data and disk files between programs. SHARE takes care of problems that arise when more than one program, or more than one computer, is making use of our disks. If one program or one computer is reading a data file and another is changing it, things can get into quite a muddle. SHARE's job is to coordinate the sharing of data so that nothing goes wrong.

All the programs that we've discussed so far are parts of DOS. The PRINT and GRAPHICS programs were introduced with the 2-series of DOS, and the GRAFTABL, KEYBxx, and SHARE programs were introduced with the 3-series of DOS. They can be used with the DOS versions that introduced them or any later version.

There are other resident programs that you can add to your system besides the ones that come with DOS. Among the most powerful and popular is Prokey, a keyboard macro program that can expand single keystrokes into large amounts of work accomplished, and Sidekick, a resident program that gives us a background calculator, note-taker, ASCII table, and other functions, all on tap in the middle of any other program—thanks to the magic of resident programs.

18

Making Software Choices

You almost certainly know by now that you don't just buy a computer. It doesn't work that way. Maybe you can just buy a car—and casually decide on things like the paint color. But for a computer, no. There are lots and lots of tricky choices that you have to make when you set up a small computer and the consequences can be far-reaching.

The choices you have to make fall into two categories: hardware and software. There is little we can give you in the way of general advice about your hardware choices, except to say don't scrimp on memory or disk storage.

But in software, there is some guidance that we can give you, and that is what this chapter is about.

At the end of this chapter, Section 18.7, I'll stick my neck out and make some personal judgment recommendations on name-brand programs.

18.1 Choosing Any Program

The best advice I can give you about buying software is to have plenty of money and be prepared to waste some. It's always good advice to have plenty of money, and I'm not being cute here. The most important thing you need to know about buying software is don't expect to pinch pennies.

I'm not saying that the best software is the most expensive. To the contrary, software pricing is a very chaotic part of the marketplace. When I look at the programs that I personally consider to be absolutely first-rate, I find a wide variety of prices: some quite high, some very modest.

Software prices don't seem to be set by its cost of production, by its worth to us, or by its quality compared to any competition. You shouldn't expect to have to pay top dollar to get the best software, nor can you choose the best by looking to the most expensive.

While you're probably already aware that getting all the software you need will probably be expensive, that is not the message we have for you. Our special secret tip to getting the right software is this: be prepared to waste some money.

If you can get all the right software on the first try, good for you. But, more often than you might expect, no matter how carefully you comparison shop and test drive, your first software purchase may not suit your needs once you really begin to use it. What do you do then? Unless your money is in very short supply, and you don't highly value the efficient operation of you and your computer together, you should buy again—this time with a clearer idea of what your true needs are.

Often, you just can't tell what features you really need until you have worked with some program in that subject area. One of the wisest things that you can do is to buy as carefully as you can, but be prepared to buy again.

I bought four different text editor programs until I found the one with which I wrote this book. Later I bought another one, just because it might be better (it was—but not better enough to be worth retraining myself to use it). My most expensive software buy ever was an accounting program that I came to hate; I gladly bought another. It was cheaper and a little better. Don't be afraid to do this yourself when necessary.

After that advice, what can we tell you about general rules for buying software? Quite a bit. There are more sound, practical principles in selecting programs than you might expect.

The first thing to look for is how well does the program fit into the rest of your system? Are its data files in a standard format, or something weird and wonderful that no other program can touch? Are the data formats well documented so that, if you wish, you can write new programs to use the data? (This is particularly important for accounting data.) And, here is an increasingly important question—is it hard-disk compatible?

For a program to work well on a hard-disk system calls for two things: first, it must be flexible about where it expects to find its data files (too many early programs were rigidly married to the use of the A and B floppy disk drives; when you're trying to work off a hard-disk C drive, that's murder). Second, does it have a copy-protection scheme that requires the use of a floppy disk?

Copy-protected programs which have to inspect their original "system" floppy disk are basically hostile to the whole philosophy of working with a hard-disk system. If you're using a hard-disk system, you need to have programs that either aren't copy protected (best of all) or that are copy protected in a way that can be permanently moved to a hard disk (a reasonable compromise). Most of

Microsoft's copy-protected programs, such as Word and Multiplan, have this kind of hard-disk-friendly copy protection scheme.

On the subject of programs fitting into the rest of your system is the question of integrated programs. Integrated programs combine several functions that traditionally have been met with separate, isolated programs. Integrated packages are a relatively new item in the software market and a very exciting one. While each part of an integrated package might provide less than all of the features you want, all the parts will work together. And best of all, the "flavor" of the program, its command structure and the way it presents displays to you, will be consistent.

Then, are the programs hostile to your system? Don't laugh—too many programs are. If a program is copy protected, then it may not allow itself to be transferred to a hard disk system or an electronic disk, and this means it will not fit into your own work flow as easily as it would otherwise, as we've already discussed. But the greatest enemies of your system are those few programs that require you to "reboot" your system to use them.

If you have to shut down the operation of your computer and restart it just to use some program, then that is a major disruption of your computer. You may not do it now, but in the future it is likely that you will have your computer doing more than one thing—working with you in the "foreground," while some other tasks are being worked on in the "background." Having to reboot your system totally disrupts this sort of multiple use of the computer. Even without this multi-tasking, a reboot of your computer is a stupid waste of time and effort, and you should avoid any programs that call for it.

If your computer system has a hard disk, as more and more of the serious user's systems do, then it is very important to you that your programs not be copy protected, or at the least they must be hard-disk friendly. The same applies if you use an electronic disk to speed up your work as I do. Chapter 16 covers the special needs of hard and electronic disks.

Menus, help-screens, and the sort of program features that are called user-friendly, are another factor. The standard wisdom is that menus—which are screen displays that list a program's options and features—are always a good thing. You might be surprised to learn that this isn't true. If a program is used only occasionally, or if it is used by relatively non-technical people, then lots of user-friendliness can be very nice. On the other hand, when you use a program a lot you'll become proficient in using it, and then menus and help-screens get in the way of your work. Example? The text editor used to write this book doesn't have a single help screen or menu screen, and I'm grateful for it.

I'M SO USER-FRIENDLY, I'M GOING TO ASK YOU A DOZEN QUESTIONS BEFORE I'LL LET YOU GET ANY WORK DONE!

There's another way of approaching menus and help-screens. The ideal, really, is for a program to feature menus and such, but keep them out of your way when you don't need them. The fifth text editor that I bought works that way, and it's one of the reasons why it's even superior to the one I use (which is flawed but familiar like one of the family).

Related to the subject of user friendliness is a program's command structure. How do you tell a program what to do? This can greatly affect how easily and efficiently you can use the program. Here again the standard folk wisdom isn't quite true. Use of function keys is slick but may not be the most efficient form of command.

The widely popular word processor WordStar uses alphabetic commands rather than function keys, because a skilled typist is disrupted by having to reach for function keys. Heed the lesson of WordStar—for a heavily-used program, different rules apply. What is efficient and friendly for a program that is used casually may be tiresome in a program that you use a lot.

When a program does use function keys, does it use them well for your particular computer? While the alphabetic part of a keyboard is very standard, the rest of it—cursor keys, function keys and all—vary greatly from maker to maker.

Fortunately for IBM PC users, the PC's keyboard sets the standard that most new software is designed around. If you have a standard PC keyboard, most programs will be well adapted to it. On the other hand, IBM's keyboard for the PC*jr* doesn't follow the PC's standard for where the function keys are, and that's important since efficient function key use is a major factor in the successful use of many programs. Also, some of the extended members of the PC family, such as Data General's DG-1 computer, use a different keyboard arrangement. Fortunately, though, most non-IBM members of the PC family, including the Compaq models, follow the PC's function key layout faithfully.

Part of the question of command structure is how menus work. Some menus let you choose from a list with a single key stroke. Others make you move through a list of options with the space bar or cursor keys, and then select your choice with the enter key; that looks slick, but is harder to use. Likewise, if you can select from a menu or from a yes-no choice with a single key stroke, do you also have to press the enter key? If you do, that's more of a nuisance to use. When a program acts directly on a keystroke (rather than also needing an enter key), the program is said to have "live keys" rather than "dead keys." Live key operation is usually better—quicker, easier, and more efficient. For dangerous operations (like anything that could destroy some of your data), a dead key approach is probably better.

The next thing to consider in selecting programs is customization. Any complex program presents you with a lot of choices. You should be able to choose some options once and be done with it. But many programs demand that you tell them what you want each time you use them. If a program can be customized, then its worth to you may multiply greatly. The best programs in this regard keep a profile data file, which records your customization.

The next best possibility is a program that is customized internally, through the use of a patcher that makes the appropriate changes in the program. If you are considering getting a patchable program, find out if the patches are done easily, say through a special-purpose patching program. Some programs can be customized through patching, but the patches have to be done by a skilled technician (usually using DOS's patching tool, the DEBUG program).

Related to customization is whether or not a program comes with its source code. The source code can be very valuable to you, for example, to make customization possible or to give you guidance in writing programs that use the same data. It isn't always appropriate to get source code, so don't expect it as if you had a natural right to it. Most source code contains proprietary programming techniques, and you can't expect program developers to give away the family jewels. If the source code is in assembly language, you have less reason to want it than if it is in BASIC. And you have more reason to expect the source code for an accounting program than for a word processor. If the source code is available, that is a factor in selecting one program over another.

Let's summarize the general things you can look for in selecting programs:

- Don't be reluctant to discard a poor program and buy a replacement; finding good programs can be an experimental process.
- Does the program fit into your use of your computer?
- Is the program part of an integrated package?
- Is the program hostile to your work flow?
- Does the program have a good user-interface?
- Is it user-friendly enough?
- Is it too user-friendly to be convenient?
- Are its commands easy to use or a nuisance?
- Is the use of special keys good or poor?
- Can the program be easily customized?
- Is the source code available (if it's appropriate to have it, which often it is not)?

After that, let's look at the specific needs in four program areas—word processors, spreadsheets, accounting, and programming languages.

18.2 Choosing Word Processors

What we all call word processing really breaks down into two separate functions, and possibly two separate programs. The two halves of a word processor are a text editor and a print formatter.

The task of a text editor is to work together with you in entering and changing your text material. The job of a print formatter is to take care of page numbering, paragraph justification, headings, footings, underlining, and in general controlling your printing device.

In the best dedicated word processing systems, these two tasks are so well integrated that the person using the system is completely unaware of any separation between the two. This is exactly how it should be. But for small personal computers, word processing programs do not live up to this standard. This means that what we use on our computers is likely to be much clumsier than what it ought to be.

There are two approaches to getting a word processor for our computers. One is to select and buy a text editor and a print formatter separately. The other is to buy a complete word processing program. The first, separate approach appears to be a very unwise one—and it is, usually. However, you may find a text editor so well suited to your working style, that it is better for you to use it separately. Also, for economy you may choose to use the text editor that comes free with your computer—such as DOS's EDLIN editor, which we'll cover in Chapter 20—and buy only an inexpensive print formatter.

Usually the most sensible thing is to buy a complete word processing program, such as the famous WordStar, or one of the many excellent competing word processors. You should at least consider the alternative.

Selecting a word processor or a text editor program is a special area, unlike the purchase of any other software. There are two main reasons for this. One is that there are more text editors and word processors to choose from than there are other types of programs. Programmers seem to love to develop text editors so the market is flooded with them. This gives you lots of programs to choose from; and frankly you need the variety, for the other thing that sets text editors apart from other programs is their complexity.

Text editors are different from most other programs because they have so many complex commands built into them—commands to insert and delete, commands to copy and move material, commands to set margins, commands to move around in the text, by line, by word, or by paragraph, and many other commands as well. All these commands have to be dealt with while still making it as easy as possible for you to type in your written text.

This is not only very complex in itself, but it also raises a tricky question: how are these commands to be given? With function keys, which vary greatly from computer to computer? With alphabetic command codes, which interfere with the typing of the text? And how is the display going to be formatted? And how is help with the complex commands to be given? With lengthy help menus? With a terse menu area on the screen?

Because of all of that, text editor programs differ widely in their user interface and in the quality of the human engineering that has gone into them. While we might be able to evaluate different text editors and word processors by some fairly objective standards, different peoples' taste in how they want to work makes a great deal of difference in how happy they will be with one editor or another.

This means that your choice of a word processor may be more difficult than your choice of any other program if a word processing program is going to be an important tool for you. If word processing is a minor thing for you, then the choice is less critical but still not an easy software choice.

Here are some guidelines to help you make an intelligent decision.

First, does the word processor work well with your particular printer? Does it make good use of any special features of your printer? There is little standardization in printer features, and some have a few features that are very valuable—if your word processor can take advantage of them.

Next, do you need lots and lots of features, or would a spartan word processor serve you well?

Then, consider the command and menu structure. For a casual, or non-expert user, menus and help screens are necessary to guide you through the complex commands. For an experienced heavy user, they are a nuisance. And then there are the commands. For an expert typist, alphabetic commands are almost certainly best—this is the approach that WordStar has taken. For other users, a function-key approach probably will work better. Consider how well the use of function keys matches your computer's keyboard. Also consider customization—do you get to choose what command is assigned to what function key? The two editors I like best on my computer can both be fully customized—that is one of their greatest strengths.

If your word processor will be used a lot, choose very carefully. The difference among word processors is greater than the difference among accounting programs or spreadsheet programs.

See Section 18.7 for my personal recommendations on word processing programs.

18.3 Choosing Spreadsheets

Spreadsheet programs, like the original VisiCalc, are designed to do routine calculations on numbers that are organized in a rectangular grid, or spreadsheet. The most common work for spreadsheet programs is business financial calculations such as budgeting and forecasting, but their use has spread far beyond that.

When we consider spreadsheet programs, we start with the granddaddy of them all, VisiCalc. There are now quite a few competitors for VisiCalc, so you are likely to have a lot of choice. Here are the factors that I think you should consider in looking at spreadsheets.

First, how advanced are its features? The original VisiCalc has been surpassed by many of its later rivals, particularly in terms of the flexible use of cells on the calculation worksheet. Multiplan, Lotus 1-2-3, SuperCalc 3, and others have gone far beyond what Visi-

Calc originally offered. When Multiplan was introduced by Microsoft, it set a new standard for convenient and advanced features, but by the time you read this there may be a new kid on the block that is even better. On the other hand, consider if you need extra features. If you will be buying template programs to use with your spreadsheet, then all you may need is the lowest common denominator, the features of the original VisiCalc.

Second, is it hostile to your system? Some spreadsheets can't be transferred to hard disk systems. Check on the spreadsheets that are available, and find out if they can be copied to other media, or if they require rebooting the system in order to use them. This is a major factor in how convenient these programs are to use.

Third, will it work with standard VisiCalc or 1-2-3 templates? There are many useful template programs on the market, which can greatly enhance the value of your spreadsheet program. Find out if yours can use them. (Very likely it can.)

Fourth, does it make use of advanced hardware? Most members of the IBM PC family can be fitted with fast floating-point processors, like the Intel 8087 arithmetic co-processor. If your use of a spreadsheet is extensive, your calculations can become lengthy. A spreadsheet program that is designed to use the 8087 might be especially valuable to you because it will calculate quicker.

Fifth, does it fit into the other programming tools that you use? If you are using a spreadsheet for some interactive what-if calculations, then you are using the spreadsheet by itself. But many spreadsheet users need to incorporate the results of calculations into reports and proposals. Find out how easily its results can be used by your word processor. This concern, by the way, is one of the strongest arguments for integrated multi-function programs, which we cover in Section 18.5.

18.4 Choosing Accounting Programs

Accounting programs are a work horse for many small business computers, and they can be a major source of problems because a business can become dependent upon them.

Only you and your accountant can judge if a program has the kind of features that you need. Unfortunately, you probably can't find out if a program meets your requirements without not only buying it, but also investing several months worth of effort into using it. This is a nasty fact of life with accounting software. It also tends to be among the most highly priced software, the clumsiest to use, and to have the most programming errors in it. In my experience with computer systems both large and small, accounting programs seem to always be a difficult area, and it is rare for a business to be fully happy with its accounting programs.

Keep this in mind when you get a package of accounting programs. Be prepared for more difficulties than you usually encounter with other programs, and take care that you don't expose your business to more danger than you can afford through premature overdependence upon an accounting package.

Besides your own particular accounting needs, here are some general things that you should look for in accounting programs.

If the program is written in BASIC, as many are, can it be compiled for extra speed? This alone could become extremely important to you.

How well can it be customized? It is with accounting packages that you are most likely to need a program to be adapted to your needs, and to have the program's questions answered once and for all, not over and over again each time the program is used.

One of the ways you might want to customize any program, especially an accounting program, is to change its use of disk drives. It is very common for the authors of application programs like accounting packages to be quite shortsighted about the use of disk drives. Often the programmers either never think that you might want to use their program with a different disk setup than they envisioned, or else they are just too lazy to do what is needed to give you a choice.

If you have the source code for the program, as is true for many accounting programs written in BASIC, you might be able to change the use of disk drives. I've done this myself with the general ledger program that I use for my own bookkeeping. Even if you can't—or daren't—change the source code for a program, it is often relatively easy and safe to patch a program to change its references to specific disk drives. In Chapter 21 we'll go over the details of how to do this.

Can it be instructed to perform a lengthy series of operations unattended, or does it demand constant human interaction? Some accounting programs will eat up the work time of their users just replying to stupid and unnecessary questions from the programs.

Is the vendor in business to stay? Your general ledger program may not need to be updated next year, but a payroll program probably will, and maybe a fixed assets program as well.

Are all the subjects you need covered included in one package? You don't want a payroll from one software vendor and a general ledger from another. What are all the parts? General ledger, accounts payable, accounts receivable, payroll, fixed assets, and inventory control. Make sure that all the parts you'll need in the future are available with the program you buy now.

Does the accounting package include some kind of general report writer? Large computer users learned long ago that they need custom reports to supplement their accounting package's standard reports. You shouldn't have to discover that your accounting package is missing a part that you didn't realize you would need.

Converting from manual bookkeeping methods to computerized methods is usually a bloody ordeal. I've personally guided companies large and small through the process, so I know what I'm talking about. The instruction manuals for the accounting package you select may be especially lacking in guidance in this area. Choose carefully. Move slowly. Get experienced help if you can.

We've advised you, in general, to be prepared when necessary to buy more than one piece of software. With computerized accounting there is a parallel to this idea. Be prepared to convert your bookkeeping more than once. You might set out with a chart of accounts that is structured one way, and then later learn that you would be better off with another structure. Or you might want to switch your receivables from "open item" to "balance forward." Be willing to reconvert your accounting if it is called for; the payoff may be tremendous, even though the work involved will probably be an extraordinary pain.

18.5 Choosing Multi-Function Packages

One of the most exciting and useful developments in program tools has been the appearance of integrated multi-function packages. Typically these packages include several or all of the functions of word processing, spreadsheet calculation, data management, and communications. The advantages of these packages are twofold. First, the functions are integrated so that work and data can flow easily from one function to another. Second, and even more important, only one command language is needed. Without an integrated package, if you need to incorporate spreadsheet calculations into a written report, you will have to use three different command languages—DOS's, the spreadsheet's, and the word processor's—each with its own style and flavor. With an integrated package, there is one style of command that works for all functions.

Since the number one problem of using a computer is learning computer skills, the number one advantage of an integrated package is that it reduces the amount of skills that you have to acquire.

Integrated packages are a relative newcomer on the computing scene, so you may not have much choice of packages for your computer. On the other hand, you might even choose your computer on the basis of the integrated programs available for it. (When VisiCalc was the first and only spreadsheet program, quite a few computers were sold just because they would run VisiCalc. When the integrated package 1-2-3 was introduced, some computer pundits were saying that this was another instance where people would buy a computer just to be able to run a particular program.)

What should you look for in an integrated package? The first thing is breadth of features. It defeats the whole purpose of an integrated package if it lacks even one single function that you expect to use a lot. What are the functions that might be in an integrated package?

- Text editing (the first half of a word processor);
- report formatting and printing (the other half);
- graph generation;
- spreadsheet calculation;
- data management (storing, organizing and searching your notes, whether they are mailing addresses, telephone numbers, or paragraphs of written comments);
- small-scale programming (for example, a program to search your mailing list for some criteria and then place the matched addresses in another file);
- data communications (sending and receiving data with other computers);
- message communications or electronic mail (keeping track of messages sent and received).

When personal computing is fully mature, we will see these services fully implemented on our computers. For now, the best we can expect is a reasonable number of them, working reasonable well. Consider the functions that you most need and look for them.

Next, consider which functions are fully provided and which are nominal. One package might have a strong spreadsheet but a weak text editor. Put your functional needs in priority and compare your list with various packages' strong and weak points.

The next thing to consider in choosing an integrated package is speed. To make it practical to include many features, the operating speed of a package might be compromised severely. It may not, but it might be. If you will be using an integrated package a lot—and the chances are good that you will—then it must work fast enough to not interfere with the flow of your work.

Next, consider communications. Communications—sending data and messages between computers—may not be part of your plans now, but as personal computing spreads communications will become more and more important. I advise you to consider communications capability to be part of your list of required features, even if you think that you will never need it.

Perhaps, though, the most important thing to consider in evaluating an integrated package is its "center." Many integrated packages will have one element that is the centerpiece of the entire package, which establishes the style, or flavor, of all the other elements. In looking at each package first, ask yourself if the package has a center (or if the parts of the package don't really have a core—which might or might not be a problem). Then ask yourself if the center is the right element, the most important element for you.

Of the two most widely known integrated packages, Lotus' 1-2-3 and Symphony is centered on a powerful spreadsheet. Ashton-Tate's Framework is centered on its idea-outlining "frame" system.

You'll find my own opinion on the best integrated package in Section 18.7.

18.6 Choosing Programming Languages

In Chapter 10 we covered the complex and interesting area of programming languages in more detail, but a little summary here won't hurt.

Don't be shortsighted. Program maintenance usually eats computer departments alive—both in the cost of doing program maintenance and in the hidden cost of program maintenance that doesn't get done. Choose a program language and programming methodology that makes maintenance practical. This argues heavily in favor of languages such as Pascal and C, and in favor of a fanatical devotion to learning and using structured programming methods.

There are many special advantages to using the BASIC language: it is universally available on personal computers; it is widely known; it is very flexible; and it can be both interpreted and compiled. This argues heavily in favor of using BASIC, but BASIC is dangerously hard to write in a structured way, and it is relatively slow even in compiled form.

There are many advantages to using an extra-high level language, such as spreadsheet templates, dBASE II/III programs, 1-2-3 macros, or Framework's "Fred" programming language. Speed may be sacrificed, but programming brevity and ease of maintenance will be gained.

When you get down to choosing, remember that the quality of the compiler (or interpreter) that you use is as important as the quality of the programming language.

18.7 Some Risky Recommendations

Things change very fast in the computer software arena, and it's a very risky business making any recommendations of one product over another. Making recommendations in a book, and not in a short-lived magazine issue, is even more risky. But what's life without a little risk?

Here I'm going to give you my own judgment on some of the major software products available.

Be forewarned that these recommendations are limited by my experience and judgment, and they are based on the software market as of the beginning of 1985.

In the word processing arena, I think that the best choices are Volkswriter Deluxe for easy-to-use everyday word processing, and Microsoft Word for take-it-to-the-limit state-of-the-art word processing. If you need special symbols for engineering, mathematical, and scientific use, Volkswriter Scientific is a clear choice.

For ordinary editor programs—for writing words or writing programs—the best choices are CompuView's Vedit (which this book was written with) and IBM's Personal Editor. For smart programming editors that incorporate knowledge of the language you're writing in, Bellesoft's ES/P editors are unique and superb.

For spelling checking, a natural adjunct to word processing, IBM's Word Proof stands out.

For stand-alone spreadsheets, there is widespread agreement that Microsoft's Multiplan is tops. For integrated spreadsheets, Lotus' 1-2-3 and, later, Symphony set the standard.

In the large, integrated software arena, there is an amazing slugfest going on, with many, many products competing. Only two seem important enough to mention though: Lotus' Symphony and Ashton-Tate's Framework. In my judgment Framework is the clearly superior product, if you truly need overall integrated software.

In the newly emerging area of windowing software, there are also many contenders, but only one sensible choice: IBM's TopView. TopView is a technically excellent product, which is fine, but essentially irrelevant. The most important thing about TopView is that IBM is strongly behind it, like no other software that has ever been introduced for the PC family. That alone makes TopView the only sensible choice for windowing software. Any child can tell you where a 500-pound gorilla sits.

For specific versions of programming languages, I recommend these two: Microsoft's Pascal (which is available under both Microsoft's brand name and IBM's; if you buy IBM's Pascal for the PC family, you're getting the Microsoft-written Pascal that I'm recommending), and Lattice's C (which is available under both the Microsoft brand name and Lattice's own brand name.) I'm not alone in recommending these two, by the way. Many others recommend them, and even IBM has given unofficial approval of Lattice C.

For data base software, recommendations are tough and I'm far from a data base expert. One expert of my acquaintance gives a thumbs-down to the popular dBASE II program. If you do not need fancy features, and can be well served by a relatively simple data base program, I can recommend PC-File from Buttonware.

Finally, for file recovery ('unerasing" files, and so forth) and disk management (coping with the huge capacity of a hard disk system) there is only one: Norton Utilities.

19

Avoiding Shortsighted Mistakes

If you are new to computing, or even if you aren't, you may be worried about making expensive mistakes with your computer. First, expect to make plenty of mistakes, and don't worry too much about it. Computing is a young field, and most of us don't have a lot of experience with it. Making mistakes comes with the territory; expect it, and be prepared for it. What we'll try to do in this chapter is to help you avoid some mistakes that are especially shortsighted or especially costly.

19.1 Hardware Mistakes

Since computer equipment is so modular and computers are so expandable, it is hard to make a mistake in getting too little equipment. If you end up needing an expansion feature that you didn't need at first, you can always get it later.

This seems to argue in favor of under-buying at first and adding onto your computer later. The simple fact is, it usually works the other way—you are usually better off buying more equipment than you think you might need. It is usually better to over-buy than to under-buy when selecting computer equipment.

Why is this so? Here is the simple reason. It is rare to buy a piece of computer equipment and then later realize that you never needed it at all. And it is a common experience for computer users to waste their time because they don't have a piece of equipment that they need—but are reluctant to add to their system—or waste their money by replacing some part of their system with better (faster, bigger, and so forth) components. The market for used parts of personal computers is weak, so if you need to replace your printer or disk drive with a better one, you may not be able to recover much or any of the cost of your first one.

Unless your budget is a severe constraint, it is wiser to over-buy in computing than to under-buy. The history of computing shows that people almost always need more, more, more as time goes by. If you get plenty to start with, you are usually better off. Obviously you shouldn't buy everything in sight and spend your money wildly. It is a simple fact of computer life that you are better off, when equipping your computer, to get more rather than less—more speed or more capacity than you might think you will need.

What mistakes are you most likely to make in under-buying? Too little memory, for one. Memory is relatively cheap so you can get plenty. On the other hand, memory is something you can add on but rarely have to replace. Usually, though, there is a large economy in buying memory in big chunks. For example, if you add 128K of memory to your system, and then later add another 128K, it will probably cost much, much more than if you had bought 256K to begin with.

Another common under-buy is too little disk capacity. Your data storage needs are likely to grow beyond anything you imagined possible. Adding disk storage is likely to mean discarding your old disk devices, so this can be a real money-waster. If you can add capacity by adding equipment, don't worry about under-buying. But if adding capacity will mean replacing equipment, you would be better off over-buying than under-buying.

The third most likely under-buy is printer quality. Printers that produce a high-quality appearance, especially what's called letter-quality printing, are usually expensive. This is a natural area for computer buyers to economize, but is also one of the most common areas for people to be dissatisfied with their equipment. Since printers can be so expensive, it is harder to blithely recommend that you buy a better printer than you may need. But think carefully. Upgrading to a better printer can be a real waste of money. In my own experience, this is where I have wasted the most money, by buying printers that were less than what I needed.

The biggest thing to consider, of course, is the computer itself. Personal computers today don't come with many limitations on them, particularly the PC family. It is only in buying game-oriented computers that you are likely to get a computer with too many limitations. If you are choosing between one model of computer and another, consider deeply the expansion options and the raw computing horsepower. The last thing you want to have to replace, and the most expensive thing to replace, is the computer itself. So if you are choosing between one computer and another, err on the side of more power and more expandability, rather than less.

IT CAN BE CONFUSING, DECIDING WHETHER TO UNDER-BUY OR OVER-BUY.

To recap, the most common and expensive shortsighted mistakes that are made in buying personal computer hardware are buying too little disk storage capacity and too low a quality of printer. An even more common mistake, though a less costly one, is to buy too little memory; this won't waste much money, but it can waste your time. Finally, the most expensive mistake of all is to buy too little in the computer itself—too little expansion capability or too little computing speed ("horsepower").

19.2 Software Mistakes

Making mistakes in buying software can be very expensive, even more wasteful of your time and effort than of your money; and your money can be wasted in basketloads if you make the wrong moves in buying software for your computer. You are more likely to make

PSSST! KID! WANNA' BUY SOME SOFTWARE?

YOU'RE MORE LIKELY TO WASTE MONEY ON SOFTWARE THAN HARDWARE.

mistakes in buying software than in buying hardware. It is easy to waste money in this area.

In Chapter 18 we covered some general rules that can guide you in selecting software. But here, let's take a short look at what are common shortsighted mistakes in buying software.

Probably the most important mistake is to underestimate how much you will want to tie your use of software together; by that we mean using one piece of software in conjunction with another. Integration is the key here. The more integrated the software, the better. This is again a strong argument in favor of multi-function packages. You may, quite wisely, want to buy the best available word processor and the best spreadsheet program. But you might be even wiser to get an integrated package that did both, even if that means having a second-rate word processor and spreadsheet. The same rule obviously applies to accounting packages. If you are going to need payroll processing in the future, then it would be very shortsighted to buy a general ledger that doesn't have an accompanying payroll module, no matter how superior the general ledger might be.

Another common software mistake is to underestimate how important speed and ease-of-use will become to you. When you start out in computing, speed may not seem extremely important. You may think that it is no big deal that it takes a few key strokes to tell one program to do some operation, while another program could do the same thing automatically through a batch processing command. As time goes by, it is likely that your use of the computer, and your dependence on it, will grow a lot. Then the speed and ease of use of your computer programs will become major factors in how efficiently you, yourself, can get your work done.

Still another shortsighted mistake in buying programs is to underestimate how important it is to be able to transfer programs to fast access storage, such as hard disks and electronic disks. As the volume of your programs grows, and as the amount of time you spend working with your computer grows, the worth of hard and electronic disks grows. When that happens, copy-protected programs, which cannot be transferred to other disk systems, become real enemies of your system.

19.3 Operational Mistakes

There are three main mistakes that you can make in organizing the operation of your computer. The first one we don't really have to hammer into you, since you will hear it from so many sources: make backup copies of your data. Again and again and again.

Computers are so thoroughly reliable that it is easy to feel that your data is quite secure. But that isn't the case. Your data is in danger in two ways. The lesser danger is from failure of the computer—or its programs—destroying your data. The greater danger is from inadvertent erasure of your data. It is extremely easy to lose your data by a mistaken DEL/ERASE command.

The solution to this operational danger is to frequently make backup copies of your data. Because this can be time consuming, it is tempting to skip doing it. The best and safest way to safeguard your data is to incorporate backup procedures into your working methods through batch files. Chapter 11 tells you more about how to do this.

The second shortsighted mistake in the operation of your computer is not taking the time to get organized. It is easy to think that you don't need to devote much effort into organizing your use of the system. But the simple fact is one of the best investments that you

YOUR BEST COMPUTER INVESTMENT IS INVESTING IN THE TIME TO GET ORGANIZED.

can make of your time is to carefully organize how you use your computer, including placing the right programs together on your disks, and especially working out the most effective batch processing files. Once you've done that, do it again when your work patterns change or you understand a better way to get organized.

The payoff in smooth, easy work is tremendous. I find that it pays off for me to take the time to refine my working procedures roughly once a month. Even after a full year of heavily using the same computer, I still reorganize every month or so; it takes me about a half-hour's effort, and then what I'm working on goes more smoothly.

The third operational mistake is neglecting to use batch files altogether. There is nothing else in the DOS operating system that can more enhance the smooth and effective operation of your computer system than automating working procedures with batch processing files. Turn to Chapter 11 for more information about batch files.

20

The EDLIN Editor

In this chapter we'll take a look at the text editing program that comes with DOS, the EDLIN program.

20.1 Introducing EDLIN

To begin, we should set the stage to tell you what an editor is for, and how EDLIN fits into the world of editing.

Ordinary written material, such as a letter or report that you or I might write, is dealt with in a special way by computers. Computers have a special format for storing written material: the format known as an ASCII text file. In Chapter 9, where we discuss file formats, you'll find some more details about how ASCII text is recorded in the computer. Here are just a few key things that we need to know about ASCII text files.

The data that is stored in an ASCII text file is the ordinary stuff of written material—alphabetic letters, numbers, and punctuation symbols like the comma and the period. The very words you are reading here are ASCII text, and they are stored in my computer in the form of an ASCII text file. ASCII text files are organized into distinct lines of text, which will become very important to us as we learn how to work with ASCII text files.

The punctuation that we put into a text file—the commas and the periods—don't mean much to the computer, but the computer adds its own special punctuation to an ASCII file. This special punctuation is used to mark the end of each line, and also the end of the entire ASCII text in a file. This special punctuation—end-of-line and end-of-file—is invisible to us. While we see our own punctuation, the computer keeps its special punctuation hidden from us, so that we don't see the end-of-line markers themselves, but we do see their results, which is the separation of our text into distinct lines.

ASCII text files are widely used in computers, and there are three uses that are particularly interesting to us: ASCII text files are used for word processing data, for the source code of programs (which is what computer programs look like when we write them), and for batch processing files. Most computer users will do word processing on their computers, many will be writing programs, and everyone should know how to create and change their DOS batch processing files—so everyone who uses a personal computer needs to know how to work with ASCII text files.

There is a special kind of program that is designed to help us enter and change ASCII text. These programs are known as editors. A word processing program is basically just an editor with many fancy frills. The frills are important in a word processor, but the heart of word processing is just the entering and revising of written text: in short, editing.

It is hard to use a computer well without an editor program on tap. Not only does much of what we want to do with the computer call for an editor, but also we need an editor to create batch processing files. The key to effective use of our computers lies in using good batch commands, and we need an editor to create the batch processing files, which define what a batch command is to do. If we want to be proficient in the use of our computers, we must be able to use an editor to create our batch files.

Editor programs are so important that most computer users buy them specially—often getting a complete word processing program that includes an editor. Having an editor is so important that DOS can't rely on your buying a separate one—so DOS includes a simple editing program, called EDLIN. If you don't have another editor, you will need to use EDLIN. Even if you do have a word processing program, you may find that you need to use EDLIN, simply because your word processor may be too powerful to be handy for simple editing tasks. You don't hunt mice with an elephant gun, and you may find that you don't want to use your word processor to create simple batch files. Even if you have another powerful editor, you probably need to learn how to use EDLIN.

There is another very practical reason why you should learn how to use EDLIN. For quick work with batch files, you should have a copy of an editor program on each of your program disks. Your main editor or word processor may be too large to fit on each disk. It is good to have a small, compact editing program available, and EDLIN fills that bill.

To use EDLIN effectively, you have to understand how it works, and that calls for a little discussion of different ways of doing editing. EDLIN is a type of editor known as a line editor (that's what gave it the name EDLIN) or a command editor. Most good editors, including word processors, are full-screen editors, which means that they show as much as possible of the material being edited on the display screen, and new material is entered in its proper place on the screen.

While a full-screen editor shows as much of the file as possible, a line editor like EDLIN conceals information, which makes working with it more cumbersome. To display any part of a file, or to do anything else, we must enter commands that tell EDLIN what to do. The commands might be to display part of the file or to make some changes to a file. Whatever we do, it is all done in terms of commands, and the commands operate on the lines of a file.

EDLIN always refers to a file in terms of the numerical order of the lines in the file. If we had a file with three lines in it like this:

```
This is the first line
This is the second line
This is the third line
```

then EDLIN would refer to these as line numbers 1, 2, and 3. To help us keep track of the line numbers, EDLIN always gives the line number when it displays lines from the file. If EDLIN were to display the above lines, they would appear like this:

```
1: This is the first line
2: This is the second line
3: This is the third line
```

The line numbers that EDLIN shows are not part of the data that is in our ASCII text file—it is just shown for reference.

Another thing that you need to know about EDLIN and line numbers is that the lines are renumbered after any change. If we delete line 2, what was line 3 (which in our example, says "This is the third line") immediately becomes the new line 2. Likewise, if we insert a new line following line 1, the old line 2 gets a new number as line 3.

To make it easier to work with, EDLIN keeps track of its current place among the lines of a file. When EDLIN displays lines, it indicates which is the current place in the file by marking it with an asterisk (*). For example, if the current location in our three-line file was the second line, then it would be displayed like this:

```
1: This is the first line
2:*This is the second line
3: This is the third line
```

When we tell EDLIN to do something for us, we can either tell it to work with some particular line number or to work on the current line.

EDLIN IS A CRUDE WRITING TOOL, LIKE A BOX OF CRAYONS.

Remember the DOS editing keys that we covered in Chapter 7. These keys are used to help us enter and revise DOS commands, and they work equally well when we are working with EDLIN. For anything we are typing into EDLIN, whether it is a command to EDLIN or data we are entering, we can use the DOS editing keys to revise it.

There is one more item we need to cover before we can move onward into the actual use of EDLIN, and that is a safety feature that is built into EDLIN and many other editors. When EDLIN is used to change a file, it does not destroy the old file. Instead, the old file data is kept under a different name—the old data is left in a file with the original filename, and a filename extension of BAK, short for backup copy. If we have made some disastrous error in editing a file, the BAK copy will help us recover from the mistake. Because of this backup convention, we can't edit a file that has an extension of BAK—if we need to work with a BAK file, then we must first rename it to something else.

Now we can move on to see EDLIN in action.

20.2 Ordinary EDLIN Commands

We begin using EDLIN by entering the EDLIN command name, followed by the name of the file we want to edit. For example:

```
EDLIN    B:FILENAME.EXT
```

EDLIN requires that we give it the name of a file to work with (many editors don't need a file name to start but EDLIN does). The file can either be an existing file that we want to change, or a new file that we want to create.

When it begins, EDLIN will look for the file we've named, and if it already exists, EDLIN will read it into memory. After EDLIN begins, it will give us one of three messages. If EDLIN doesn't find the file, it will report:

```
New File
```

If we knew that we were creating a new file, that's dandy. If we thought that we were changing an existing file, this means that EDLIN wasn't able to find it—perhaps we misspelled the filename. Another possibility is that the file we want to edit does exist, but it's not in the current directory. If that's the case, we need to quit EDLIN and either change directories to the one that contains our file (which we do with the CD or CHDIR command), or else we can give EDLIN the pathname that will lead it to the file along with the file name.

If EDLIN finds the file, it will read it into memory if there is enough room for all of the file. It would be a little unusual for us to be using EDLIN with a file that is bigger than will fit into memory, but it could happen. If EDLIN has enough memory space for the file, it will report:

```
End of input file
```

This message tells us that EDLIN did find the file, and that there was room for all of it. If there isn't room for the entire file, then EDLIN will give no message at all. This is a little cryptic (which is the sort of thing that makes EDLIN a weak editor), but if we know how to read EDLIN's signs, no message means "the file was found, and it's too big to fit into memory." When a file is too big to fit into memory, EDLIN does not use all the memory available—it keeps a cushion of about 25 percent to give us some working room.

When EDLIN is up and running, it tells us that it is ready for a command by giving its command prompt, which is a simple asterisk (*). To help distinguish when we are working with EDLIN from when we are working with DOS or any other program, EDLIN has this distinct asterisk prompt. After EDLIN gives us one if its three messages ("New File", "End of input file", or no message, meaning "File found and partially read into memory"), EDLIN will give us the asterisk command prompt.

Since we've learned how to start using EDLIN, we might as well make our first order of business learning how to end it. There are two different commands used to end EDLIN's operation. One, E (for end), will write the file from memory to disk, replacing the old file with a new version (and saving the old version as a BAK file, meaning that it will have .BAK for the filename extension). So E-for-end writes the file and then ends operation. To have EDLIN carry out the E command, we type in the single letter, following EDLIN's asterisk prompt, and press the enter key, which tells EDLIN to act on the command we have typed.

The other way to end EDLIN's operation is Q (for quit). Q-for-quit is used when we want to stop using EDLIN but we don't want to write a file back to disk; perhaps we haven't made any changes and don't need to write the file, or perhaps we've make some mistakes in our changes and we want to discard them. Whatever the reason, if we want to throw away the copy of the file that we have in memory we use the Q command. As a protection against accidentally losing some work we have done, EDLIN will ask us

```
Abort edit (Y/N)?
```

and unless we answer "Y" for yes EDLIN will continue operation.

Be careful to keep these two commands straight or you may write a bad file when you don't want to or throw away changes that you wanted to keep. E is end, including writing the changes, and Q is quit, without writing any changes to the disk copy of the file. If you've been tinkering with a file and have made a mess of it (deleting lines that you need to keep or whatever), then be sure to use Q-quit, not E-end, so that you discard the changes that you don't want to make a permanent part of the file.

Both of the commands that we have seen so far are given as single letters—E and Q. All of the EDLIN are single letters, which makes it very quick and easy to type them in as long as we can remember the right letter to use. We always press the enter key to tell EDLIN to carry out our commands, just as we do in entering DOS commands.

While the two commands we've seen so far are used by themselves the other DOS commands take some parameters, which tell them what and where to act. For example, the D-for-delete lines command needs to know which lines to delete. Before we go into the details of each command, let's see how we specify which lines to act on.

When an EDLIN command needs us to tell it what line to act on, we have five different ways we can indicate which line we want to use:

1. We can put in the specific line number, such as 27 or 32500. If we put in a line number that is too big (beyond the end of the lines in memory), then EDLIN acts just as if we had put in the next number after the last line.

2. We can explicitly refer to the line after the last line in memory by typing in a pound sign (#). This has the same effect as entering a line number that is too big.

3. We can indicate that we want to use whichever line is the current line by putting in a period (.). A period means, "use the current line number." Remember that EDLIN indicates the current line by marking it with an asterisk; after some experience with EDLIN, you'll be able to easily keep mental track of where the current line is, although at first you might be a little confused about it.

4. We can leave the line number blank and EDLIN will use some default line number that will vary with what makes the most sense for each command.

5. Unless we're using a 1-series version of DOS, we can indicate a line number relative to the current line by entering a plus or minus sign and a number, such as "+25" or "−200". This will refer to the line that is that number of lines before (−) or after (+) the current line.

With that background, let's look at some more commands.

To add some lines to a file, we use the I-for-insert command. The command is given like this:

*line-number*I

For example, to start inserting at the beginning of a file, before the first line, we would use the command

1 I

This sets us up to begin inserting lines into the file. The insertion begins before the specified line number. If we leave the line number off, the insertion goes before the current line.

If we are creating a new file, then there is nothing in the file and we have to use the I-insert command to start entering lines into the file. You might expect that with a new file we'd automatically start off inserting information, but EDLIN doesn't work that way. With a new file the first command that we give EDLIN is the I-insert.

When we give EDLIN the insert command, it sets itself up to let us enter not just one line but line after line, which is very convenient. At the end of each line, we press the enter key to signal the end of that line and the beginning of the next. EDLIN will accept our new lines endlessly. What do we do to stop entering new lines? We give EDLIN the break or Control-C command, and EDLIN then knows to stop taking in new lines.

(Recall that on the standard IBM PC keyboards, break is keyed in by holding down the Ctrl shift key and pressing the key marked ScrollLock/Break. On the PC*jr* keyboard, the same operation is done by pressing Fn (function) followed by B (for break). On any keyboard, Control-C does the same job.)

When we enter break, EDLIN will switch back into command mode waiting for our next command. To signal this EDLIN will show its command prompt, the asterisk. One special warning about breaking out of insert mode—you should press break only after you have pressed enter for the last line you inserted. If you press break with a line partly entered, it will be thrown away. Keep that in mind—losing the last line you've entered is very easy to do until you're familiar with EDLIN's rules.

The opposite of the I-insert command is the D-delete command. D-delete removes one or more lines from the file we are editing.

To delete one line, we enter the command like this with one line number:

*line-number*D

For example, the command **3D** deletes line number 3.

When we press enter that one line will be deleted. Naturally, all the following lines will be renumbered. If we want to delete a group of lines, we give two line numbers separated by a comma, like this:

*starting-line-number,ending-line-number*D

Both of the lines specified, and any lines in between, will be deleted.

For example, the command **1,10D** will delete all lines from the first line through the tenth.

You'll recall that we can always leave a line number specification blank and a default will be used. If you enter just a D without a line number, like this:

D

then the current line is deleted. With the range form, if we leave out the first number, like this:

```
,ending-line-numberD
```

then lines are deleted from the current line through the line specified. The reverse doesn't work. If you specify

```
starting-line-number,D
```

it will only delete one line, and not (as we might think) a range of lines from the starting point to the current line.

We can't do our editing of a file blind. We need to be able to see what we are doing. The L-list command lets us list (that is, display on the screen) lines from the file. Remember that EDLIN doesn't reveal anything about the file we're editing voluntarily. It will only show us exactly what we ask to see, nothing more. (Full-screen editors show much more information.) The L-list command has a format similar to the D-delete command. We can enter it with no line number, one line number, or a range of lines, like these examples:

```
L
line-numberL
starting-line-number,ending-line-numberL
```

As we mentioned each command has its own defaults, which are tailored to what makes the most sense for it. The defaults are quite different for L-list than they are for D-delete. If we give no numbers, then EDLIN lists 23 lines centered on the current line—it will show 11 lines before and 11 lines after the current line. This is an easy and convenient way to get a quick snapshot of our current region in the file.

If we enter only the first line number with or without a comma, EDLIN also shows 23 lines but starting with the specified line, no matter where the current line is. If you put in just the second line number (with a comma before it to indicate that it is the second number), then lines are displayed from 11 lines before the current line, up to the specified line.

Do you find this a little confusing? One of the problems with EDLIN is that its rules are too complicated (they are even a little more complicated than what I explained). This is unfortunate, but with a little practice you'll find that the commands like L-list are reasonably easy to use.

The next thing we need to learn about EDLIN is how to make changes to a line that is already in the file. Say we've used the L-list command to find the part of the file we're interested in, and we are ready to make changes. We can delete lines and insert new lines, but how do we just change existing lines?

Changes are made with the edit-line command. For this command we don't have a letter of the alphabet to signal the command—we just enter the number of the line we want to edit. In response, EDLIN displays a copy of the line, as it exists, and then gives us a (seemingly) blank line with the same line number. We can then use the DOS editing keys to make changes to the line, including copying any part of it that we don't need to change. When we have the line the way we want it, we press enter and the line is changed. If we decide we don't want to make any changes to the line, we can just press enter without typing in any changes and the line will be left as it is.

The edit-line command has a default line number, just like any other command. If we press enter with no line number EDLIN will assume that we want to edit the current line. When EDLIN gives us the asterisk command prompt, if we press enter the current line will be displayed and then it is set up for us to change, which we can to with the DOS editing keys.

If we just repeatedly press enter, EDLIN will switch back and forth between command mode (with the asterisk prompt) and editing the current line. Each time we switch the current line location is moved down one. This makes it possible for us to move through the file, line by line, by just repeatedly pressing enter. As each line is set up to be edited, we have the option of changing it or moving on to the next line. This is a convenient and quick way to go through a small file, making changes as we need to.

One of the things that an editor needs to be able to do is search through a file to find the location of some text we are interested in. EDLIN has two commands to do this: the S-search command and the R-replace command (which is really a search-and-replace command). We'll start with the S-search command. There are several variations on the S-search. The simplest one is like this:

`starting-line-number,ending-line-numberSwhat-to-search-for`

The search command searches through the range of lines looking for the "what to search for." If it is found, then the line with the information is displayed (and made the current line). If EDLIN doesn't find what it is searching for, then it will report with a message "Not found." Each of the three parameters is optional. If the starting line is left off, the search begins with the line following the current line. If the ending line is left off, the search goes on to the end of the file in memory. If the "what to search for" is left off, then EDLIN uses whatever we last gave it as a "what to search for." These three default values make it very easy to continue a search after one instance has been found. After we have had the search command search once, entering the command S with no more parameters will continue the search from where EDLIN left off.

EDLIN will only report exact matches of the information that we asked it to search for. If we are searching for the word "when", like this:

```
Swhen
```

then EDLIN would find the word in the middle of a sentence, but it wouldn't find it when the "W" is capitalized at the beginning of a sentence. Some editors can make matches in either upper- or lower-case but EDLIN does not—it requires exact matches.

There is another variation on the S-search by putting a question mark just before the S. For example:

```
1,35?Swhere
```

S-search is prepared to search repeatedly when the question mark is used until we find the instance that we are looking for. Each time EDLIN finds what it is looking for, it displays it and asks us

```
O.K.?
```

If we answer N for no, then EDLIN will go on looking. If we answer Y for yes, then EDLIN will stop looking so that we can work with the line that was found. Here's another opportunity for confusion. To me, this yes/no convention seems backwards. Whether you find it logical or not, remember the rule: Y-yes means stop and work here; N-no means no searching.

Related to the S-search command is the R-search-and-replace command. This command is entered like the S command, including the optional question mark. Replace is designed to replace what it finds with something else. We have to enter two sets of characters after the R-command. The two items are separated by a special character, Control-Z. This separator is the same Control-Z character we discussed as the end-of-file marker in Chapter 7. Remember that we can enter it either by holding down the Ctrl shift key and pressing Z, or we can use the F6 DOS editing key. When DOS is interpreting our keystrokes, F6 means the same thing as Control-Z.

To see what the R-command looks like, here is an example (our example will show a 'carat' character, "^", before the Z—that's also the way a Control-Z appears on your screen, but the two together represent the one Control-Z character):

```
1,200Rold information^Znew data
```

The S-search command stops at the first instance that it finds, so that we can do whatever we want with what we found. But the R-replace command has something active to do, so it will automatically repeat its search-and-replace operation all through the range of lines that we give it. In our example, every time EDLIN finds "old information" anywhere in lines 1 through 200, it will replace it with "new data." Each replacement is displayed so that we can see what is going on.

While the ordinary form of the R-replace command will replace each instance that it finds, the question mark version will stop each time and ask us OK? If we answer Y for yes, the replacement is performed; if we answer N for no, the line is left as it was, unchanged. The search-and-replace continues even if we answer N for no. You will notice that this is an important difference between S-search and R-replace. With S-search, answering yes stops the search while no continues it. With R-replace, answering yes lets the replacement take place while no prevents that one replacement, but the search still continues with either a yes or a no answer. So while these two commands are very similar, they respond very differently to the yes-or-no answer.

As you might imagine, it is very easy to make an accidental mess out of using the S and R commands. You should proceed cautiously until you are comfortable with them.

There are two more commands that are used in that special case when a file is too big to fit into memory. These commands are used to write out some of the file onto the disk to make room and then to read in more.

The W-for-write command is used to write some lines out of memory onto disk. The command is given like this:

*number-of-lines*W

As many lines as were specified are written, from the beginning of the lines in memory. If we don't specify a number of lines, then EDLIN will write just enough lines to get the 25 percent working cushion that it likes to have. After the lines are written, the part of the file that remains in memory is still numbered from line one. Our line numbers don't tell us where the lines are relative to the beginning of the entire file, but only relative to the beginning of what is in memory.

When some space has been freed by writing out part of a file (or by deleting some lines), we can then read in more of the file into memory from disk. This is done with the A-for-append command. A-append is given just like the W-write command:

*number-of-lines*A

If there is enough room, then EDLIN reads as many lines as we have asked it to. If we don't specify the number of lines, then EDLIN will automatically read until memory is 75 percent full leaving a 25 percent cushion of working space.

If EDLIN finds the end of a file while reading it with the A-append command, it will report it with the message

```
End of input file
```

just as it will when it first starts editing a file that fits into memory.

As you can probably tell from this outline of the ordinary EDLIN commands, EDLIN is not really a convenient and easy editor to use. In practice EDLIN is very clumsy and inconvenient to use, except when you are using it with very tiny files. That, is the one thing that I recommend using it for—creating and changing batch files. Little work like batch files are just EDLIN's speed. With anything larger you should use a more serious editor.

What we have seen so far with EDLIN concerns the commands that are available in all versions of DOS. Later versions of DOS also have four additional advanced commands that are very useful, which we'll cover in the next section.

20.3 Advanced EDLIN Commands

From the commands that we've seen so far, EDLIN doesn't have any way to move data around or to duplicate it. If we need to rearrange our file data we would be stuck, except for three special commands that were introduced with DOS 2.00. These commands are C-copy, M-move, and T-transfer. They can be used with any version of DOS in the 2-, 3-, or 4-series (but not with the 1-series, which predates the introduction of these advanced commands).

The C-copy command lets us duplicate some lines, copying them to another part of the file. There are four parameters in this command:

```
starting-line,ending-line,where-to,how-many-timesC
```

Each of the four parameters is optional, except for the "where to" specification, which must be given. If either the starting or ending lines are left off, then the current line is assumed. If the number of times is left off, then only one copy is made. The copied material is placed before the specified "where to" line, just as it is with the I-insert command.

For example, the command **1,5,24C** will make a single copy of lines 1 through 5, and place it right before 24.

Usually we would use this command just to duplicate a bunch of material once, but there are times when we might want to use the "how many times" parameter to make several copies. As an example, if we were creating a table or list in a file we might create a skeleton line (with all the repeated information), copy it as many times as needed, and then fill in the details in each line. Every table and list that you see in this book was created that way (even though I used another editor, not EDLIN).

For example, if you created a skeleton heading for a series of five tables, and that heading occupies lines 1-3, you can make the other four copies of the heading with the simple command "1,3,3,4C". This places four more copies of the heading right after the original copy. Then you can go about the work of filling in the details of each table. You can see many ways that this sort of thing can be very useful.

The M-move command performs a similar function to the C-copy command, but it acts as a move to takes lines out of their current place and put them somewhere else. With a C-copy the original copy stays in place; with M-move it is gone. Duplication makes sense for a C-copy command but not for M-move, so M-move doesn't make multiple copies. There are three parameters for M-move:

*starting-line,ending-line,where-to*M

As with C-copy, the third parameter, "where to," is required and not optional. The starting and ending line numbers will default to the current line if they are not specified.

The third special command that can be used to rearrange data is the T-transfer command. T-transfer is used to read the contents of another file and to place it into the file being edited. The command is given like this:

*line-number*T *file-name*

The contents of the file are placed in memory ahead of the specified line number (just as it is with I, C, and M). The file must be specified, naturally enough, but the line number is optional. If it is not specified, then the current line indicates where the new data is to go.

For example, suppose we've created a skeleton or "boiler plate" model for some work you do repeatedly , and put it into a file called OUTLINE. If we are editing another file and find that we need to include the outline material, say following line number 150, then we would use this command:

150TOUTLINE

There is one further advanced command that EDLIN provides, the P-page command. The P-page command is intended for browsing paging) through a file, and it works just like the L-list command with one handy exception. L-list leaves the current line unchanged, which might be far from what is being displayed on the screen. The P-page command makes the last line displayed the current line so the working location in the file follows what is displayed.

21

DEBUG—A Technical Tool

In this chapter we jump into the deep end of the pool and get in way over our heads. Our topic is the DOS programmer's tool command, DEBUG. DEBUG is quite an advanced tool and it is not intended for the ordinary user of DOS. But DEBUG may provide capabilities that you need, or you may just want to know what can be done by DEBUG. Here is a low-level introduction to DEBUG.

If you don't need to know about technical matters like this, or you're not interested in them, don't feel you have to plow through this chapter. If you don't need it, you won't be cheating yourself—this is technical material for those who need to know everything about DOS.

21.1 Some DEBUG Background and Hex

Freight trucks aren't built like passenger cars, and for good reason. Cars are intended for easy, comfortable driving by ordinary people; trucks are built for more rough-and-ready use, for professional use by qualified drivers.

Almost everything in DOS is designed for civilian use by the likes of you and me. But there are some special things that need to be done by qualified, technically expert people, and DOS's DEBUG is designed to provide the means to accomplish many important tasks that can't be done except with a sophisticated and complicated tool.

In order for a truck to be able to accomplish its purpose, it can't be made as pretty or as easy to drive as an ordinary car. So it is with DEBUG. Much of what DEBUG works with is technical in nature, so the use of DEBUG is equally technical and complicated. This isn't to say that DEBUG is necessarily over your head; you can judge that for yourself. I can assure you that it is substantially more complicated and technical than any other element in DOS.

The details of using DEBUG are closely tied to the details of the particular microprocessor that is in your computer. Our discussion here will be based on the Intel 86 series of microprocessors, which are used in the IBM PC. Most of the features of DEBUG require a rough understanding of the microprocessor, and some of them call for a very thorough understanding.

The first thing you need to know about DEBUG is that it does all of its work in hexadecimal arithmetic. Unfortunately, DEBUG doesn't even give us the option of using decimal numbers—everything in DEBUG is done in hexadecimal or hex as it is called.

Hexadecimal arithmetic uses 16 as its base, or radix, instead of 10, which we normally use. Deep in their hearts, all computers work with binary numbers so they need to be given, in one way or another, binary numbers. Hexadecimal is simply a shorthand for binary, with each hexadecimal digit standing for four separate binary digits (called "bits"). While our decimal arithmetic uses the ten digits 0 through 9, hexadecimal arithmetic uses sixteen digits, which are represented by 0 through 9 followed by A (with a value of ten) through F (with a value of fifteen).

Here is a table giving a quick outline of the hexadecimal digits:

Hex digit	Decimal equivalent	Binary equivalent
0	0	0000
1	1	0001
2	2	0010
3	3	0011
4	4	0100
5	5	0101
6	6	0110
7	7	0111
8	8	1000
9	9	1001
A	10	1010
B	11	1011
C	12	1100
D	13	1101
E	14	1110
F	15	1111

Hex numbers are interpreted like decimal numbers, but with a base of sixteen rather than ten. If we interpret "12" as a decimal number, it would be in words as:

one times ten, plus two equals twelve

but the same "12" interpreted as a hexadecimal number would be

one times sixteen, plus two equals eighteen

Numbers can be up to four hexadecimal digits long so they can range from 0 to FFFF, which is equivalent to the decimal number 65,535.

The use of DEBUG involves memory addresses (every position in memory has a numeric address). For computers like the IBM PC family that are based on the Intel 8086 family of microprocessors, complete memory addresses are five digits long, but they have to be represented by numbers no longer than four digits. This is accomplished by using two numbers to represent an address. The first number, called the segment part, is treated as if it were shifted one place over, the equivalent of multiplying it by "10." The second number, called the relative part, is added to the segment part (shifted over) to get a complete address. It is done like this:

```
1234
 5678
179B8
```

When addresses are written out, they are shown with the two parts separated by a colon, like this:

```
1234:5678
```

When DEBUG shows us addresses, it always shows them in that form. When we give DEBUG addresses, we can type them in that way or we can leave off the segment part and the colon and give only the relative part. In that case, DEBUG will use a default segment value.

There is one other way that we can specify the segment part of addresses. The microprocessor has registers, which are used to hold numbers for addressing memory. Each of the registers has a symbolic name. For example, CS is the name of the code-segment register, which customarily provides the segment portion of addresses within a program itself (as opposed to the program's data). Any of the standard symbolic register names can be used if you know and understand them.

There is a more technical summary that we might go into, but rather than lay it all out here we will let it emerge as we discuss the commands that DEBUG can perform.

21.2 The DEBUG Commands

We begin operating DEBUG in one of two ways. We can give the command name, DEBUG, and DEBUG will begin operation by showing us its command prompt, which is a hyphen (-). DEBUG like

EDLIN has its own command prompt, which is different than the main DOS command prompt. when we see a "-" we know that DEBUG is asking us for a command.

The other way to start DEBUG is to give the name of a file after the command, like this:

```
DEBUG    A:FILENAME.EXT
```

When we begin DEBUG this way, it will start by reading the file into memory so that we can work with the data in the file.

After we've started DEBUG, we need to know how to stop it. The Q (for quit) command is used to tell DEBUG to end its operation. In response to DEBUG's hyphen command prompt, we type Q, press the enter key, and DEBUG ends. As it is for the EDLIN editor, all of DEBUG's commands are single-letter abbreviations.

The first thing we might want to do with DEBUG is to display the information stored in some of memory. Displaying is done with the D-display command. We have to tell DEBUG what we want displayed, which is always a part of our computer's memory. DEBUG needs to know two things about what to display from memory—where to start and how much to show. We must specify where to start as an address (which we saw how to enter in the last section).

There are three ways to tell DEBUG how much to display—we can leave this part of the command blank and DEBUG will show a standard amount, say 80 bytes. Or we can give a second address (relative part only), and DEBUG will display through that address. Or we can indicate the number of characters we want displayed by keying in L (meaning we're specifying the length we want displayed), followed by the number of bytes (which, unfortunately, must be given in hexadecimal). Here are examples of all three ways of invoking the D-display:

```
D    F000:6000              display from an address, default length

D    F000:6000   6800       display from one address through another

D    F000:6000   L 100      explicit length for 100 (hex) bytes
```

These three ways of specifying a section of memory are collectively called a range, and several more of the DEBUG commands use ranges. Whenever we indicate that DEBUG needs a range, you can give it to DEBUG in any of these three formats.

As a convenience, D-display keeps track of where it was displayed last so that just entering the D command, with no parameters, will display successive parts of memory, which is convenient for browsing.

The information shown by D-display shows the contents of memory, in both hexadecimal and character formats, so you can read what is there either way. (The U command, which we are coming to, gives us another way to see memory.) Here is a typical D-display:

```
-D 0:0

0000:0000  43 31 E3 00 3F 01 70 00-C3 E2 00 F0 3F 01 70 00  C1c.?.p.Cb.p?.p.

0000:0010  3F 01 70 00 54 FF 00 F0-47 FF 00 F0 47 FF 00 F0  ?.p.T..pG..pG..p

0000:0020  A5 FE 00 F0 87 E9 00 F0-DD E6 00 F0 DD E6 00 F0  %~.p.i.pf.pf.p

0000:0030  DD E6 00 F0 60 07 00 C8-57 EF 00 F0 3F 01 70 00  f.p'..HWo.p?.p.

0000:0040  65 F0 00 F0 4D F8 00 F0-41 F8 00 F0 56 02 00 C8  ep.pMx.pAx.pV..H

0000:0050  39 E7 00 F0 59 F8 00 F0-2E E8 00 F0 D2 EF 00 F0  9g.pYx.p.h.pRo.p

0000:0060  00 00 00 F6 86 01 00 C8-6E FE 00 F0 F2 00 71 05  ...v...H~~.pr.q.

0000:0070  53 FF 00 F0 A4 F0 00 F0-22 05 00 00 00 00 00 F0  S..p$p.p"......p
```

The information from D-display, and all other DEBUG commands, appears only on your computer's display screen. You can save a record of it several ways. One is to turn on your computer's echo-to-printer switch, which we discussed in Chapter 7. Another is to redirect the output of DEBUG to a file. The display shown above is actual DEBUG output, which was captured in a file using redirected output and then incorporated into the text of this chapter.

Besides displaying memory, DEBUG also lets us compare two parts of memory with the C-compare command. To work, C-compare needs a range to indicate the location and length of the one part of memory, and a second address to indicate the location of the other part of memory. DEBUG will then compare them, byte for byte, and report any differences to us.

Similar to the C-compare command is the M-move command, which will copy the data in one part of memory to another. Like C-compare, M-move needs a range to indicate the move-from locations and an address to indicate the move-to locations.

Since we have to use hexadecimal numbers with DEBUG, it would be nice to have some aids. Unfortunately, DEBUG gives us no help in converting between decimal and hexadecimal, but it does give us a tool to do addition and subtraction in hexadecimal—the H-hex-arithmetic command. To use the H command, we key in H followed by two hex numbers. H will then display their sum and their difference—this gives us easy access to hex addition and subtraction, something that is very useful in working with addresses.

For example, if we gave DEBUG the command

    H 1234 ABCD

it would reply with

    BE01 6667

which is the sum and difference of the two numbers we gave—all in hexadecimal.

But for converting from hex to decimal, we are on our own. To do that, we must turn to a programmer's pocket calculator, or to BASIC (which has easy ways to convert decimal and hex) or to counting on our fingers and toes.

Naturally, we may want to make changes to the information that is stored in memory. DEBUG gives us two ways to do this—the E and F commands. The E-enter command lets us make direct changes to memory. There are two ways to use the E-enter command, one that lets us enter data without comment and the other lets us see what we are changing first.

The first way to use E-enter is like this:

    E *address list-of-data*

The list of data is stored in memory, starting at the address and continuing until everything in the list has been placed in memory. For our convenience, the list-of-data can be any mixture of character data and hexadecimal data. If we use characters, then we have to enclose them in quotes to make them distinct from hex numbers. Here is an example:

    E 0F32:0100 32 "Peter Norton" 32 73 74 69 6B 73 ", doesn't he?"

The other way to use E-enter is interactive, with DEBUG showing us the old contents of each byte of memory before we change it. This is very important and useful, because it provides a safeguard against changes being made to the wrong part of memory. Occasionally you may receive patches, which are changes that need to be made to a program. Patches are often given in the form of DEBUG's interactive E-enter commands, so that you can confirm that you are changing what you are supposed to be changing and not something else.

The interactive form of E-enter is invoked by giving E an address but no list of data to store. E-enter will then display, in hex only, the data at that address and wait for you to key in a new value, also in hex. You either key in a new value or press the space bar to leave the value unchanged.

DEBUG will continue, presenting you with byte after byte to change until you call the process to a halt by pressing enter. You can confirm the changes you made either by later using D-display to show where you made the changes or by using another feature of E-enter, the hyphen. While you are using the interactive form of E-enter, keying in a hyphen will move you back one byte (just as pressing the space bar will move you forward one). This makes it easy to back up and confirm what you have done. The F-fill command can also be used to change the contents of memory. F-fill is used like the automatic form of E-enter, except that we specify a range of memory and not just a single starting memory address, like this:

```
F range list-of-data
```

The reason for the range is that F-fill will duplicate the list-of-data as many times as necessary to fill up the range of memory. The list of data can be as long and complicated as you wish, but the most common use for F-fill is to set a block of memory to one byte value, like zero.

For example, if we wanted to clear all of the working memory to zero, we could do it with this F-fill command:

```
F 0 L FFFF 0
```

We can search through memory for some particular data with the S-search command. S-search needs the same kind of parameters as F-fill: a range (indicate what part of memory to search for) and a list of data in hex or character formats. S-search will report the address location of each set of data in the range that matches the data list. If you are using DEBUG for snooping and patching—two of the most popular uses of DEBUG—then the search command is definitely for you.

For example, you could find out how many times the name "IBM" occurs inside DOS's command interpreter, COMMAND.COM, by using DEBUG's S-search command, like this:

```
DEBUG COMMAND.COM
S 0 L FFFF "IBM"
```

Besides the main memory your computer also has registers, which it uses to hold working addresses and temporary results of arithmetic operations. DEBUG provides the R-register command so that we can display and change the register values. If we enter the R command by itself, DEBUG will display the contents of all the computer's registers along with some related information. If we enter R followed by the name of one particular register, then DEBUG will display its contents and give us an opportunity to enter a new value, similar to the way the interactive E-enter command works. To successfully use this command, you must understand how registers are used by your computer and also how DEBUG uses the registers when it is working.

One of the ways that your computer talks to its various parts and also to the world around it is through an element known as a port. Ports are data paths into and out of your computer's microprocessor. There are many possible ports and your particular computer will use some of them for special purposes. Generally, you must have a very detailed knowledge of your particular computer's inner workings to be able to understand and use ports. Each port has an address that identifies it. These port addresses are similar to, but completely distinct from, memory addresses. Each port can pass data in or out, which is its role in life. DEBUG gives us two commands to move data through ports. I-in reads data from the port and displays it. O-out sends data out the port. The commands are used like this:

```
I port-address
O port-address data
```

While DEBUG gives us the means to display and change data in memory, often our real goal is to display or change data that is on disk. DEBUG provides us with a way to read and write disk data to and from memory. The L-load and W-write commands are used for this. L-load and W-write work in two distinct ways. They can either read and write entire files or specific parts of the disk storage. Let's cover the file part first.

As you'll recall from the beginning of this section, when we start DEBUG we can either start it by itself or with the name of a file that we want DEBUG to read into memory automatically. If we make changes to the file's data in memory, how do we write it back to the disk? The W-write command, without any parameters, will write the memory copy back to the disk replacing the original disk copy of the file. Suppose we want to read another file into memory? How can we do this? It takes a combination of two commands, oddly enough. The first command, N-name, tells DEBUG the name of the file to be read; the second command is L-load, without any parameters (just like writing a file is done with W-write, with no parameters). To read a file, we do something like this:

```
N  A:FILENAME.EXT
L
```

and then the file is read into memory, just as it would be if we had used that file name when we started DEBUG.

The "naked" form of L-load and W-write is used to read and write complete files, but another form of these commands is used to read specific parts of the disk data. In this case we specify the memory address we want the data read into, and what part of the disk we want to read from. The command is like this:

L *address drive-number sector-number sector-count*

The address is the location in memory the data is to be placed to. The drive-number is the equivalent of the letter that DOS uses to identify disk drives, with zero representing the A-drive, one the B-drive, and so forth. This indicates which disk drive the data is to be read from. The sector-number indicates what part of the disk is to be read; the exact number used depends upon your particular computer, the particular disk format, and also the version of DOS. The sector-count indicates how many disk storage units, called sectors, are to be read into memory.

Writing to specific locations on the disk is done with the W-write command using the same kind of specifications used for a L-load command. Everything that we have discussed so far has been about and has been working with abstract data. DEBUG also has the ability to work with programs in several interesting ways.

With the D-display command we saw how to display data in a combined hex and character format. That is fine if what we are displaying is data, but it doesn't tell us much if the information is part of a program. To translate raw programs into a more intelligible format, DEBUG uses the U-unassemble command. U-unassemble translates the hexadecimal of machine language programs into the form of assembly language. Ordinary civilians still won't be able to comprehend it, but anyone who can at least stumble through assembly language programs will be able to decipher some or all of what is being done. Here is an actual example of a U-unassembly done on my computer:

```
F600:0000 E98F7E          JMP     7E92

F600:0003 E8A76B          CALL    6BAD

F600:0006 CB              RETF
```

The display, as you can see, includes the address locations, the data in hex format, and the equivalent assembly language instructions, like "JMP" and "CALL". The assembly language format does not strictly follow what is needed to create an assembly program, but it is closely equivalent.

DEBUG also provides the flip side of U-unassemble, the A-assemble command. A-assemble allows us to key in assembly-like instructions, like the "JMP 7E92" that appears above, and have them translated into machine language and stored into memory. While any of us can use the U-unassemble command, and some of us will also be able to understand it as well, only those who are fluent in assembly language can use the A-assemble command successfully. It is more difficult to use DEBUG's A-assemble command than it is to write ordinary assembly programs, since an assembler provides more aid and assistance than DEBUG can. A-assemble is only for proficient experts.

There are two more program-oriented commands that DEBUG gives us. Both of them are quite advanced and are really only for use by very proficient assembly-language programmers. Even then, these two commands are used only in fairly extreme circumstances, when programming problems can't be solved by more routine methods. These two commands are T-trace and G-go.

The T-trace command is used to execute a program step by step. With a program ready in memory, T-trace will execute the program's instructions, one at a time, and display the status of the computer as reflected in its registers. T-trace can be told to stop after each instruction or to continue for a number of instructions but displaying the results of each one. T-trace is mostly used when a programmer is uncertain about the exact results of some instructions, or of a very small part of a program. T-trace is too laborious to be effective for extensive program testing.

The G-go command also executes a program, but without tracing its results. G-go will execute or carry out a program as quickly as DEBUG is able to. With the G-go command, we can specify locations in the program, called break points, where DEBUG will stop executing it. This is the difference between executing a program by itself and executing it under the control of DEBUG's G-go command. With break points set, we can run a program and then stop to check the results when an interesting or important part has been reached.

This has been a quick, and slightly technical, overview of what the facilities of DEBUG are. In the next section we'll look at how to use DEBUG to patch or change programs.

21.3 Using DEBUG to Patch

Whatever else we might do with DEBUG, there is one common use that most of us might be using DEBUG for: modifying or patching programs.

There are two different kinds of patching that we might be doing with DEBUG. One is making actual detailed changes, in hexadecimal, to correct a program or alter its operating characteristics.

For example, some editing and word processing programs are patched with DEBUG to customize the way that they operate. When we do this kind of patching, we should be following very careful and detailed instructions that tell us how to make the patches.

The other kind of patching is patching that we might do on our own. This is patching where we don't have to know the exact details of the program that we are changing. Instead, we want to change something more obvious and easier than a change to the program code. One petty example of this kind of patching is changing a message that a program displays. Another, which we have referred to at several points in this book, is to change a program so that it does not tie itself to using specific disk drives.

In order to illustrate how this is done, let's dream up a typical example of how such patching might be done. Suppose we have a program, which we'll call SUPER, and we find that this program really is super in every respect but one: SUPER insists on reading its data from our disk drive B but we want it to use whatever default disk drive DOS is currently using. If we can change SUPER so that it doesn't specify a disk drive, then we can move SUPER's data to a hard disk, an electronic disk, or any disk other than the B drive that SUPER insists on.

Here is what we would do to try to change SUPER. We don't know in advance if this is going to work—the method is experimental, but there is a very good chance that we will succeed and do no harm in the process.

First, we find the SUPER program. It should be in a file named SUPER.COM or SUPER.EXE. If SUPER happens to be a BASIC program, it might be stored in a file named SUPER.BAS. Whatever the name, we find it and copy it to a separate disk (so that we can safely change it without endangering our main copy). In the process, we should note the size of the program file. Next, we have to consider one picky detail. If the program file has an EXE extension, then DEBUG will treat it in a special way that makes it possible for DEBUG to use the T-trace and G-go commands. We don't want this for reasons that are rather technical. The main thing is, if we have an EXE file we don't want DEBUG to know about it. If the file has an EXE extension, we use the DOS command RENAME to change its extension to anything other than EXE. Let's assume that SUPER is an EXE file, so we will rename it like this:

```
REN  SUPER.EXE  SUPER.XXX
```

Next, we start DEBUG and tell it to load the program file. The command is like this:

```
DEBUG  SUPER.XXX
```

At this point, DEBUG now has a copy of the SUPER program file in memory. We suspect that inside this program file are specific references to the B drive in this form: "B:". We are going to ask DEBUG to search for them. To use the search command, we have to tell it how much to search, which would be the length of the SUPER.XXX file. If we can translate decimal into hexadecimal we can figure it out. If we can't, we'll tell DEBUG to search as much as possible. Here is the S-search command that we will use:

```
S 0 L FFFF "B:"
```

Step-by-step, this is what we are asking DEBUG to do: "S" says we want to search for something. "0" says to look from the beginning of DEBUG's working memory. "L" says that we want to search for some length. "FFFF" says to search for as many bytes as possible; if we knew the exact length of the file (in hexadecimal) we would substitute it here. The last part, in quotes, tells DEBUG that we want to look for the drive specification of "B:".

In response to this command, DEBUG will report where it found "B:". If it doesn't report it anywhere, we are out of luck (sorry) and have to give up. Instead, DEBUG is likely to report one or even several addresses. If we want to, we can display the data following each address. If DEBUG reported an address like this:

```
04EF:0220
```

then we would use the D-display command to show information from there:

```
D 04EF:0220
```

using exactly the same address that S-search gave us.

When we do this display, we may see only the "B:", but more likely we will see a complete filename with the "B:" at the front. We'll probably see something like this:

```
04EF:0220  42 3B 46 49 4C 45 4E 41-4D 45 32 32 32 32 32 32    B:FILENAME
```

The combination of the "B:" and the filename is a tip-off that we have found what we want. Our goal is to remove the "B:" part. We can use the E-enter command to replace it with blank spaces, which we do like this:

```
E 04EF:0220 "  "
```

We repeat this process for each memory location that the search command reported that it found "B:". When we are done, we write the file back to disk with the W command.

Now we have our modified program file and are ready to test. If we renamed it from an EXE file, we need to change its name back:

```
RENAME   SUPER.XXX   SUPER.EXE
```

Finally, we are ready to test it to see if it works. To be safe we need to make copies of any current data that SUPER uses, just in case the new, modified version gets up to any mischief. We'll test the new SUPER with one copy of our data, knowing that if anything goes wrong we have another, undisturbed copy. Then we try running the SUPER program and see if it looks for its files on the DOS default drive we have pointed to instead of the B drive. If the test works, then we can start using the modified program with our ordinary data.

The same methods described here can be used to locate and change messages that are built into programs. I can think of two plausible reasons why you might want to do this sort of thing. One would be to replace DOS's starting message with your company's own logo. If you want to do that, you'll find the DOS starting message located in the COMMAND.COM file. Another reason would be to translate program messages from English into another language. Whatever your reason, you can use the techniques that we have covered here to make any kind of reasonable changes that you want.

If you have no real reason to do this sort of patching work, you might want to give it a try simply to learn how to do it. It's a skill that might come in handy some day.

Making patches or changes to programs like this is a potentially dangerous process—we may end up making a program unusable due to some error on our part or some trick in the program. You need to proceed with caution when you do this kind of work. Under normal circumstances what we have described works just fine, and is surprisingly easy to do.

22

Reference Summary of Commands

In this chapter we'll give you a quick reference summary of the commands that DOS provides along with some guidance about their use.

22.1 Separate Commands

ASSIGN ASSIGN reroutes references from one disk to another. One of the main uses of ASSIGN is to fool programs that expect to work with two diskettes into working with one hard disk.

ATTRIB ATTRIB allows you to set the read-only attribute of a file, which protects files from being changed or erased. This command does not apply to the 1- or 2-series of DOS.

BACKUP BACKUP makes copies of hard disk files onto floppy diskettes for backup purposes. Unlike the COPY command, BACKUP can treat many floppies as a single storage unit. See the RESTORE command.

BREAK BREAK controls how often DOS will check for the break, Control-C, key-command, which interrupts a program. With BREAK OFF, DOS will check only when output is being written to the display, or when input is being read from the keyboard; with BREAK ON, DOS will check as often as it is able to. This command does not apply to the 1-series of DOS.

CD CD is another name for the CHDIR command, which changes directories. This command does not apply to the 1-series of DOS.

CHDIR CHDIR, or CD, changes the current directory from one location in the directory tree to another. The current directory can be set independently for each disk drive the computer has. If CHDIR is not given a new directory to switch to, it will simply display the pathname of the current directory. This command does not apply to the 1-series of DOS.

CHKDSK CHKDSK will inspect the status of a disk and report how many files there are, how much space there is, and how much space remains available. CHKDSK will also report how much memory is available (which has nothing to do with the disk). If CHKDSK discovers any errors in the disk's directory or space table (called the FAT), it will report them and fix them.

CLS CLS will clear the display screen, which is useful for removing extraneous information. This command does not apply to the 1-series of DOS.

COMP COMP will compare the contents of two files and report any differences.

COPY COPY will copy files with several variations. Individual files can simply be copied from one disk to another; a group of files can be copied, under the control of wild card filenames; one or more files can be copied under new names; and finally, files can be combined, or concatenated, into one file.

CTTY CTTY is used to redirect DOS's "console" from the keyboard and display screen to another device—typically a communications line. The main purpose of CTTY is to allow remote control of your computer. This command does not apply to the 1-series of DOS.

DATE DATE is used to change DOS's record of the current date. It will also display the date, including the day of the week. Normally DATE is used only once when DOS is started up.

DEBUG DEBUG is a multi-function tool designed to perform technical programming functions related to the "debugging" of programs. DEBUG can be used to inspect the contents of memory and disks, to change them, and to execute programs under close control. DEBUG is oriented to the technical needs of advanced programmers, and it is not easy to use. DEBUG has a number of subcommands that are outlined in Section 22.3.

DEL DEL, or ERASE, is used to delete one or more files from a disk. When a file has been deleted, it cannot be recovered by ordinary DOS methods.

DIR DIR is used to display a list of the files in a directory on a disk. DIR will display the entire directory or a portion selected by filename. The information displayed by DIR includes the file name and extension, the size, and the date and time of the file.

DISKCOMP DISKCOMP is used to compare disks to see if they match exactly. DISKCOMP cannot tell if two disks are functionally equivalent (which they would be if they have the same files with the same data). It can only report if they are exact copies of each other, including details that are functionally irrelevant.

DISKCOPY DISKCOPY is used to make a complete and exact copy of a disk. Although you will often be recommended to use DISKCOPY, the best way to copy data from one disk to another is with the COPY command.

ECHO ECHO is used to control whether batch file commands will appear on the display screen. ECHO ON, which displays the commands, allows you to see exactly what is happening; ECHO OFF suppresses the command display, which may be irrelevant and confusing. This command does not apply to the 1-series of DOS.

EDLIN EDLIN is a simple editor for working with ASCII text files. EDLIN has numerous subcommands that are listed in Section 22.2.

ERASE ERASE is another name for the DEL command, which erases files from disk.

EXE2BIN EXE2BIN is used to convert programs from the "EXE" format into the "COM" format. This command is intended for use by program developers only—usually only assembly language programmers.

FDISK FDISK controls the partitioning of a hard disk so that it can be divided among more than one operating system. This allows DOS to use one part of a disk and other parts to be used by other systems, such as XENIX or PC-IX.

FIND FIND is a filter command used to locate those lines in a stream of display data that contain some particular data. This command applies only to the 2-series and later.

FOR FOR is an advanced batch file command used to repeat some batch operations for each item on a list of names. This command does not apply to the 1-series of DOS.

FORMAT FORMAT is used to prepare disks for use. The disks may or may not be formatted to include a working copy of DOS.

GOTO GOTO is an advanced batch file command used to jump to another part of the file. GOTO can be used to skip over an unwanted portion of the commands, or to skip backwards to repeat commands. GOTO is often used with the IF command. This command does not apply to the 1-series of DOS.

GRAFTABL GRAFTABL establishes the extended ASCII character set for use in graphics modes. This command does not apply to the 1- or 2-series of DOS.

GRAPHICS GRAPHICS loads a resident program that is able to print a copy of a graphics display screen. This command does not apply to the 1-series of DOS.

IF IF is an advanced batch file command used to test for some logical condition (such as the existence of a file or an error in a previous program), and then carry out a command based on the test. The command controlled by an IF is often a GOTO command. This command does not apply to the 1-series of DOS.

KEYBxx The KEYBxx commands are resident programs that provide keyboard translation for use in countries other than the United States. This command does not apply to the 1- or 2-series of DOS.

LABEL LABEL controls disk volume ID labels. This command does not apply to the 1- or 2-series of DOS.

LIB LIB is used to control program libraries of the kind that are used by the compilers of languages such as BASIC, Pascal, C, COBOL, and FORTRAN. LIB is intended for use by advanced programmers, and it is usually distributed with programming languages (rather than with the rest of DOS) although it is actually a part of DOS, like the command LINK.

LINK LINK is used in the development of most programs (other than interpretive BASIC programs). LINK is used to combine program parts, including parts taken from a compiler's library. LINK will be used by all programmers, beginning and advanced.

MD MD is another name for the MKDIR command, which creates directories. This command does not apply to the 1-series of DOS.

MKDIR MKDIR, or MD, creates new subdirectories as part of a disk's directory tree. This command does not apply to the 1-series of DOS.

MODE MODE controls the mode of the printer, display, or communications line.

MORE MORE is a filter command used to keep display output from rolling off the screen before it can be properly studied. This command does not apply to the 1-series of DOS.

PATH PATH is used to instruct DOS about where to look for command program files. PATH can be used to tell DOS to search in several directories and also to search on several disks. This command does not apply to the 1-series of DOS.

PAUSE PAUSE is a batch file command used to display a message and wait for a keyboard response.

PRINT PRINT is used to send disk data files to the computer's printer, while allowing the computer to be used for other purposes. PRINT is a primitive form of print spooler. This command does not apply to the 1-series of DOS.

PROMPT PROMPT changes the DOS command prompt. This command does not apply to the 1-series of DOS.

RECOVER RECOVER is used to check individual files for damage and to reconstruct the directory of a disk if it has been damaged. RECOVER is a very limited but potentially very useful file recovery command. This command does not apply to the 1-series of DOS.

RD RD is another name for the RMDIR command, which removes directories. This command does not apply to the 1-series of DOS.

REM REM is a batch file command used to display a message on the display screen.

REN REN is another name for the RENAME command.

RENAME REN, or RENAME, is used to change the name of one or more files.

RESTORE RESTORE restores files that have been saved with the BACKUP command. This command does not apply to the 1-series of DOS.

RMDIR RMDIR, or RD, is used to remove a directory from a disk's directory tree. RMDIR is the opposite of MKDIR and it is analogous to DEL and ERASE. This command does not apply to the 1-series of DOS.

SELECT SELECT allows you to set the keyboard and date/time formats among several international standards. This command does not apply to the 1- or 2-series of DOS.

SET   SET is used to create or display equations in DOS's environment. SET is an advanced command, which can be used, in conjunction with suitable programming, to control the action of programs. This command does not apply to the 1-series of DOS.

SHARE   SHARE is a resident program that controls file sharing. This command does not apply to the 1- or 2-series of DOS.

SHIFT   SHIFT is an advanced batch file command used to shift batch file parameters over one place. SHIFT makes it easier for a batch file to process a list of parameters that can vary in number. This command does not apply to the 1-series of DOS.

SORT   SORT is a filter command used to rearrange lines of display data in alphabetical order. SORT can be used independently of its filter role to simply sort the contents of a file. This command does not apply to the 1-series of DOS.

SYS   SYS is used to transfer the hidden files (which are part of DOS) to a disk. The main function of SYS is to transfer DOS to a copy-protected disk or to update the version of DOS on a disk.

TIME   TIME is used to display or change DOS's record of the current time of day. Normally the TIME command is used only once each time DOS is started.

TREE   TREE is used to display the complete directory tree from a disk. This command does not apply to the 1-series of DOS.

TYPE   TYPE is used to display the contents of an ASCII text file on the display screen.

VER   VER is used to display the version number of the version of DOS that is being used. This command does not apply to the 1-series of DOS.

VERIFY   VERIFY is used to instruct DOS to check or not check that any data written to disk was written correctly. For most purposes, it is completely unnecessary to verify the data written to disk. This command does not apply to the 1-series of DOS.

VOL   VOL is used to display the volume label on a disk. Labels can be placed on disks when they are formatted. This command does not apply to the 1-series of DOS.

22.2 EDLIN Commands

number—edit a line   Sets up to review and change lines already in the file. Use of the DOS editing keys is particularly useful with this command.

A—append   Reads more file data from disk. Used only when a file is too big to fit into memory at once; used together with W-write, which will make room by writing out the beginning of the file, from memory to disk

C—copy   Duplicates lines from one part of the file to another. This command does not apply to the 1-series of DOS.

D—delete   Deletes lines from the file.

E—end   Writes the file to disk and ends the operation of EDLIN.

I—insert   Begins the process of inserting or adding lines to a file. If you are creating a new file, your first command should be I-insert so that you can start entering the data for the new file.

L—list   Displays a group of lines from the file together with their reference line numbers.

M—move   Moves a group of lines from one location in the file to another.

P—page   Displays a group of lines similar to the L-list command, but also moves the current location within the file for convenience. This command does not apply to the 1-series of DOS.

Q—quit   Ends the use of EDLIN without writing the file back to disk. Used if too many mistakes have been made, or when EDLIN is used to browse through a file rather than to change a file.

R—replace   Searches for some data in a file and replaces it with other data.

S—search   Searches for some data in the file and indicates its location.

T—transfer   Inserts the entire contents of another file into the file that is being edited.

W—write   Writes part of the file being edited to make room in memory for more lines from the file. This command is mostly used together with A-append for files that are too large to fit into memory.

22.3 DEBUG Commands

A—assemble   Accepts assembly-like commands and translates them into machine language. For knowledgeable, advanced users only. This command does not apply to the 1-series of DOS.

C—compare   Compares two areas in memory and reports any differences.

D—display   Displays the contents of an area of memory in both hexadecimal and character formats.

E—enter   Places data into memory; used when patching programs; interactive form displays old data before new data is accepted for greater safety.

F—fill   Places data into memory, duplicating as needed; mostly used to clear memory to zero or some other value.

G—go   Starts executing a program from a particular address. For advanced users only.

H—hexarithmetic   Does addition and subtraction of hexadecimal numbers.

I—in   Reads from the computer's ports and displays the data read.

L—load   Reads from the disk into memory. Can load from particular disk locations or load an entire file.

M—move   Moves (copies, really) data from one area in memory to another.

N—name   Accepts the name of a file for later use by the L-load command.

O—out   Sends data out of the computer's ports.

P—proceed   Proceeds with statements after a jump.

Q—quit   Ends the use of DEBUG and returns to DOS for the next command.

R—register   Displays the contents of the registers or makes changes to their values.

S—search   Searches memory and reports the location of some particular data.

T—trace   Executes a program with controlled break points. For knowledgeable advanced users only.

U—unassemble Displays the contents of memory in the form of the equivalent assembler instructions. Requires knowledge of assembly language to understand.

W—write Writes data from memory to disk, the reverse of L-load. Can write either to particular disk locations or to an entire file.

23

Narrative Glossary

This narrative glossary is intended to provide a very brief rundown of the most common and fundamental terminology used in discussing computers. You can use this narrative glossary in two ways—either by reading it all or by scanning the word list for the terms you are interested in, and then reading the surrounding discussion.

Numbers and Notation

binary

bit

Computers work only with *binary* numbers; that is numbers made up of zeros and ones (0's and 1's). Binary digits are called *bits*, for short. No matter what a computer is doing, it is working with bits. Even if the subject matter is alphabetic characters, or decimal arithmetic, the method is binary numbers.

hexadecimal

Writing many bits, for example 0101010011101010101, is inconvenient, so several short-hand notations have been developed. The most common is *hexadecimal*, or base-16, notation. Hexadecimal digits have 16 possible values, from 0 through 15. They are written as 0 through 9, followed by A (representing the value ten), B (meaning eleven), and C through F (with a value of fifteen).

hex

Hexadecimal digits, also called *hex*, represent four binary digits, or bits, at a time. (Another notation, called *octal*, uses the digits 0 through 7 and represents three bits at a time.)

octal

The bits that a computer uses are grouped in-to larger units. A group of eight bits is called a

303

byte

nibble
nybble
nybble

character

alphanumeric

ASCII

Extended ASCII

EBCDIC

ASCII data

text data
ASCII file

byte. Since hex notation represents four bits at a time, it takes two hex digits to represent the value stored in a byte (hex digits are sometimes whimsically called *nibbles* or *nybbles*). A byte can be used to store two to the eighth power of values—256 different values. The values can be interpreted as numbers or as *characters* (such as letters of the alphabet). One byte can hold one character; therefore, the terms bytes and characters are sometimes used interchangeably. The letters of the alphabet and the ten digits, together, are called the *alphanumerics*, although the term is sometimes used loosely to mean any text data.

When bytes are used to hold characters, some code must be used to determine which numeric value will represent which character. The most common code is the American National Code for Information Interchange (*ASCII*). In ASCII, the capital letter A has the value 65 (in hex notation, 41), B is 66, and so forth. ASCII includes codes for letters, numbers, punctuation, and special control codes. ASCII proper has only 128 different codes, and needs only seven bits to represent it. Since ASCII characters are almost always stored inside 8-bit bytes, there is room for the 128 ASCII codes and another 128 codes. The other codes are sometimes called *extended ASCII*. ASCII codes are standardized, but extended ASCII will vary from computer to computer. Traditionally, IBM computers have not used ASCII coding to represent characters—they use *EBCDIC* (the Extended Binary Coded Decimal Information Code). *ASCII data*, or an ASCII file, is data that consists of text—that is, letters of the alphabet, punctuation, and so forth—rather than numbers or other data. Sometimes the term ASCII is used loosely to mean *text data*. Properly speaking, an *ASCII file* not only contains the ASCII codes for letters, spaces, punctuation, and so forth, but also contains the standard

ASCII codes for formatting, such as carriage return and end-of-file.

When a byte is used to represent a number, the 256 different byte values can be interpreted as either all positive numbers ranging from 0 through 255, or as positive and negative numbers, ranging from -128 through 127. These are referred to as *unsigned* (0 to 255) or *signed* (-128 to 127) numbers.

unsigned number
signed number

word

To handle larger numbers, several bytes are used together as a unit, often called a *word*. For different computers different meanings are given to the term word, but most often it means either two bytes (16-bits) or four bytes (32-bits). For the IBM PC family of computers a word usually means a two-byte, 16-bit, number.

A two-byte word has two to the 16th power different possible values. These can be used as unsigned numbers, with a range of 0 through 65,535, or signed numbers, with a range of $-32,768$ through 32,767.

floating-point

Integers, or whole numbers, are not satisfactory for some tasks. When fractional numbers are needed, or a very wide range of numbers is needed, a different form of computer arithmetic is used, called *floating-point*. Floating-point numbers involve a fractional portion, and an exponent portion, similar to the "scientific notation" used in engineering. To work with floating-point numbers, computers interpret the bits of a word in a special way. Floating-point numbers generally represent approximate, inexact values. Often more than one format of floating-point numbers are available, offering different degrees of accuracy, common terms for this are *single-precision* and *double-precision*. Floating-point numbers are sometimes called *real numbers*.

single-precision
double-precision
real numbers

zero-origin

Due to the nature of computer arithmetic and notation, items are often numbered starting from zero for the first element. This is called *zero-origin*. Counting from zero is usually done when figuring a memory location relative to some starting point. The starting point can be called many things, including *base* and *origin*. The relative location is most often called an *offset*. Starting from any base location in memory, the first byte is at offset zero, and the next byte is at offset one.

base
origin
offset

Computer Fundamentals

hardware

All of the mechanical and electronic parts of a computer system are called *hardware*. The programs that a computer uses are called *software*.

software

memory
storage
location
address

The idea of a computer starts with the concept of *memory* or *storage*. A computer's memory consists of many *locations*, each of which has an *address*, and can store a value. For most computers, including the PC family, each location is a byte; for others, each location is a word.

The addresses of the locations are numbers. The values stored in each location can be either discovered (read) or changed (written). When reading or writing a value, the address of the location must be given.

page

Some computers organize their memory storage into large modular units, often called *pages*. IBM PC computers do not use pages, but for addressing purposes they divide their memory into units of 16 bytes, called *paragraphs* (a term that was chosen to suggest a smaller division than a page). The memory addressing mechanism for these computers uses two parts—a *segment* value, which points to a paragraph boundary, and a

paragraph

segment

displacement

vector

relative value, which points to a byte located at some displacement, or offset, from the segment paragraph. The two values, segment and *displacement*, are needed to specify any complete address; together, they are sometimes called an address vector, or just *vector*.

K

Amounts of computer memory are frequently referred to in units of 1,024, because 1,024 is a round number in binary notation, and almost a round number in decimal notation. The value 1,024 is known as *K* for kilo; 64K is 64 units of 1,024, or exactly 65,536.

When referring to general capacity, K almost always means 1,024 bytes. However, when referring to semiconductor "chips," K means 1,024 bits. When magazine articles refer to 16K and 64K chips, they mean 16K bits (equivalent to 2K bytes) or 64K bits (equivalent to 8K bytes).

operations

A computer has the ability to perform *operations* on the values stored in its memory. Examples of these operations are arithmetic (addition, subtraction) and movement from location to location. A request for the computer to perform an operation is called an *instruction* or *command*.

**instructions
commands**

**program
code**

A series of computer instructions that together perform some work is called a *program*. Programs are also called *code*.

processor

microprocessor

The part of the computer that interprets programs and performs the instructions is called the *processor*. A very small processor, particularly one that fits onto a single computer chip, is called a *microprocessor*. The development of microprocessors made personal computers possible. Properly speaking, a computer is a complete working machine that includes a processor and other parts; but the processor part of a computer is sometimes also called a computer.

The memory of a computer is used to store both programs and data. To the memory there is no difference between programs and data. To the processor, however, only those stored values that represent valid instructions can be a program. The processor reads and writes from its memory both to carry out a program and to access the data that the program uses.

registers

To help it carry out its work, a computer may have a small amount of very specialized memory, which does not have addresses. This specialized memory is referred to as *registers*. Registers are used to make arithmetic more efficient or to assist in handling addresses.

stack
push
pop
LIFO

Many modern computers, including the PC family, use a push-down *stack* to hold status information. Data is *pushed* onto and *popped* off of the top of a stack, on a *last-in-first-out* (or *LIFO*) basis.

bus

When a computer uses a common data path to pass data from one part to another this path is called a *bus*.

peripherals

adapter

controller

The memory and processor are the internal part of a computer. There are many external parts, generally called peripheral equipment, or *peripherals*. Most peripherals must be connected to a computer through some supporting electronic circuitry called an *adapter*. For a complex peripheral, such as a diskette drive, the adapter will include some special logical circuitry called a *controller*. A controller is often a specialized computer in its own right.

storage

diskettes
hard disks

Peripherals may be of many kinds, but they fall into a few simple categories. *Storage* peripherals are used to hold programs and data that can be moved into the computer's internal memory. Examples of peripheral storage devices are floppy *diskettes*, cassette tape recorders, and high-capacity *hard disks*. (For more on this, see the disk vocabulary section below.)

Other peripheral equipment is used to communicate with people. The equipment used to communicate between people and computers are usually called *terminals*. A terminal most often consists of a typewriter-style keyboard, and a TV-like display screen, called a *CRT* (for cathode ray tube). A printer of some kind may be used instead of a CRT. A display screen is called a *monitor*, or simply a *display*. A color display may accept its color signal information in a combined form, called *composite*, or separated into its red, green and blue components, called *RGB*.

Large computers may have many terminals, but small personal computers usually work with only one terminal, which may be built right into the computer system. Having only one terminal is a large part of what makes a *personal computer* personal.

Other kinds of peripherals, besides storage and terminals, are printers and telephone connections. Connections between computers and telephones are referred to by the names of some of their parts, such as *modems* and *asynchronous* adapters. All of these terms, in general use, refer to the entire computer-telephone connection, which is generally called *communications*. The most common format for communications connections follows a design standard known as *RS-232*. The speed, or data rate, of a communications line is measured in *baud*, which is bits-per-second. Three hundred baud is a common speed for personal computer communications; 300 baud is about 35 or 40 characters per second. On personal computers, an RS-232 connection is also called *serial*, since it transmits data one bit at a time. A *parallel* connection can transmit more than one bit at a time.

terminals

CRT

display monitor

composite
RGB

personal
computer

modem
asynchronous

communications

RS-232
baud

serial
parallel

**dot-matrix
letter-quality**

Computer printers come in many varieties. Many personal computers use an inexpensive *dot-matrix* printer, which creates its printed results by writing a series of dots. *Letter-quality* printers produce results comparable to good typewriters. Most letter-quality printers use a print element that is either a flat disk, called a *daisy-wheel*, or one that is shaped like a large *thimble*.

**daisy-wheel
thimble**

ink-jet

There are two new exciting kinds of printers that are being used in place of traditional dot-matrix and daisy-wheel printers. One is *ink-jet* printers, which squirt very tiny drops of ink and paint their information with these small dots. Some ink-jets print as crudely as dot-matrix printers, while others print as finely as a typewriter that uses a fabric ribbon. The other new printer technology is grandly called laser printing. A *laser printer* is essentially a computer-driven photocopier, but where a photocopier gets its image from taking a camera-like picture of something we're copying, a laser printer creates an original image of what we want to print. A computer-controlled laser beam paints the image inside the photocopier, which then prints the image onto paper.

laser printer

interface

An *interface* is a connection between any two elements in a computer system. The term interface is used both for connections between hardware parts and software parts, as well as the human interface.

I/O

Much of the equipment that can be connected to a computer is generally referred to as input/output equipment, or *I/O*.

chips

The smallest physical parts that make up a computer may be called *chips*. Chips and other parts are wired together electrically and held mechanically on boards. If there is one principal *board*, it is called the *system board*, or *mother board*. Openings for the addition of

**board, system
board
mother board**

slots   more boards are called expansion *slots*, into which are placed memory boards, disk boards, asynch comm boards (telephone connections), and other expansion or peripheral boards.

port

interrupt

external interrupt

internal interrupt

software interrupt

A microprocessor interacts with its world through three means, memory accesses, interrupts, and ports. *Ports* have a port number or port address, and are used for passing data to or from peripheral devices. *Interrupts* are used to get the computer's attention. There are three kinds of interrupts (although all three are handled the same). An *external interrupt* is from the outside world (for example, from a diskette drive). An *internal interrupt* reports some exceptional logical situation (for example, division by zero). A *software interrupt* is a request from a program for some service to be performed. A software interrupt is an alternative to using a call to activate a subroutine. Memory accesses are used to read or write from the computer's memory.

RAM

ROM

memory-mapped

The computer's memory can be of several types. Ordinary memory, which can be read or written to, is called *RAM* (random access memory). Memory that contains permanent data is *ROM* (read only memory). Memory can be dedicated to some use, for example, to hold the data that appears on the computer's display screen. If a display screen uses the computer's memory to hold its information, then it is a *memory-mapped* display.

Programs and Programming Languages

program
subroutine

function

Series of computer instructions are called *programs*. Parts of programs that are partially self-contained are called *subroutines*. Subroutines may be procedures if they only do some work, or *functions* if they also result in a

procedure

subprogram
routine

value ("open the door" is analogous to a *procedure*; "tell me your name" is analogous to a function). Subroutines are also called *subprograms* and *routines*.

Many subroutines use parameters to specify exactly what work is to be done. For example, a subroutine that computes a square root needs a *parameter* to specify what number to use. Many subroutines will indicate how successful their operation was through a *return code*.

parameter

return code

machine language

Computers can only execute programs that appear in the detailed form known as *machine language*. For the convenience of people, however, programs may be represented in other forms. If the details of a machine language program are replaced with meaningful symbols (such as the terms ADD or MOVE), then the programming language is known as *assembly language* (also called *assembler*, symbolic assembler, or *macro assembler*).

assembly
language
macro assembler

low-level

Assembler is called a *low-level* language, because assembly programs are written in a form close to machine language. Other forms of programming languages are more abstracted, and produce many machine instructions for each command written by the programmer. These are called *high-level* languages. Examples are BASIC, Pascal, FORTRAN, COBOL, PL/I, C, and FORTH. Programs that translate high-level language programs into a form usable by the computer are called *compilers*; for low-level languages the translators are called *assemblers*. There is no real difference between a compiler and an assembler—they both translate from a human programming language to a form of machine language.

high-level

compiler
assembler

source code

When a person writes a computer program, the form it takes is called *source code*, or

object code

link editor
load module

source. When the source code is translated (by an assembler or compiler), the result is often called *object code*. Object code is nearly ready to be used but it has to undergo a minor transformation, performed by a *link editor*, or linker, to produce a *load module*—which is a finished, ready-to-use program.

debug

An error in a program is called a *bug*, and the processing of trying to find errors, or trying to fix them, is called *debugging*.

algorithm

There are usually many ways to accomplish an objective with a computer program. The scheme, formula, or method that a program uses is its *algorithm*. For many tasks—even as simple a one as sorting data into alphabetic order—there are dramatic differences in the efficiency of different algorithms, and the search continues for better and better methods.

variable

type

string

file

A program works with symbolic entities called variables. In effect, a *variable* is the name of a place that can hold data of some type. Specific data can be moved into and out of a variable, and the purpose of the variable is to provide a mechanism for manipulating data. Variables usually have a fixed *type*, which indicates what sort of data it can accommodate. For example, integer type, single- and double-precision floating-point, and *string* (a collection of text characters). In a program, a *file* is just a special kind of variable, one that can be connected to a diskette file or some device such as the display screen.

Human Roles

On a personal computer, one person may do everything that is to be done. However, in traditional large computer systems, there is a division of labor separating human involvement with a computer into various roles. Users of personal computers may wonder about the meaning of various job titles used.

user

The *user*, or end user, is the person for whom computer work is done.

analyst

The systems analyst, or *analyst*, determines the details of the work that the end user needs done, and decides on the general strategy of how a computer will perform the work.

programmer

The *programmer* converts the analyst's general strategy into the detailed tactics and methods to be used. This usually includes writing (and testing) the actual program. However, actually writing and testing the program is sometimes left to a coder.

coder

The *coder* turns the programmer's detailed methods into the program instructions.

operator

The *operator* runs the program on the computer to produce the results needed by the user.

Data Organization

file

record

field

Data is organized and viewed differently, depending upon who or what is looking at it. To the computer itself, data consists of just bits and bytes. To programmers who manipulate data, there are some traditional logical boundaries for data. A complete collection of related data is a *file* (as an example, a mailing list file). One complete unit of the information that is in a file, is called a *record*. In a mailing list file, all of the information connected with one address would be a record. Finally, within a record are *fields*, the information of one type. For example, the zip code would be one field in an address record in a mailing list file.

logical record
physical record

The records that a program reads or writes are *logical records*. Logical records are placed in the storage medium's *physical records*—which are the pieces actually read or written to a diskette. A program sees logical records, while the operating system performs any translating necessary between logical and physical records. On a diskette, a physical record is called a sector.

data base
data base manager

The terms data base and data base manager are used, and abused, so widely that they have no precise meaning. When data is large, complex, and spread across several files, it might be called a *data base*. A *data base manager is a program*—usually large and complex in itself—which can control and organize a data base. Full-scale data base management is far beyond the capabilities of a personal computer.

Diskette Vocabulary

sector

Data on a diskette is stored on *sectors*, which can be individually read or written. Typically for DOS a sector is 512 bytes. Sectors are the diskette's physical records—the units that are actually read or written. A *track* is the collection of sectors that will fit into one circle on a diskette. A typical disk format has eight sectors in a track. If there is more than one surface on a disk or diskette drive, then a *cylinder* is all of the tracks that are the same distance from the center. Sectors that are in the same cylinder can be read without moving the disk drive's read/write mechanism. Moving the read/write heads from one track/cylinder to another is called *seeking*, and it is relatively slow. Typically there are 40 or 80 tracks on each surface of a diskette.

track

cylinder

seeking

directory

A diskette needs a table of contents for its files, called a *directory* in DOS. On some other

VTOC

FAT, file allocation

boot record

systems, a directory is called a *VTOC* (Volume Table Of Contents). Some means must be used to keep track of used and unused space on a diskette. With DOS this is done with the *FAT* (File Allocation Table). The first sector of each diskette is dedicated to holding the first part of the operating system's start-up program, called the bootstrap loader or *boot record*. On each diskette there are four kinds of sectors—boot record, FAT, directory, and data space (where files are stored).

floppy

flippy
hard disk

fixed disk
hard file

Winchester

A diskette is flexible, thus it is called a *floppy*. A diskette that can be turned over to use the other side is a *flippy*. (Double-sided diskettes are not turned over.) A *hard disk* has a rigid platter in place of the flexible plastic of a floppy. The rigid shape allows more precise data recording, and thus higher density and more capacity. IBM's terminology for hard disks in their personal computers is *fixed disks*; everyone else calls them hard disks or *hard files*. The sort of hard disks installed on personal computers today use a collection of methods called *Winchester* technology, so they are also called Winchester disks.

mini-diskette

high-capacity

There are other sort of diskettes as well. While standard-sized diskettes for personal computers are 5 1/4 inches across, a new type of diskette, called a *mini-diskette*, is only around 3 1/2 inches across—small enough to fit into a shirt pocket. Also, advanced technology has made it possible to pack much more information into a standard-sized diskette. These are called *high-capacity* diskettes.

Operating Systems

operating system

An *operating system* is a program that supervises and controls the operation of a computer. Operating systems are complex and consist of many parts.

BIOS

One element of an operating system is its *BIOS*, or Basic Input-Output System. The BIOS is responsible for handling the details of input-output operations, including the task of relating a program's logical records to a peripheral device's physical records. At the most detailed level, the BIOS contains routines tailored to the specific requirements of each peripheral device; these routines are called *drivers*, or *device handlers*.

**driver, device
handler**

**logical I/O
physical I/O
services**

Usually an operating system is organized into a hierarchy of levels of services. At the lowest level, the device handlers insulate the rest of the operating system from the details of each device. At the next level, relating *logical data* to *physical data* is performed. At a higher level basic *services* are provided—such as accepting output data from a program to be placed into a file.

**loader
relocation**

error handler

Besides device and data handling, an operating system must supervise programs, including *loading* them, *relocating* them (adjusting their internal addresses to correspond to their exact location in a memory), and recovering from any program errors, through an *error handler*.

**command
processor**

Another element of an operating system is the *command processor*, which accepts and acts on commands given by the computer's user. Commands usually amount to a request for the execution of some service program.

Index

Related Resources Shelf

Inside the IBM PC, revised & enlarged   Peter Norton

This best-seller has been thoroughly updated and expanded to include *every* model of the IBM microcomputer family! Detailed in content, yet brisk in style, INSIDE THE IBM PC provides the fascinating tour inside your machine that only the renowned Peter Norton can give. He'll lead you into a complete understanding of your IBM—knowing what it is, how it works, and what it can do. First review the fundamentals, then move on to discover new ways to master the important facets of using your micro to its fullest potential. Definitive in all aspects.

☐ 1985/384 pp/paper/0-89303-583-1/$21.95

Creating Utilities with Assembly Language: 10 Best for the IBM PC & XT
Stephen Holzner

With assembly language as its foundation, this book explores the most popular utility programs for the IBM PC and XT. For the more advanced user, this book unleashes the power of utilities on the PC. Utilities created and discussed include PCALC, ONE KEY, CLOCK, FONT, DBUG SCAN, DSKWATCH and UNDELETE. The author is a regular contributor to *PC Magazine*.

☐ 1985/352 pp/paper/0-89303-584-X/$19.95

Artificial Intelligence for Microcomputers: A Guide for Business Decision Makers   Mickey Williamson

This book discusses artificial intelligence from an introductory point of view and takes a detailed look at expert systems and how they can be used as a business decision-making tool. Includes step-by-step instructions to create your own expert system and covers applications to cost/benefit analysis, personnel evaluations and software benchtesting.

☐ 1985/224 pp/paper/0-89303-483-5/$17.95

Assembly Language Programming with the IBM PC AT   Leo J. Scanlon

Author of Brady's best-selling IBM PC & XT ASSEMBLY LANGUAGE: A GUIDE FOR PROGRAMMERS (recently revised and enlarged), Leo Scanlon is the assembly language authority. This new book on the AT is designed for beginning and experienced programmers, and includes step-by-step instructions for using the IBM Macro Assembler. Also included is a library of 30 useful macros, a full description of the 80286 microprocessor, and advanced topics like music and sound.

☐ 1985/464 pp/paper/0-89303-484-3/$21.95

To order, simply clip or photocopy this entire page, check your order selection, and complete the coupon below. Enclose a check or money order for the stated amount or include credit card information. Please add $2.00 per book for postage & handling, plus local sales tax.

Mail To: **Brady Books, c/o Prentice Hall Press, 200 Old Tappan Road, Old Tappan, NJ 07675.**

You may also order from Brady directly by calling 800-624-0023 (800-624-0024 if in New Jersey).

Name _____

Address _____

City/State/Zip _____

Charge my credit card instead: ☐ MasterCard   ☐ Visa

Credit Card Account # _____ Expiration Date _____ / _____

Signature _____
Dept. Y   D5831-BB
Prices subject to change without notice.

1227 Warren St.

R. W. 94063.

(415) 369-7722

8M
1831
88
5

13 20 21 32 37 42